Words of Praise for H

This is a wonderful book to give to someone who is seeking the truth and asking the hard questions. It is honest, thought-provoking, witty, at times very moving, and is truly written by someone who can say "been there, and done that."

—Ray Comfort
TV co-host and bestselling author

If ever you've wondered if the God who waylaid Jacob in his scheming, or interrupted Balaam in his cursing, or ambushed Paul in his crusading, or accosted Hagar in her despairing is still on the job, read this: Kitty's tale of God's surprising and abrupt pursuit of her, hard on the heels of her beloved mother's death, is a wonder of storytelling and a testament of grace. What joy and terror it evokes, to know this God is out there and on the loose, able to turn even the stoniest heart to flesh.

—Mark Buchanan
Author of *Your God Is Too Safe* and *Hidden in Plain Sight*

Typically people formulate opinions, gather allies, and then maybe sort through the evidence. It is true on both sides of the evolution debate, as well as the global-warming, crime-and-punishment, and existence-of-God debates. [Foth-Regner] studied the evidence before she decided which side she wanted to play for. This book may or may not persuade you, but you should read it.

—Michael Cronin

As a former Methodist Sunday school teacher who had been baptized Presbyterian, and someone who has coasted through the various stages of wonder and doubt as an agnostic, atheist, secular humanist, and follower of the Just-in-Case denomination, I find my consciousness has been raised by Foth-Regner, in ways that make me think I must re-examine what I believe.

—Victoria Powell, editor/writer

Unlike those of us who have lived within the arms of Christianity since infancy, Kitty had to fight for her faith, inch by grueling inch. Her journey, battling years of skepticism and headstrong refusal to listen to the Voice shouting in her ear, is an inspiration to all Christians. You will make a mental list of people you want to give this book to.

—Kathleen Winkler
Author of *College Bound: A Guide for Christian Students*

Heaven Without Her is a compelling read that grips the reader from the opening line and doesn't let go until the closing word! Those who have struggled to embrace God as He is portrayed in the Bible will find in Kitty Foth-Regner a faithful and compassionate guide for the journey from skepticism to full-orbed faith.

—Sam Horn, PhD New Testament Theology
Senior Pastor, Brookside Baptist Church
Vice President for Graduate Studies, Northland Baptist Bible College

Talk about a Godsend. Kitty Foth-Regner's book should be read by any woman (like me) who thought she found all the answers by becoming "liberated." Kitty's story is one of heartbreaking loss, but also of victory and joy, which she found when her study of the Bible ultimately led her to the real truth—in the Lord. I highly recommend it.

—JoAnn Petaschnick, writer/editor

If you think that science has proven God unnecessary and the Bible irrelevant, you owe it to yourself to read this book. It offers powerful proof that even a committed Betty Friedan feminist can find her way to eternal truth if she's willing to follow the evidence wherever it leads.

—John D. Morris, PhD
President, Institute for Creation Research

This is a fantastic book about one woman's journey from feminism to faith, told in a transparent and captivating life story. You will leave no page unturned! She rationally analyzes the philosophies and religions advocated to her throughout her all-consuming and heart-wrenching journey for the truth—and in the end proves that it is found only in Jesus Christ! This book would be a great gift for others who are searching for the truth.

—Attorney Lana Lee McLario Helm

I believe this memoir mirrors the experience of so many women who are left spiritually empty-handed at the end of the day. And it will resonate especially with anyone who, in grieving, has wondered about the realities of heaven. The author grants us an intimate and poignant view of her own loss and spiritual struggle. Then, with the tenacity of a bestselling crime-solver, she sorts through and compiles evidence for faith in Christ that ultimately cannot be dismissed. This book is a must read for the discriminating seeker.

—Jennifer Reese, MS

Kitty Foth-Regner's account of her conversion to Christ is a profound testimony of what happens when the Holy Spirit goes to work through the Word and the faithful witness of other believers. The author's life story is a ringing tribute to the power of the risen Christ.

—Ingrid Schlueter
Host, *Crosstalk* Radio Talk Show
VCY America Radio Network

Exhaustively revisiting and cataloging the events of her own life, Foth-Regner concludes that the problem that had no name actually has one—namely, separation from God—and its solution is faith.

I admire the literary thoroughness of Foth-Regner's entry into faith. She reads today's popular Christian canon—everything from C. S. Lewis to Josh McDowell and the writings of the creation debate—in her determination to build a real faith out of the scraps of her yearnings.

—Patty Kirk
Author of *Confessions of an Amateur Believer*

Like the author, I spent more than three decades believing I was free and unbound by limitations because I had chosen a path that entitled me to pursue, achieve, and conquer anything my heart desired. And like Foth-Regner, I found myself empty and unsatisfied with all my conquests and achievements. It was a thrill to be invited into this delightful memoir of the determined, analytical search of one who, with all her heart, desperately wanted to know the truth, and who inevitably found it in the God who has revealed Himself in the Holy Bible.

— Paula M. Haberman (nee Sobczyk)

Heaven Without Her is just the sort of page-turning memoir I wait for and savor. A candid, moving, funny, beautifully written journey of one daughter's climb out of radical feminism and empty agnosticism on the backs of brilliant Christian thinkers, and the loving legacy of her mother's faith. Simply profound.

—Becky Freeman Johnson
Author and co-author of twenty-six books,
including *Help! I'm Turning into My Mother!*

Heaven Without Her is a fascinating chronicle of a seeker's journey to faith in Christ. This is a real page turner, not only because Foth-Regner has written in such an engaging style, but because she has written about what everyone is looking for—God, meaning, and eternal life. This is a great book to give to intelligent seekers!

—Dr. N. Allan Moseley
Professor of Old Testament and Hebrew and Dean of Students,
Southeastern Baptist Theological Seminary
Author, *Thinking Against the Grain*

Witty and penetrating, this conversion story will give you fresh insights into how to communicate your faith. Kitty Foth-Regner offers a poignant account of her grief over her mother's death, which sent her on an intense spiritual search. But her irrepressible spirit bubbles up in hilariously funny conversations with her worldly friends as she explores religious questions and discovers that there are good reasons for accepting God's Word as true.

—Nancy Pearcey
Scholar of Worldview Studies, Philadelphia Biblical University
Author of *Total Truth: Liberating Christianity from Its Cultural Captivity*

If you've ever found yourself privately wondering whether there might be something beyond the here and now, or whether the ancient Christian faith holds any relevance for today, I urge you to read Kitty's account of her own spiritual journey. It has relevance to all of us.

—Shaunti Feldhahn
Nationally syndicated newspaper columnist and Public speaker,
Bestselling author of *For Women Only*

Heaven Without Her

A Desperate Daughter's Search
for the Heart of Her Mother's Faith

Kitty Foth-Regner

THOMAS NELSON
Since 1798

NASHVILLE   DALLAS   MEXICO CITY   RIO DE JANEIRO   BEIJING

Published in Nashville, Tennessee, by Thomas Nelson. Thomas Nelson is a registered trademark of Thomas Nelson, Inc.

Unless otherwise noted, Scripture quotations are taken from The New King James Version. © 1982 by Thomas Nelson, Inc. Used by permission. All rights reserved.

Scripture quotations marked KJV are from the King James Version

Scripture quotations marked NASB are taken from the NEW AMERICAN STANDARD BIBLE®, © Copyright The Lockman Foundation 1960, 1962, 1963, 1968, 1971, 1972, 1973, 1975, 1977, 1995. Used by permission.

Scripture quotations marked NLT are from *HOLY BIBLE*, New Living Translation. © 1996 used by permission of Tyndale House Publishers, Inc., Wheaton, Illinois 60189

Thomas Nelson, Inc., titles may be purchased in bulk for educational, business, fund-raising, or sales promotional use. For information, please e-mail SpecialMarkets@ThomasNelson.com.

Published in association with the literary agency of WordServe Literary Group, Ltd., 10152 S. Knoll Circle, Highlands Ranch, Colorado 80130.

Library of Congress Cataloging-in-Publication Data

Foth, Kitty.
    Heaven without her : a desperate daughter's search for the heart of her mother's faith / Kitty Foth-Regner.
        p. cm.
    Includes bibliographical references and index.
    ISBN: 978-0-7852-2744-1
    1. Foth, Kitty. 2. Christian biography. 3. Apologetics. I. Title.
BR1725.F68A3 2008
277.3'083092--dc22
[B]

2007045962

Printed in the United States of America

HB 09.13.2018

To Dr. John Whitcomb and the late Dr. Henry Morris,
for showing me the truth about where we came from,
what we're doing here, and where we're going.
And to the late Reggie White, for leaving it all
on the field for the Lord.

CONTENTS

I look forward to death,
except for one reason only.
How can I possibly live in a world,
no matter how heavenly it may be,
if my little agnostic Kitty is not there?

—*Ethel Boehm Foth*
March 5, 1993

CHAPTER 1

Through a glass, darkly:
Face-to-face with forever

4:30 p.m., May 30, 2000, Milwaukee, Wisconsin

*T*he last time I talked to my mother, she was lying in a morphine-induced coma in her room at the nursing home where she'd lived for the last eight years. We were not alone; my husband, Dave, was there, along with my oldest sister Carrie and her husband, David, an Episcopal deacon. Random nurses and aides floated in and out of a scene so dreamlike that it still doesn't seem quite real to me.

I do remember David delivering what he called the last rites, a swarm of prayers that sounded very dire to me. He has one of those deep-as-a-grave voices, a voice that resonated as he gestured over her body and spoke of "God's servant Ethel" and how she was "lying in great weakness" and how much she needed His mercy.

I wanted to say, "Um, excuse me? She's dying, right? She needs a cure, not mercy. Try calling a doctor instead of your imaginary friend."

"Comfort her with the promise of life everlasting," he boomed in a pitch that was a perfect match for his shirt, an ominous black garment with a peek-a-boo square of white at the throat.

I thought briefly of all the promises I'd broken. No comfort there.

1

"That it may please You mercifully to pardon all her sins," he added.

I glared at him: how dare he accuse my mother of sin? No one noticed my anger; all heads were bowed but mine. I quickly dropped my eyes again, fearful that I might have broken some spell he was casting, half-expecting him to launch into something along the lines of "double, double, toil and trouble . . ."

Instead, he rambled on about God's mercy and love.

Empty words, all. If his God really existed, which I sincerely doubted, He apparently had no problem ripping my heart out. What good was a God who would do a thing like that?

When he had finished, we sat there silently for a long while. I remember wishing they'd all leave so I could be alone with my mom. But it was such a personal request that I didn't have the nerve to ask them to get out. And they didn't seem to be doing a very good job of reading my mind. I finally settled for kneeling next to the head of her bed and whispering in her ear.

"You can let go now, Mom," I said, crossing my fingers. I said it only because someone had told me it's the kind thing to say to a dying parent.

"I'll be okay," I added. I didn't mean that either, even though she was eighty-seven, and I was forty-seven and, from what some very smart people have told me before and since, I had no business viewing her impending death as anything more than a sad but inevitable incident in my life.

She didn't respond. I knelt there, looking at her supremely peaceful countenance, listening to her steady breathing. I fumbled for something else to say.

Finally it came to me: "I'll see you there, Mom."

It was a promise, one that I intended to keep. Of course, I had no idea what this could possibly mean. But as Dave and I left the room moments later—I couldn't handle the death watch, and clearly she wasn't going to know whether I was there or not—I decided it might be a good time to find out. After all, everyone else seemed to have a pretty good idea of what the afterlife had in store for her, telling her slumbering form that she was about to embark on a great adventure. And telling her this with great gusto and cheer, like travel agents who have just sold a client a really expensive vacation package: "Ho, boy, don't we all wish we were going with you!"

I kissed her good-bye—a quick peck on one soft check, as if this were an everyday "see ya later" parting—and headed for the door, pausing only to grab my purse. Dave followed me out.

"She sure would've liked this little gathering," I said bitterly as we walked briskly down the hall to the nearest exit. Normally crawling with aides, nurses, and housekeepers, the place was eerily vacant. "Surrounded by people she loves, with everyone for once focused on her."

"And it's not even Christmas," Dave said.

Then he wisely shut up. Maybe he was sad, knowing he'd probably never have another teasing conversation with my mom. Or maybe he recognized that I was just a sympathetic word or two away from a total meltdown and feared what might follow in its wake.

With good reason, as it turned out.

꒷

THERE WAS ONE thing I was pretty sure of, even then: in her final alert hours, my mother had undoubtedly been overjoyed to be heading home at long last.

Her faith had been formed early, thanks to a mother and grandmother with rock-solid Christian convictions. Their generations had apparently been unfazed by the scientific revolution Charles Darwin launched in 1859 by publishing *Origin of the Species by Means of Natural Selection, or the Preservation of Favored Races in the Struggle for Life.* Christianity was truth, as far as they were concerned, and it permeated everything they did, said, and even thought. They held, in short, what is today called a "biblical worldview."

For instance, women of this era didn't believe that marriage was all about being happy, although I daresay that most were happy enough with their husbands. If yours was nasty to you, you were to respond with love because the Bible told you to do so. End of discussion.

Nor did they believe financial gain was to be had at any cost. If a shopkeeper gave you too much change, and you didn't notice it until you got home, then you marched right back to return the excess. Thou shalt not steal, after all, even if your gains *were* the result of someone else's honest mistake.

So thoroughly did this worldview permeate their lives that my grandmother's only surviving cookbook—handwritten in a spiral notebook—included generous helpings of advice from the Old and New Testaments. There between recipes for Ruth Niles' Butterscotch Brownies and Mrs. Martini's Potato Salad would be a solution for discouragement:

> Hast thou not known? hast thou not heard, that the everlasting God, the LORD, the Creator of the ends of the earth, fainteth not, neither is weary? there is no searching of his understanding. He giveth power to the faint; and to them that have no might he increaseth strength. Even the youths shall faint and be weary, and the young men shall utterly fall: But they that wait upon the LORD shall renew their strength; they shall mount up with wings as eagles; they shall run, and not be weary; and they shall walk, and not faint.[1]

Dealing with sorrow? Between her instructions for Ann's Noodle Dish and Happy Day Cake, this grandmother I'd never known had given a place of honor to the ultimate comfort food:

Let not your heart be troubled: ye believe in God, believe also in me.
In my Father's house are many mansions: if it were not so, I would
have told you. I go to prepare a place for you. And if I go and prepare a place for you, I will come again, and receive you unto myself;
that where I am, there ye may be also.[2]

My grandmother's generation—and my mother's—apparently
had no need for shrinks or anti-depressants or self-improvement
books. They had another source of help in times of trouble.

I'd never been much interested in these things. But that was about
to change forever.

CHAPTER 2

When I was a child:
A healthy fear of hell

5:00 p.m., May 30, 2000

The good news was that I didn't have to worry about my mom being in pain any longer, or sinking into dementia, or losing her limbs or vision. Her favorite nurse had assured me that, thanks to the morphine, she was now pain-free and wouldn't wake up again this side of eternity.

That left me free to focus on my own despair as I sat at my craggy pine kitchen table, smoking Viceroys and nursing a Miller Lite.

The trouble was this: I couldn't imagine living in a world without my mother. She had been the one constant source of strength in my life, the one who'd joined hands with my father to give me, the baby of the family, an idyllic childhood. She was the only person who'd loved me nearly unconditionally no matter how horrifying my behavior had become, and the one I would have rescued had my entire family been drowning around me. (I'd actually spent a great deal of time thinking about this as a child, and my answer had never changed.)

Just how was I supposed to live without her?

Even worse, I was not at all convinced she was headed anywhere but to oblivion. I'd not seen a shred of evidence that heaven was anything

6

more than wishful thinking. Not that I'd really *looked* for that shred, but I'd certainly given the matter some thought over the years.

My conclusion: who could know what happens after we croak?

My family, on the other hand, seemed to think they each had, in hand, a one-way ticket to the Great Beyond. For instance, if you'd asked her a few days earlier, before the morphine had kicked in, my mother would have told you she was a heaven-bound Christian, like just about everyone else in our family.

I suppose some might say that even I had once been a Christian, at least until I grew old enough to decide for myself at age five or ten or whenever it is that one is supposedly able to make an informed choice about such things. Whatever that magic age, my decision had been a rousing "No way!" It seemed clear to me that religion had been designed specifically to ruin my good time, and although my folks took me to church and Sunday school every week until I went off to school, I never paid a bit of attention to the Bible stories served up by the earnest men and women who taught our classes.

That's probably why I found myself, that dark day in May of 2000, thinking that a final destination of oblivion was about as likely as any other scenario. And if that was the case, then the nihilists were right, and despair was the only appropriate response to life.

As a youngster, I had as much faith in God as the next kid—enough to survive the ramp-up of the Cold War, anyway, without undue fear.

People think that the children of the 1950s were sheltered from the real world, and in some ways that may be true. Where I grew up, in small-town Green Bay, Wisconsin, the biggest scandal we ever got wind of was the rumor that a divorced woman lived in a dreary, gray apartment building on Monroe Street. (Of course, no one had ever seen her, so we couldn't be sure.)

But then in 1960, Nikita Khrushchev disrupted our small-town utopia by pounding his shoe on a table at the UN and promising to bury us all. He even walled the evil West permanently out of the Communist workers' paradise he was building in Eastern Europe. By age nine, my little neighborhood friends and I knew from eavesdropping on our parents' discussions that tensions were running high between America and the Soviet Union; my mom and dad and older sister Andy had, in fact, been in Berlin in 1961 on the day that Khrushchev slammed the gates shut, escaping on one of the last trains out because my German-born father sensed that they'd best get out while the getting was still possible.

We also heard scary predictions from a completely unlikely source: Mrs. G., the mother of one of our playmates.

"Listen up, girls," she told her daughter and me and our friend Rosie one day as we sat on the narrow covered porch fronting their comfy little house. Her tone was ominous, but she'd hemmed us in with her considerable girth so that we had no choice but to stay and listen. "You need to know that one of these days, buses are going to pull up in front of your schools to take you away."

"Away?" Rosie repeated nervously. "What do you mean?"

"Forever," Mrs. G. added with gut-wrenching finality.

She leaned forward conspiratorially, her clasped hands dangling between her knees against the faded blue housedress, and raised one perfectly arched eyebrow at Rosie.

"They'll take you up north," she said, referring to the wilderness of northern Wisconsin, "and keep you there. And then the Russians will bomb Green Bay to kingdom come, and all us parents will be dead."

Mrs. G. didn't say why our parents would be unable to escape with us, and we were too afraid of her to ask directly. Later on, Rosie and I wondered about this.

"Maybe there wouldn't be enough buses for all of us if our parents came along," she suggested.

"Or maybe they figure our parents won't be able to keep the secret," I said without specifying who "they" were, since I didn't have a clue. "Maybe they know our moms would get all scared and tip the Russians off that we were trying to escape."

Neither answer was satisfactory, not even to a nine-year-old mind, but they were the best explanations we could come up with. We didn't question Mrs. G.'s prediction; she was a parent, after all, and if there was one thing we knew for sure, parents didn't lie or make up outrageous stuff just to scare us kids. Instead, we kept a lookout for those school buses. There weren't many in Green Bay in those days; every kid we knew lived close enough to walk to school, even in bad weather. But once Mrs. G. had delivered her dismal prophecy, my stomach lurched every time I saw a lumbering yellow bus.

The specter haunted Rosie too. She and I discussed the subject often in the ensuing months. I can remember sitting with her on the porch of our big old, red-brick Victorian on Quincy Street one evening in the autumn of 1962, talking until well after dark about how the Communists would probably kill us all in the end. It seemed inevitable. Not that Mrs. G. had taken us to this logical conclusion, but just as we knew parents didn't lie to you, we were pretty sure they avoided telling you the really bad stuff.

As if that weren't frightening enough, Rosie and I then got into a discussion of the afterlife and whether we'd end up in heaven or the other place. This subject was especially horrific for me, because Rosie had been taking catechism.

"Let's face it," she said that autumn night, "if you aren't Catholic, you're going to hell."

I stiffened. "That's not true."

"Uh-huh, it is," she said, nodding so vigorously that her short, black braids bounced on her shoulders. Rosie was as dark as an

Indian, and her already blushing complexion always flushed red when she was passionate about a topic, as she was about hell. "Not that all Catholics are going to heaven, but if you're good enough, you will. But if you're not Catholic, you're going to hell—I know that for sure."

I could hardly believe this. I couldn't recall that this subject had ever come up in my Congregational Sunday school classes. Surely someone would've warned us if being Protestant meant certain hell?

The next day, while Mom was putting together my favorite tuna casserole, I ventured a question on the subject.

"Oh, honey, you don't have to worry about that," she said, sprinkling crushed potato chips over the top of her creation. The sight made my mouth water. "You don't have to be Catholic to go to heaven. I know they believe that, but—well, it's too complicated to explain, and I don't want you arguing with Rosie about it. Just be nice to her, and believe in God, and everything will be fine forever and ever. I promise."

But there was something about Rosie's claim that worried me in spite of Mom's assurances. I started having nightmares in which my mom and dad and I were driving in Dad's big Buick, laughing and singing, when the landscape began to change from Wisconsin countryside to total darkness; then a red glow appeared on the horizon, and within moments we found ourselves driving under flaming bridges and between crumbling buildings, all of us frightened into total silence.

As the years rolled on, I tried to replace that mental image with thoughts of a kinder, gentler God and a kinder, more tolerant afterlife—most often, with considerable success. The afterlife was all theoretical in those days, and it's easy to shape theory into the fantasies of one's choosing. Especially when you recognize no higher authority than self.

I was only seventeen when the theoretical became reality. But my position on the afterlife and higher authorities didn't budge. After all, I was just beginning to discover how much fun could be had when you were your own boss.

CHAPTER 3

Willfully ignorant:
Turning on and tuning out

5:30 p.m., May 30, 2000

I fought the urge to call Mom's room. Various friends and relatives were probably there, maintaining the death watch, and I didn't feel like talking to any of them. I really didn't feel like talking to anyone who was unable or unwilling to stop this madness.

"She's led a good, long life," one of the nurses had said to me a couple days earlier, after explaining that they were going to start hospice care.

It had taken every last ounce of my willpower to simply smile sadly and nod at this nurse. What I really wanted to do was scream at her: "So what? Why is that supposed to comfort me? Instead of standing there making these *stupid* comments, why don't you do something to save her life?" And to be honest, I probably would have thrown in a few cuss words, too.

But for once I bit my tongue. I did it for my mom—first, because one of her favorite sayings was "I have scars all over my tongue." And second, because it seemed like a really dumb time to insult one of my mother's primary caregivers.

Besides, I didn't trust myself. This despair was disorienting; I felt drunk with fear, and well beyond the reach of any human help.

IT HAD BEEN nearly three decades since I'd felt this heartsick.

It was on September 1, 1970, three days after my parents had settled me into my dorm room at little Ripon College in central Wisconsin, that death left the realm of the theoretical for me.

I had just returned to my beautiful old dormitory after lunching in the cafeteria, and made a beeline for the mailroom, thinking there might be a letter from home waiting for me. Instead, I practically ran over the white-haired housemother of our freshman dorm.

"The dean of women wants to see you, Miss Foth," she said. We talked that way in those days, never calling people of a different generation by their first names unless we were invited to do so. "Right away. Do you know where to find her?"

Of course I did; everyone knew where to find the dean of women. She was reputedly the administration's toughest disciplinarian, and I don't think I was alone in fearing her. I went straight to her office, housed in one of the century-old buildings on the hill overlooking the campus. I was pretty nervous, truth be told; freed from the constraints of home and curfew, this wild child had been out partying with some new friends the night before and anticipated a lecture on behaving like a young lady.

So when the office secretary let me into the dean's mammoth office, I was surprised to see not her Deanship but my dad's dear friend Haydn. He was perched nervously on a loveseat in the artfully arranged room, a cup of coffee untouched on the table before him.

"Mr. Evans," I said, fighting panic. I was nuts about him, but he had no business here in the dean's office, and I didn't want to see him here, not now, because it was scaring me silly.

He looked up at me, his countenance sagging in anguish. It would strike me later that although he'd always reminded me of a favorite old hound dog, I had never before seen him wearing anything but a big smile on his face.

"Sit down," he said. "And brace yourself."

I sat stiffly in the armchair nearest him.

He didn't beat around the bush.

"Your father had a heart attack this morning," he said. "He's dead."

I sat silently, riding waves of horror.

Then: "I have to get home to Mom." Because this was a mistake, of course—my beloved Daddy, dead? It simply wasn't possible. She needed me there to help her sort it out. "Now—let's hurry."

I don't remember much about the rest of that day, or those that followed. I do recall Mr. Evans trying to make small talk throughout the ninety-minute drive home.

"How's school going?" he asked. "How's the food? I really want to know."

I'd been annoyed. This was just the way my father had quizzed me when he picked me up from boarding school in the late '60s, but that was different. I'd loved having a father who found even the food I ate the most fascinating subject in the world.

But there was something wrong about Mr. Evans asking me these things. They were my dad's questions.

It never occurred to me, self-absorbed as I was even then, that Mr. Evans was trying to keep his mind off the fact that he'd just lost his best friend.

※

THE FUNERAL WAS held a few days later at the sparkling new Congregational church that my parents had helped build. It was sort of a colonial style, I guess you would say, with all the woodwork painted white and nary a sign of stained glass, not even in the sanctuary. A church for pilgrims, which just happened to be its name: Pilgrim Congregational.

The building looked too bright and cheery for a wake and a funeral. And yet that's exactly what went on there that September day, as my father's body lay in the garden room, in a nook created by the bay window overlooking the newly planted garden. I looked at him again and again in disbelief; I'd never seen a dead body before, and he really did look like he was just sleeping. Except that it was a hot day and there was no air conditioning, and toward the end of the visitation period, the makeup the funeral home had applied to his face seemed to be melting.

⁂

BUT THEN, LIFE itself seemed to be melting away that week, as the mind-numbing denial and shock wore off, leaving me with the absolute certainty that nothing would ever be right again.

From the earthly perspective, it never really was, at least for my mother and me; my sisters were already adults, immersed in their own lives. That left Mom and me alone to battle this horror of life without the man who'd promised to take care of us always.

What exactly are you supposed to do when that fairy tale has ended, when happily ever after is no more? No one had warned me about this.

"Now do you understand how important it is to believe in God?" Mom asked me a few days after the funeral, as she helped pack my things for my return to school.

We were in the big, bay-windowed middle bedroom of the house on Quincy Street, the room that had finally been deeded over to me a few years earlier, when Andy had officially grown up and left home. It was a bright and cheerful room with flowered wallpaper and window seats and bookcases holding everything from a complete set of

Nancy Drews to respectable collections of the Black Stallion and Tom Corbett Space Cadet series.

I didn't respond. It was hardly the time or place to discuss religion, in my opinion; as far as I could see, this God of hers had failed her big-time.

She sighed softly, sat down on the bed, and gazed out the window. I concentrated on arranging my best dress neatly in the red suitcase, one of the set my parents had given me just a few months earlier as a high school graduation gift.

"I'm so sad," she said finally, almost to herself.

Indeed, she looked as though she had been weeping for days, although I hadn't seen much of it; women of her era apparently kept their grief to themselves.

"But I know that your father is in heaven now," she added, returning to the task at hand by folding my favorite pair of Plushbottoms jeans, "and it's better there than anything we could possibly imagine. And I'll be there with him one day. We'll all be with him again."

"I suppose," I said, letting her have her little fairy tale. But in my heart, I refused to buy into it. I knew there was no proof that any of it was truer than what the Brothers Grimm had imagined. After all, science had shown that there didn't even have to *be* a God at all. Hadn't evolution been proven the mechanism that brought everything into being? And if there was no God, there would be no heaven, which meant my dad had probably just plunged into non-existence, which in turn meant that I would never see him again and that life was, in the end, futile.

Thanks to thoughts like these, I didn't handle the aftermath of my father's death any better than I handled the fact of it. I used it as an excuse to turn my back on my hometown boyfriend and friends and just about anyone and anything capable of reminding me that there had even been such a dream of living happily ever after, somewhere out there.

Except Mom, of course; you can hardly leave your mother behind.

※

LIFE GOES ON, we liked to say in those days, and I applied myself to getting right back into it. I returned to college and immersed myself in the oh-so-cool hippie culture that began engulfing American college campuses in the late '60s. I hung out with girls who wore ragged blue jeans and army boots and went without bras or makeup and spent their free time getting high on marijuana or hashish or LSD— girls who talked about philosophy and Vietnam and how, once they'd graduated from this candy store, they were going to open a drug-paraphernalia shop or rent a farm with their "old men" or go on for their masters' degrees and PhDs.

Eager to be a part of the more intellectual hippie set because it seemed to attract the cutest guys, I studied Russian history and art history and read Chekov and Sartre and fancied myself a disciple of Vladimir Lenin (my professors didn't mention petty details like Bolshevik bloodbaths or Stalinist purges). I smoked pot brazenly with my new friends after lunch and dinner, often while sitting outside on the grassy slope above the student union, a slope encircled by a mishmash of lovely nineteenth-century buildings and cold modern structures. We sat and smoked there for any passersby to see, because we could; the school had reportedly declared our campus off-limits to the local cops. On weekends we did more of the same, often dropping LSD and then hitchhiking out into the country to smoke some more and watch the sun set or rise, depending on what time our adventure had begun.

I learned a lot at Ripon. I learned, for instance, that not everyone had grown up in a storybook family like mine. That some kids' parents were divorced and that it was nothing to be ashamed of—that it was, in fact, something to rejoice over, because the missing parent was usually a guilt-ridden ticket to luxuries like an on-campus BMW. I learned that absolutely no one planned to follow in their parents' footsteps except for a couple of kids from Southern California, one with a famous screenwriter for a father, and the other with a mother who was a moderately well-known movie actress.

Every few weeks, I left the cool kids and hallucinogens behind and took a Greyhound home to visit my mother. She did not complain to me, nor did she cry over my dad, that I can recall, but I was devastated nonetheless by what I perceived to be the loss of her entire life. I wanted desperately to comfort her, to make it up to her by moving home and learning to be a good and obedient daughter.

And yet I was terrified at the prospect of doing that, of loving her too much, because then she would surely die too, and I would then be the one left alone. So I headed back to Ripon and smoked more dope and popped more pills and somehow managed to avoid flunking out.

Occasionally, I contemplated my future. The choice seemed clear: be a housewife like my mother, devote my entire life to a husband and kids, and end up alone and awash in sorrow. Or get a job and work my way through an endless series of casual relationships in pursuit of a fun, happy, and pain-free existence.

I was pretty good at hiding my extracurricular activities from my mother. She was far from dumb, but being a child of the 1920s instead of the 1960s, she also was clueless when it came to recreational drinking, drugs, and sex.

The closest I came to getting busted was the summer between my freshman and sophomore years. I'd come home from an LSD-filled long weekend with college friends and slept for twenty-four hours straight. Before crashing, I'd written a letter about our escapades to another girlfriend, signing and sealing it and leaving it on the front-hall table with my mother's outgoing mail, never worrying for a moment that she would be tempted to invade my privacy.

But apparently a little thing like sleeping for twenty-four hours trumps a mother's respect for privacy. She not only opened my letter and read it; when I finally crawled out of bed, she also confronted me with it, almost beside herself with horror and anger, and apparently not in the least embarrassed by her snooping. The letter was pretty bad, filled with careless references to blotter acid and birth-control pills and hitchhiking around central Wisconsin. But I'd already spent years honing my excuse-making skills. I insisted that my letter was a lie, that I'd just been trying to fit in with this crazy girlfriend's crowd by implying that I did these things too. Seeing uncertainty in her eyes, I sealed my victory by bursting into tears.

"How can you even think I'd do anything like that?" I wailed. "How stupid do you think I am?"

"Oh, honey," she said, her rage vanishing as she wrapped her arms around me. "I don't think you're stupid. Just falling in with the wrong crowd, that's all. I just don't want you to ruin your life."

"I won't," I promised, with a young adult's certainty that I was immortal and omniscient, and she was still intent on ruining my good time.

And then she started to cry.

"I don't want to lose you too," she sobbed. "Can't you understand that?"

I didn't really get it. I suspected that if anyone was going to suffer another loss, it would be me.

Still, I cut way back on the drugs and hitchhiking after that episode and quit them entirely, along with Ripon College, at the end of my sophomore year.

Not that I was admitting that there was any real danger in my psychedelic hobbies. But she'd been hurt enough by my dad's death, and I really didn't want to take any chances of adding to her pain.

❧

I DIDN'T WANT to add to my own pain, either. But it seemed as though the entire music industry was conspiring in those days to remind me that life was hopeless and that sorrow would always be the rule. Amid all the bubble-gum ditties and drugged-out rock of the early 1970s were heart-wrenching songs like James Taylor's "Fire and Rain" and Gilbert O'Sullivan's "Alone Again (Naturally)."

And then in 1974, Helen "I Am Woman" Reddy released "You and Me Against the World"—a song in which a mother is apparently telling her daughter that, once one of them has died, it's pretty much over: "Then remembering will have to do, our memories alone will get us through. . . ."

What marketing types now call the "takeaway" was pretty clear: one day death will separate us, and that'll be it—memories only, no hope for an eternal reunion.

I played that song over and over again late into the decade, trying in vain to cry the sorrow out of my system once and for all.

CHAPTER 4

In the beginning:
How I came to be so lost

6:00 p.m., May 30, 2000

*A*s my mother drifted relentlessly toward a bleak, blessed, or nonexistent eternity, I sat at my kitchen table with the morning *Milwaukee Journal-Sentinel.* By the time the grandmother clock in the next room struck six, I'd read just about every article, taken a stab at the crossword puzzle, and scoured the night's TV listings. There was nothing worth watching on TV. Reading a book was out of the question; I knew without trying that I'd be unable to concentrate on anything that couldn't be digested within a matter of minutes.

Threatened with being left alone with my thoughts or sharing them for the thousandth time with Dave, I grabbed another Lite from the old refrigerator in the garage and headed outside with our three dogs. Our cocker, the Beaver, and yellow lab pup, Shadow, ran off to the far corners of our fenced-in yard. My basset hound, Woody, and I planted ourselves in a secluded spot next to the shed, hidden from the world by a stand of mature evergreens and a curtain of self-seeded clematis vines cascading from the branches of a wild cherry.

I sat on a boulder that had once been a carefully chosen and positioned architectural element of my garden but now served solely as a spot for me and Woody to escape. A few late purple tulips were blooming at my feet, but mainly we were surrounded by foliage. Late May had long been a challenging period for me as a gardener—too late for most spring bulbs and, in Wisconsin, at least, too early for summer perennials. But for the first time in years, I didn't care; if the lab pup had decided to dig up my prize roses that evening, I would not have stopped him.

"Hey, old guy," I said, stroking Woody's silky cheek as he snuggled up against my leg. "You won't believe this, but you probably won't be seeing your grandma again."

He didn't seem concerned. Labs lick your face when you're crying, and cockers watch you with eyebrows puckered in worry, but aging bassets respond to just about everything by napping. True to form, Woody snoozed. It crossed my mind that maybe he knew something about death that had escaped me—like maybe he was sure we'd all be together again soon on some distant shore.

The idea was silly but vaguely comforting. I blew my nose—Rhett Butler's final farewell to Scarlett O'Hara had taught me to always carry tissues during times of crisis, so I'd stuffed the pockets of my blue jeans with Kleenex before going to see my mother that day—and determined to look into this afterlife thing just as soon as Mom was gone and I'd recovered from this completely unacceptable heartache.

"I thought losing Thumper was the worst," I told Woody, summoning up an image of the ancient yellow lab who'd been his best friend until we'd put him down the previous May, ending, at last, his valiant battle against cancer. "But that was nothing compared to this."

Thumper had been my mom's favorite, the only one of our animals that never tried to jump into her wheelchair with her, the one who would instead rest his head in her lap and gaze up at her adoringly whenever she came to visit. Wondering if she'd possibly be seeing him again soon, I remembered our conversation the day I called her to announce that we'd just had him put to sleep.

"Dear Old Gentleman," she'd said sadly. "But at least he won't be in any more pain. And who knows? He's probably already with God in heaven, waiting for you."

I would realize later that she'd once again been trying to sweeten the God pot for me, giving me another good reason to turn to Him. But at the time all it did was unleash my tears once again.

"My goodness," she continued, when I said between sobs that I'd have to call her back. "I hope you're this upset when I die."

As I sat on my boulder, petting Woody and replaying her words in my head, I thought: *You got your wish, Mom. And then some.*

And then it hit me: maybe she'd known exactly how I'd feel. Maybe she'd really been saying, "Just wait—when I'm dead and gone, you'll be sorry you didn't spend more time with me." Whereupon I finally allowed my anger to kick in, barely stifling the words I'd longed to scream at her that afternoon: HOW DARE YOU LEAVE ME?

TRY AS WE might to ascribe human emotions to our pets, they simply don't understand anger or abandonment or grief. At 6:15, the dogs reminded me loudly that it was long past their suppertime. I dragged myself inside to feed them and asked Dave if there'd been any calls.

"None," he said, looking up from his paperback, some thriller he'd be putting on my "to read" stack in a matter of minutes.

I thought it odd that there had been no word from the nursing home, after the flurry of morning calls that had come into the spare bedroom I use for my freelance copywriting business. It seemed like every time I picked up the phone, there was a nurse on the other end, delivering dire news.

RN Mary had called at 8:45 a.m., for instance—the time neatly recorded in my phone log for the day, along with her key words—to report that my mother was now unresponsive.

"Her skin is turning dusky and bluish," Mary said matter-of-factly.

"What does that mean?" I asked, not really wanting to know.

"It indicates a lack of circulation," she said. "Your mother's heart is beginning to shut down."

"Oh," I said.

"She's almost in a coma."

"Oh."

To this day, I can remember what it felt like, hearing these things. No chills ran up my spine; instead, I felt again the same waves of terror that had washed through me thirty years earlier, when Mr. Evans announced that my father was dead. Relentless waves, starting in the depths of my bowels and racing up my throat and into my sinuses to sting my eyes. Over and over again.

By 11:00 a.m., the nurses' calls had come to an abrupt stop. I continued answering the phone instead of letting voice mail pick up, but for most of the day, the only calls that came in were about business. My #1 client called from Florida to discuss corrections to a news release. A graphic artist phoned to tell me which of several direct-mail concepts he had selected and to ask me to e-mail him the copy ASAP. Another client called to talk over a new project, an operator's manual for his company's flagship product, with the only catch being that he needed the text in a month.

Through it all, I didn't mention my mother. I couldn't. Apparently I sounded normal, because no one asked me if anything was wrong.

Then I actually did some work. As my mother lay dying in a nursing home just a couple of miles away, I corrected the news release. Wrote the direct-mail piece. Drafted an article on the perinatology applications of a breakthrough ultrasound system.

At 3:02 p.m., a nurse named Cathy called to update me.

"Your mother's blood pressure is down to 86 over 54," she said.

The numbers were meaningless to me, but from her tone of voice, I knew this wasn't a good sign.

"It won't be too much longer, Kitty," she added, perhaps to encourage me to rush to my mother's bedside. It was an impossible thought: How could I sit there and watch her die? How could people *bear* watching a loved one die?

It must have been after that conversation that I found out about the last rites deal.

It seemed important that I be there for this ritual, although I didn't know what it entailed; I didn't think Congregationalists went in for stuff like that. I found Dave puttering in the garage and told him about these plans. He had been raised Roman Catholic, so he understood the significance of that ghastly phrase.

We'd climbed into his pickup truck and headed over to the home.

⁂

AND NOW HERE I was, several hours later, update-free. The shape of things to come.

That night Dave took over for me, feeding the dogs as well as our two cats. He also offered to feed me—ordinarily an invitation I jump at, since he's a great cook. But not that night. Instead, I popped open another beer, pulled a box of sourdough pretzels out of the cupboard, and sat down at the kitchen table once again.

"Try this," he said, placing in front of me a stack of untouched issues of the *Conservative Chronicle*. I hadn't been able to concentrate on politics lately, my mother's illness having driven my long-held libertarian ideology down to a distant second in my heart. My *Chronicles* were piling up.

I picked up the issue on top of the stack and looked up Linda Bowles, my favorite of the dozens of writers featured each week. She delivered an immediate and powerful fix. Her column was about life after the Clintons, one of my favorite topics. She entertained me for a good five minutes or more with lines like "Proud men and women who would never be a slave to another person are conditioned to willingly put their heads in the yoke and become a slave to Big Government" and "history may record that the legacy of the Clinton presidency was that its classic wretchedness awakened the American people from a soul-numbing moral stupor.

"The Lord moves in mysterious ways."[1]

The Lord.

Somehow those words didn't bother me the way they once had. Although it was hardly the first time I'd noticed this phenomenon, it still shocked me a little. I couldn't explain it, except to suppose that I'd been reading the columns of conservatives like Linda Bowles and constitutional lawyer Phyllis Schlafly for so long that their stances were beginning to make sense.

Or maybe they were simply brainwashing me. When it came to social issues, after all, they were big-time traitors to our gender. If they hadn't so brilliantly and consistently displayed intelligence in economic affairs, I would have simply shrugged them off as chicky fluffs.

But their essays *were* brilliant, and so, increasingly, their ideas about everything else were gaining credibility in my eyes. Even the stuff about the Lord.

Nope—no chicky fluffdom here.

※

I DON'T THINK I ever thought of my mom as a chicky fluff, exactly. True, she'd never had a real job; and, true, she'd never been interested in having one. But in my mind, a real chicky fluff lacked not only the desire but also the ability to earn her own living; and I always figured my mother was smart enough to have brought home the bacon if it had ever become necessary.

Still, once my feminist consciousness had been raised and then ratcheted up in the mid-1970s, most of the values my mom had instilled in me went undercover, leaving in their wake only a self-righteous and conspicuous commitment to honesty and charity. The rest of my newfound ethical system kept us from being on the same wavelength for the last quarter century of our lives together.

I'd been plenty rebellious and wild as a teenager. But the real schism between us occurred when I, in my early twenties, stumbled across a book that would set the direction for most of my adult life: Betty Friedan's *The Feminine Mystique.* It was the late autumn of 1974, not long after I'd enrolled in journalism school at the University of Wisconsin–Milwaukee and moved into my studio apartment on Milwaukee's hippie-esque East Side. I can still hear the radiators hissing mightily against the chill seeping through the drafty windows that lined the north wall of the place. I'd set aside my college texts long enough to crack open Betty's book, which I'd picked up that afternoon at a musty used bookstore.

I don't know that I'd ever heard of Betty or her book before that day. The title piqued my curiosity, I suppose, and then the title of the opening chapter—"The Problem That Has No Name"—must have reeled me in.

But it was probably Betty's opening line that persuaded me to risk the dime the shopkeeper wanted for the book: "The problem lay buried, unspoken, for many years in the minds of American women. It was a strange stirring, a sense of dissatisfaction, a yearning that women suffered in the middle of the twentieth century . . ."[2]

Yearning? I could certainly identify with that. Buried in the minds of American women? So it wasn't just me? Suffering? Yes, of course I was suffering!

And so it was that I'd settled back on my beautiful red sofa bed—a gift from my mother, and just about the only new item in my apartment—lit a cigarette, and started learning about this strange new worldview that would soon become my own:

> If I am right, the problem that has no name stirring in the minds of so many American women today is not a matter of loss of femininity or too much education, or the demands of domesticity. . . . It is the key to these other new and old problems which have been torturing women and their husbands and children, and puzzling their doctors and educators for years. . . . We can no longer ignore that voice within women that says: "I want something more than my husband and my children and my home."[3]

To this day, I believe Betty was right about one thing: we women *do* need more than husband and children and home. The only problem, I now know, was that she couldn't have been more wrong about what that something was. It was not, as she insisted, a career and income of one's own.

Alas, it took me more than a quarter century to learn that the most dangerous lies are those that contain a healthy dose of truth. But that day in 1974, I happily embraced the values Betty espoused—and learned shortly thereafter, to my delight, that my professors, classmates, and new big-city friends seemed to share them too.

And so I danced into adulthood, quite sure that making myself perfectly successful and, therefore, perfectly happy was the only goal worth pursuing. The only goal worth even thinking about, in fact.

This point of view worked almost perfectly for me for close to twenty-six years. But it took just one terminally ill little old lady to blow it all to kingdom come.

CHAPTER 5

Professing to be wise:
A life worth the living

6:30 p.m., May 30, 2000

I smoked and sipped beer and straightened out the newspapers on the kitchen table. That made me think about the mess of papers in my mother's room—papers I'd have to go through once it was all over. There was a ton of junk, direct-mail pieces and magazines and catalogues she'd never gotten around to ordering from. But there were some good things, too, including articles and poems she'd written in the sixty-some-years since she'd graduated from the University of Wisconsin with her journalism degree.

Except for a poem or two, she'd never had much of anything published, though she'd sent out plenty of query letters and verses and collected plenty of rejections. She'd shown the rejections to me a few years ago, having found a slew of them tucked away in an old vinyl briefcase embossed with my dad's name. The few that were personalized were kind, suggesting that there were magazines that would welcome her work—just not theirs.

I wondered if she'd thought about those rejections in her last coherent moments, if she'd regretted having put most of her energy into us rather than what might have been a fruitful writing career.

But maybe she'd managed to get vicarious satisfaction from Carrie and me, who'd actually become professional writers. She seemed to have been proud of us, anyway. Between the two of us, we'd written scores of corporate brochures and video scripts and white papers, and we'd been paid well for our efforts, and she had always shown tremendous interest in the latest example of our work, even if it *was* about cattle auctions or health insurance or barium enemas.

What's more, I had actually broken into the realm of fiction by winning a local contest with a medical thriller called *The Cure*. Even though it carried the endorsement of final judge Sue Grafton, the published book had been an astounding failure in the few stores that carried it. Only 150 copies were sold, two-thirds of them to people I knew; but it was dedicated to my mom, and she had bragged it up to everyone who would listen, and later, when the going-out-of-business publisher gave me the 350 leftover volumes, she'd sent copies to everyone she knew.

Still, neither Carrie nor I had shown any signs of becoming wildly successful journalists or novelists or poets. And so I wondered: Did my mom get enough vicarious pride from our reams of corporate copy and one sad little thriller to make up for the fact that her career had never taken off?

Hope as I might, the answer had to be negative.

I vowed to start another novel just as soon as she was gone and I'd figured out what was what in the cosmic scheme of things. I didn't want to wind up with nothing to show for *my* life.

✳

MY 1974 READING of *The Feminine Mystique* opened up a whole new world of possibilities and pleasures for me. I was soon spending much of my free time reading the philosophers who were emerging to promote this new way of looking at womankind.

There was Shulamith *The Dialectic of Sex* Firestone, the feminist who called for the abolition of family and parenthood.

There was Germaine *The Female Eunuch* Greer, who diagnosed our problem as being sexually repressed.

There was Marilyn French, whose novel *The Women's Room* would for years top my list of favorite books because it proved that smart women look to themselves, not men, for happiness.

And there was Gloria Steinem, who taught me that women had an inalienable right to reproductive freedom—including, naturally, the then-new and already sacred right to abortion.

With instructors of this caliber, it didn't take me long to make the most important aspects of radical feminism my own—all the me-centered principles that made *my* ambitions, *my* feelings, *my* intellect, and *my* freedom my number one priorities. I wrote A+ papers blasting the beauty-obsessed women's magazines of the day. I bashed marriage and married people and supported organizations defending the *Roe v. Wade* abortion-rights decision. I looked forward to the day when we women could be freed forever from the fear and burden of pregnancy without having to pop pills or submit to surgery.

But somehow the perfect feminist mind-set eluded me. I could point to a lot of causes—a great Econ 101 professor who transformed me overnight from a McGovern-era socialist into a Barry Goldwater conservative, an aversion to being seen without mascara, and a persistent obsession with men, to cite just a few examples.

But the main thing that kept me from being totally absorbed by radical feminism was my reluctant admiration for my mother and the life she led. This was something I didn't acknowledge to my friends, of course: How could I admit to admiring a woman who'd been perfectly content to raise children and let her husband take care of her? How could I do anything but scoff at her?

I kept these thoughts to myself most of the time. During my frequent weekend visits to Green Bay, I simply burrowed into the warmth of being home with her again—even though home, after my father's death, was no longer the big old house on Quincy Street, but cheesy newer rental units on the other side of town, closer to her church.

And there was more. She and I continued spending all our holidays together, with the rest of the family popping in as time allowed. We talked frequently and at length via long-distance, not an inexpensive proposition in those predigital, precellular days. We even took several glorious low-budget trips to Europe together.

Somehow I managed to set my feminist principles aside during these interludes. But the story was different when she drove down to Milwaukee to visit me "for a few days." That meant staying with me in my studio apartment, sleeping on that beautiful sofa bed she'd bought for me, just six feet from my own bed. And it meant that I invariably turned into a total shrew within hours of her arrival.

"How about we go to the zoo the weekend after next?" she would ask cheerfully as we headed downtown for a little shopping a day or two into her visit. She was apparently oblivious to the fact that I might have some sort of social life to attend to before then.

"We'll see," I would say, my grip tightening on the steering wheel of my brand-new Audi 100LS—a purchase made possible by a small inheritance from my father, and my mother's willingness to let me blow it on something so lavish, simply because I convinced her he would've wanted me to have a car that was as much a German immigrant as he had been.

"So," she would say after a while, trying to make conversation, "your sister Andy is doing very well. That husband of hers is so crazy about her—he still calls her his little bride."

I would be silent, but the implied comparison of our relative abilities to attract worthy men—subtle though it was, I heard it!—demanded a response.

"Andy," I would respond with a heavy sigh and a good heavenward roll of the eyes, "is a housewife." Never mind that she had her master's degree in German and also spoke French and Italian fluently. Her current occupation made her an airhead in my Betty-built book.

"There are worse things," my mother would reply, sighing at the obvious slam on her own life, or maybe at my undisguised hostility for just about anything she seemed to say during her Milwaukee visits. She would then sit in hurt silence, making us both uncomfortable. Whereupon I would vacillate between feeling guilty and feeling peeved that her apparently open-ended visit was keeping me from going out with my friends. Feeling peeved usually won out; guilt is such an unpleasant emotion, and feminists of that day refused to entertain it.

"I'm not going to waste *my* life like that," I would add.

"You'll meet a nice young man," she would say kindly.

"A woman without a man is like a fish without a bicycle," I would snap, knowing that whoever my current squeeze was, he probably wouldn't fall into her "nice young man" category. This sort of comment usually left her speechless.

But then I would start feeling bad about my surliness and would try to make up for it. "Besides," I would say, "they don't make them like Dad anymore. You got the last one."

I always meant that. And I didn't think that she was like a fish who'd once had a nice bicycle. In fact, I thought she'd had the best life in the world until my father died. And even though I hated being stuck with a widowed mother night after night when friends were waiting at some great bar just minutes away, I loved her more than anyone in the world.

But I couldn't admit this, not even to myself; feminists of my era were very proud of their boundless independence. We reserved our love (or what we thought of as love, anyway) for men who were unobtainable for one reason or another—men who would never threaten our independence, which we thought of as *hard-won* and *precious*.

"You're right," my mother would agree, certain that there was not in all the world another man like my father. "And you really need to marry someone who's capable of taking care of you. Every woman needs a man like that."

In those days, I would sneer silently at a comment like that, longing for a way to escape this reactionary thinking (if indeed such ideas deserved to be called "thinking"). She would then drop the subject with a sad sigh, and I would drive on just a little bit more recklessly, thinking about what my friends would be doing that night while I spent yet another lifeless evening playing gin rummy with my aging mother.

⁂

SO WE HAD our squabbles, my mother and I—my fault, I now admit, the result of my anger and impatience and unrelenting self-centeredness. But we had good times, too, even after she moved down to Milwaukee in the summer of 1990 and, within a matter of months, into a nursing home not far from our house.

With no long-distance charges to consider, we began talking daily, jabbering about anything, lingering especially over the good old days in Green Bay, when I was a child and she wasn't a widow, when we both thought we had all we could ever want on Quincy Street.

One of my favorite conversations involved touring our old house together in our minds.

"Window seats," my mother would say. "Whoever designed that house stuck them wherever he could, as if he knew a worried mother would one day spend her nights waiting up for her wayward daughter."

"Yes," I'd laugh. "My favorite one was the one in the front hall downstairs, next to the closet. Do you remember the little ring handles on the tops?"

"Yes! And when you pulled them open, you were overwhelmed by the smell of rubber," she would say, immediately reminding me of the boots we stored there, not only Dad's plain black galoshes but also high-fashion winter boots with fake-fur cuffs that you'd slip on over your shoes.

We liked to talk about everything in that house, down to the doors.

"The back door, Mom, remember that funny lock?"

"I do—you just pushed a little button, and the deadbolt would slam closed."

"Remember how the door squeaked? When Dad had a late meeting, I used to wait all night to hear the back door squeaking, and when it finally did, I'd know all was right with the world."

"And you would run to hug him hello."

"And he always smelled so good. He smelled like the night air."

"The front closet door squeaked, too, remember? And remember its big mirror?"

We could go on for hours like that, going through each room and lingering over its contents, laughing and longing for those golden days, the happy life that no one else could possibly understand.

But we didn't spend all our time in the past. We talked about current events and our current lives too. I presented her with my problems, and she gave me solutions that actually worked (or would have, had I listened to her). In return, she presented me with her problems, which I didn't find nearly as interesting. I usually advised her to be sunnier with the nurses' aides and realize they had tough lives themselves. Very helpful, I'm sure.

By then, I'd moved a bit beyond my libertarian-laced feminism. Maybe I was mellowing with age, having passed the forty-year mark. Or maybe the success of my freelance writing business had given me the confidence to be politically incorrect, and therefore forgiving of women who'd chosen another path—even trite, housewifely paths. I no longer sneered at the sentiments that had allowed my mom to write such old-fashioned poems as this:

Kitty Foth-Regner

Legacy
My grandma was little,
Demure and blue-eyed,
She left me a message
The day that she died.

"To my only grandchild —
To lead a good life,
You must be a lady,
You should be a wife.

"Be quick to request
But slow to command.
Wear your heart on your sleeve
and gloves on your hand.

"Two things you must have
But hide well," she wrote.
"A brain that is swift
And a starched petticoat."

And when I met you,
The world sang with the birds.
T'was then I remembered
My grandmother's words.
And it worked! She was right!
My grandmother knew!
I did as she said,
And I'm married to you!

—Ethel Boehm Foth

In fact, I'd even grown to find Mom's story of how she'd snared my father through subterfuge as charming as my friends did.

"Tell me again how you met your husband," someone would ask.

"Again?" she would say, smiling at both the request and the memories it stirred. "Well, okay. I was a student at the University of Wisconsin," she would begin, her entire face softening as she returned, for a brief moment, to Madison and that lovely time when happily ever after seemed almost within reach. "This was in the early 1930s, and we didn't have any money. It was the Lord who made it possible for this hick from Wausau to graduate from the University . . ."

By the '90s not even such nagging public-service announcements for God bothered me much.

"Herbert was fresh off the boat from Germany, and I heard him speak at an International Club meeting. That was it: I knew immediately that he was the one for me. He was a soccer player—they'd brought it with them from Germany—and so I offered to cover it for the school newspaper. Whereupon he offered to teach me all about it!"

My girlfriends loved this story. So, I must admit, did I.

I'm sure that the leaders of feminist thought would've disapproved. But I couldn't view Mom with purely feminist eyes; I was, in the end, a daughter long before Betty Friedan had put her ideas in my head. And my mother had done what Betty had not: she'd nabbed my perfect father, and together they'd built the kind of Ward and June Cleaver life that so many people strive for and then, falling short, dismiss as petty bourgeois.

The only problem was that it had all come to an end. Which was perhaps the real reason I had embraced feminist thought to begin with. After all, if utopia can be snatched away overnight, then living for one's own happiness and pleasure is the only sensible way to go.

BUT IN MAY of 2000, as my mother lay dying, Betty & Company were certainly proving useless to me. Of course, I couldn't see that this theoretical God was doing anything to comfort me, either. Here I was, with instant access to husband, family, friends, and a houseful of adoring pets, and I'd never felt so alone in my life.

The fact that such pain occurred at all had long been one of my more potent arguments against the existence of God. After all, He was supposed to be all-loving, wasn't He? And all-powerful? Well, 'splain that one, then: Why did He allow suffering in this world? How could He have taken my father away from my mother? And how could He even *think* about taking my mother away from me?

It would take me months to learn, and comprehend, that there was a lot more to this God than love and power, and that His plans for us were a bit more complex than keeping us fat and happy.

A few weeks later, I came across an observation that provided at least a partial answer to these questions. I wish I could remember who made it, but maybe it's an idea almost as old as time itself:

We can only see the stars at night. They're there during the day, when the sun bathes our world with light. But we can't see them until the sun slips away, plunging us into darkness.

This idea went right over my head when I first encountered it.

But I get it now. Because it suggests that we can see the extent of God's glory only when we're going through dark times. That, in fact, the darker our nights, the brighter His glory shines.

People say that the Bible, which describes this God, is full of contradictions. I would eventually learn that this isn't true, that there are, in fact, no contradictions that can't be explained, just paradoxes that serve to confuse before they illuminate: To live, we must die. To be the most, we must be the least. To have all, we must give all away.

And to get our first real glimpse of His incredible love, some of us have to be lost in blinding darkness.

CHAPTER 6

The whole creation groans:
But let's pretend everything's okay

7:00 p.m., May 30, 2000

S till no word from the nursing home. I popped open another beer and smoked a few more cigarettes and wondered if things could've worked out differently if we had made different medical decisions over the past decade.

In the mid '90s, my mother had undergone surgery for colorectal cancer. The surgeon said he thought he'd gotten it all, but naturally couldn't make any guarantees, especially since she had refused chemotherapy. It was a worrisome time, to be sure, but she came through it with flying colors, and a couple of follow-up colonoscopies had shown her to be cancer-free. By the time the decade was drawing to a close, I'd almost forgotten about it; she'd been undergoing a series of hospitalizations for other health problems, from "adverse drug events" to hip and leg fractures, and we were focused on helping her get through these episodes.

In April of 2000, she landed once again in nearby Elmbrook Memorial Hospital, this time with pneumonia. I didn't freak out—I was confident that she would pull through once again. This hospitalization was odd only in that they were keeping her an awfully long time. The days melted into weeks, and we ended up celebrating Mother's Day in her stark room on Elmbrook's fifth floor. Still, I simply continued my policy of visiting her daily when she was hospitalized—it was impossible to leave her all alone in a room containing nothing that couldn't be sterilized—and tried not to lose any sleep over the length of her stay.

Except, as it turned out, this time *was* different.

It was toward the end of the third week in May when the girl at the nurses' station stopped me on my way out of her room to say that my mother's surgeon wanted to talk to me. Not even aware that a surgeon was involved in her case, and experiencing once again what I'd felt back in the dean's office thirty years earlier, I sat at a tiny table in a tiny conference room and tried not to cry.

The surgeon, a fellow about my age, swept in, sat down, and got right to the point.

"Your mother's cancer is back," he said, staring intently at the report he'd brought in. "It's inoperable," he added.

I was stunned. I knew she would refuse chemo and radiation, just as she had the first time around. If it was inoperable, then—

"How long does she have?" I asked.

"No one can really say," he replied, still studying his report.

"Come on," I said. "You can give me some idea."

"Six months to two years, maybe."

That wasn't so bad, then. With that much time, I could talk her into chemo. Besides, this surgeon didn't know what he was talking about. This was no ordinary woman; this was Ethel Boehm Foth, and there was no way she was going to leave me!

⁂

JUST TEN DAYS later, on May 29th, my mother and I had what would turn out to be our last conversation.

Our moods were fairly lighthearted. After a month in the hospital, she seemed happy to be back at the nursing home. Hers was a big, bright, private room with pink-flowered wallpaper and pictures of her three girls on the wall, and clutter everywhere. The nurses kept telling me to get rid of some of it before the fire inspector closed her room down, but after initially agreeing to some pruning, she would invariably refuse to part with much more than the junk mail.

But now she was smiling once again, and I was overjoyed to see her looking so chipper. Even though she was confined to her bed, she was wearing one of her prettiest floral nightgowns, someone had fluffed up her white curls, and she'd actually put on some lipstick. She looked like Mom again.

As far as I knew at that time, she was aware of neither diagnosis nor prognosis. I certainly hadn't told her what the surgeon had said. I don't know if he told her. I had asked him not to—a rotten request, I now understand, but at the time I just didn't want her to be terrified, which in my mind was the only logical response to a death sentence.

I would later learn that she was well aware of everything. She had left an audiotape, recorded a day or two before this last conversation of ours, on which she had told everyone good-bye and I love you.

But I didn't know this during that last conversation, and so I acted happy and carefree. Which wasn't all that hard, since she'd been given an injection of some kind just before I got there and was getting goofier by the minute.

She wanted to watch a movie on her "VRC" (as long as she'd owned one, she never *had* been able to get its acronym straight). And not just any movie: it had to be *The African Queen*. I set the tape up and continued chatting with her a while. Finally I rose and said I had to get back to work. She just smiled.

"I love you, Mom," I said, kissing her casually on the forehead, just as I had been doing for years.

"I love you too. Start the movie."

"Okay. I'll talk to you tonight, okay?"

"Start the movie."

⁂

THAT NIGHT, I let Mom's phone ring at least two dozen times before giving up and calling the nurses' station.

The nurse who answered put me on hold long enough to run and check on her. She was resting comfortably, the nurse said. Was there anything else she could do for me?

"Would you hold the phone next to her ear so I can talk to her?"

A heavy sigh. Clearly, my call was a great inconvenience for her.

"I really don't think that would be useful," she said. "She's resting."

It is a testament to how frightened I was that I accepted this rebuff, that I didn't let this uncooperative nurse have it with both barrels—something I'd never hesitated to do when I thought we were being treated like anything less than paying customers.

⁂

AND NOW, TWENTY-FOUR hours later, as I sat smoking and drinking and replaying these events in my head, hound-dog Woody shook me from my reverie with a loud snore.

It was 7:09. I was still sitting at my kitchen table. And my mom was still dying. At least, no one had called to tell me otherwise.

I could hear the TV playing in the living room, faintly; our house is compact enough that I should've been able to make out the program that Dave had on, but I could only hear some sort of music that was heavy on the violins. It made me queasy, like I used to feel as a not-really-sick third grader who'd stayed home because the itinerant music teacher, Mrs. Graf, was coming in that day to make us sing alone in front of our classmates. By 3:30, when the theme song from my Granny's favorite soap opera could be heard drifting out from her bedroom, I'd be awash in regret at being unable to go outside to play, and fear over having to return to school the next day, and guilt over the lie that was separating me from those I loved, at least for today.

I felt sick. Sick enough to realize it was time to quit wondering and take some action. I had to know if there was any validity to my mother's idea—my entire family's, really—that she would soon wake up in a heaven of some sort. Whether it was a Christian, New Age, Buddhist, or Muslim heaven really didn't matter to me. I just wanted to know if she'd be someplace where I'd be able to find her again one day.

For the first time in my adult life, I was acknowledging the possibility that the truth about our ultimate and final destinations *might* be knowable—perhaps as knowable (and conceivably even as delightful) as any destination on earth.

CHAPTER 7

Where you go, I will go:
Just leave me the directions

7:15 p.m., May 30, 2000

*A*s the grandmother clock struck the quarter hour, I realized with a wave of panic that I couldn't picture my mother's face—she was already slipping away from me forever.

I pulled my ratty old red photo album off the bookshelf in the corner of the kitchen and flipped madly through its yellowing pages.

Ah, there they were, my favorite pictures of her, taken back in the '70s during our first trip to Europe together without my father. There she was, on our Rhine cruise, perched on a table on the boat's outside deck, a red bandana tied around her gray curls, a crazy grin on her face. And there she was, posing next to a bronze statue of a warthog in Frankfurt, laughing at some long-forgotten joke. And here, a shot of us in our wash-and-wear travel knits, examining a German songbook.

And there were others, each one a bittersweet reminder of how much fun we had had even after I'd welcomed Betty Friedan and *The Feminine Mystique* into my life.

IT WAS A Saturday in July 1975, and Mom and I were in her rented town house in Green Bay, planning our first big solo adventure.

"I vote for 'Europe Slow and Easy,'" she said, as she ignited the gas fireplace in the corner of her living room. It was a cozy room with olive green shag carpeting and a slash of rustic gray siding on the fireplace, a room stuffed with the best of her Quincy Street furniture.

She returned to her favorite red velvet chair and grinned at me. Behind her were floor-to-ceiling bookcases that she'd had built to hold her favorite books, those she couldn't bear to part with when Quincy Street had been put up for sale. There was nothing scholarly; she liked historical romances and mysteries, especially Agatha Christie, and suspense by women like Daphne du Maurier, Phyllis Whitney, and Helen MacInnes. In fact, this trip of ours had been inspired by our recent reading of MacInnes's *The Salzburg Connection*.

"Sure 'slow and easy' will be exciting enough for you?" I asked, teasingly. We had been up late the night before, poring over glossy brochures on escorted European vacations, too cowardly to make this first journey of ours without benefit of a tour guide at least as expert as my dad had been. We'd finally given up at 1 a.m., deciding only to postpone our decision until morning. "Does that one go to Salzburg? It won't be much of an adventure if it doesn't."

"Definitely," she said, flashing the full-color map in the Caravan brochure my way. "And it's the only one that uses trains instead of buses, remember. How can you have an adventure if you travel by bus?"

"Okay, that's it, then," I said. "So—a couple weeks on this tour. Then what?" I leaned back on her Chippendale-style couch in preparation for another butterfly-inducing discussion of potential destinations. We had already determined that our airfares would be lowest if we stayed at least twenty-one days; as a public-relations secretary/writer for a tiny agency, I had to watch my pennies, even in an era when favorable exchange rates made Europe cheap for Americans. "Budapest? Leningrad?"

"Siegen," she said. "Let's go to Siegen."

THREE MONTHS LATER, having completed an enchanting (but hardly "slow and easy") two-week Caravan tour of cities from London and Munich to Salzburg and Venice, my mother and I huddled together in the otherwise empty compartment of a TEE train racing east out of Paris.

Our destination was Siegen, Germany, eighty miles northwest of Frankfurt. My dad's childhood friend Waldemar had settled there after the war; he would be waiting for us at the depot to bring us home to his family for the last seven days of our vacation.

We were in full-blown panic.

"What were we thinking?" my mother wailed. "How could we even *imagine* spending a whole week with people we barely know? They can't possibly be happy about our moving in with them for that long!"

True to form, I was less concerned about them than I was about us. I summoned up the worst-case scenario: "What if *we* can't stand *them*?" I demanded. "What if we're *bored*?"

When the train pulled into Siegen, we dragged ourselves to the baggage rack, slowly collected our things and hesitated atop the TEE train's stairwell, peering out onto the platform with trepidation.

Whereupon we saw Waldemar beaming up at us; Waldemar with his beautiful blonde wife, both of them beaming up at us as though our arrival had made their lives complete.

We knew instantly that we were home at last.

I THOUGHT OF that perfect week now, as I waited for the nursing home to call me with news of my mother's death. I remembered our fears on the TEE train and the joy that had washed over us as we let our friends' boundless hospitality send those fears fleeing. And I remembered that, for one week at least, as we basked in their love and listened to Waldemar speak in his Daddy-esque German/British accent about their childhoods in Pomerania, we had the feeling that all was right with the world once again.

After that first visit, Mom and I returned to Germany twice more. And our friends had in turn visited us in Wisconsin.

At first, we corresponded with them regularly. But then time and distance and the distractions of real life got in the way, and as the years rolled on, we were in touch less and less frequently. By May of 2000, I think it had been a decade since we'd heard from these precious people.

And now my mother was dying and, if he was still alive, Waldemar would be in his nineties.

I really couldn't bear the thought of hearing the end of this story. It would no doubt prove once and for all that happily ever after really is wishful thinking, even in Siegen.

At least in this life.

Sitting at my kitchen table that night in May of 2000, my heart aching for those beautiful days, I was beginning to understand that this hypothetical heaven was truly my only hope. And I admit it: I wanted Christianity to be true because it pointed to the heaven that so many in my world already claimed as their own. It no longer mattered that if they were right, it would mean living for eternity with the God who had spent decades trying to ruin my good time. All that mattered now was getting to the truth just as quickly as possible.

IT DIDN'T HURT that, just a few days ago, I'd received what felt like a supernaturally inspired nudge from my thirty-something niece Jenny, who was some sort of weird Christian—one of those Bible-thumping holy rollers, I'd heard.

Jenny and I were sitting at my kitchen table, and I'd let my guard down in the face of her quiet compassion.

"I just don't want her to be afraid," I said tearfully.

Jenny looked at me, genuine surprise on her beautiful and supremely peaceful countenance.

"Oh, but, Kitty," she said, "it's going to be so wonderful!"

Her assurance stunned me. I immediately envied her. I wanted to feel that way—to be so sure.

Then a few hours later, hovering near my mother's bed, I was aimlessly straightening out the papers and books on her bedside table when I noticed her old white Bible. I opened its fragile cover and read what she'd written inside, penciled in her tailored hand:

"Jesus Christ is the light of my life and I see my way clearly."

It's not like this was the only thing she'd written on the book's flimsy flyleaves; there was a quote about death, a lengthy one, penned in bold blue ink, along with notations like Romans 5 and 15:4 and Mat 4:6 and 1 Cor 2:9. But it was this Jesus line that leaped out at me that day.

Jesus. One of my favorite expletives, truth be told. Sometimes delivered with what I figured to be His last name, Christ. "Blasphemy" was not in my vocabulary in those days.

At first I felt like I had stumbled across something intensely personal in someone's diary. My *mother's* diary, for Pete's sake. But later, when I thought about it, I decided that she'd written it there with the intention of someone reading it. Maybe even me.

And—I now actually *wanted* to admit to this possibility—maybe they all really *did* know something that I had somehow overlooked. I dreaded the thought of acknowledging that I'd been wrong about this single most important issue of human existence, but I figured it would be worth it if I could only get myself on a path that would one day reunite us forever.

⚘

IT'S TOUGH TO believe in Santa Claus once a sibling or friend has blown his cover. It's equally tough to believe in a supreme being in a culture that has, at best, shrugged off His existence—and at worst portrays Christians as weak-minded or psychopathic.

I'd seen the original 1962 *Cape Fear,* starring Robert Mitchum, and its 1991 remake with Robert De Niro. Somehow, between 1962 and 1991, the Max Cady character that these two actors played had been transformed from a plain old bad guy into a religious monster who spoke in tongues and whose car advertised a bumper-sticker theology. Repeated at every turn, the message of pop-culture vehicles like this was clear: go to church if you must, but don't go nuts over it, and for goodness' sake, don't even think about trying to force your views on anyone else.

By the 1990s it had, in fact, become rude to talk about religion in a positive or exclusive light. You could discuss your sex life—were encouraged to do so, in fact—but to mention the Christian God was to brand yourself a sexist, racist homophobe with the IQ of a chipmunk. And the situation isn't getting any better. One organization studied prime-time TV and its treatment of religion between September of 2003 and 2004; nearly nine out of ten references to religion were negative.[1] No wonder agnostics seeking the ultimate truths of life have trouble finding them; popular culture has rendered those truths too shameful to mention.

I like to think that it was such cultural restraints that had prevented me from seeing any evidence for the existence of the

Christian God (or any other god, for that matter)—that it was Hollywood's fault, or the news media's. But in truth I had not ever bothered looking for any such evidence; I had been way too busy making money and having fun to waste my time on anything as unknowable, and potentially inhibiting, as religion.

But now, here we were, at a crossroads. My mother was about to set off down this unknown road without me. And I would be left standing alone, faced with the decision of a lifetime.

There was no contest. I was all set to trot along after her just as soon as I could get myself packed.

Assuming, of course, that I could verify both the route and the destination.

CHAPTER 8

**Be not afraid, only believe:
At first, it's a lot to swallow**

7:30 p.m., May 30, 2000

The silence continued. It was making me crazy, but there wasn't much I could do about it. There wasn't anyone I felt like talking to except Mom, and she was in no shape to listen.

I looked outside: Darkness wouldn't descend for another hour or so. I decided to try a little weeding, always great therapy for high-stress workdays. I grabbed my favorite Packer jacket and headed out to the front yard.

Our house sits maybe thirty feet above and seventy-five feet back from the road, and I'd planted the south-facing slope between the two with all kinds of plants. There was more in bloom out here than in back: my neon-blue *brunnera* had seeded itself all over the place, dainty white anemones carpeted the soil beneath two ancient spruces, my pagoda dogwoods were wearing their modest pale yellow flowers, and the Korean spice viburnum at the front door was washing the garden in heavenly perfume.

Ordinarily, I loved this time of year, with the garden on relentless upswing and the weeds obvious only to the gardener who knew precisely what she had, and had not, planted in previous years.

I dropped to my knees beneath the Camperdown elm at the top

50

of the slope and started pulling young dandelions with my bare hands; a veteran of the weed wars, I didn't need a fork to make clean extractions this early in the season.

But while weeding was a great antidote to nearly every other kind of unhappiness, it didn't seem to help sorrow. After just a few minutes of plundering the cold, wet earth, I retreated to the crumbling flagstone retaining wall fronting the house.

It was a nice perch; I could watch the people passing by on the street below, most of them walking dogs or pushing strollers, without being noticed myself. And I could look out over the landscape sloping down to Greenfield Avenue a half mile south of us and watch the cars creeping along, carrying their owners home from a long workday or late meeting or a nice dinner out. People leading normal lives, most of them without a clue that the rug could be pulled out from under them so suddenly and so completely that they could hardly keep themselves from crashing.

Mother Nature wasn't comforting me, either. I went back inside and tried to figure out what to do next.

☬

I WAS OUT of options, it seemed. There was only one thing left to do that desperate night, with my mother "resting comfortably" at the nursing home, and that was to officially launch my investigation into heaven. It would begin with a book as potentially life changing as *The Feminine Mystique*: a little paperback called *Mere Christianity*, written by my sister Carrie's favorite Christian writer, the late C. S. Lewis.

"Read this," she had said over lunch one day in late 1997, whisking a slim volume out of her briefcase and placing it triumphantly on the paper place mat in front of my Miller Lite. "Lewis explains everything so much better than I ever could."

"Oh, thanks," I said. The title was set in enormous type, and I imagined everyone in the room could see it. I pretended to look for our waitress, giving myself a few extra seconds to think so I could be polite without making a promise I had no intention of keeping.

We were at Zorba's, a dark and cavernous Greek family restaurant where they made your American fries extra crispy and used tuna packed in oil and mushed up the feta cheese in their Greek dressing so that it was extra thick and uniformly tart. In less than two years, Zorba's would be replaced by a clean and bright steakhouse bearing the name of Joe Panos, former Philadelphia Eagles offensive lineman. I would cry the last time I walked out of Zorba's—with good reason, as it turned out; the new place uses tuna packed in spring water. But for now it was still Zorba's and still the place, next to my own little nest, that I felt most at home.

"You'll read it?" Carrie asked eagerly.

Ah, there was our waitress with my feta cheese omelet and rye toast. She set the toast plate down on top of the book, hiding its title. A good thing, I thought; Zorba's was no place to have a book on religion sitting out in plain sight.

"Sure," I said, guzzling my beer. "Just as soon as I have time."

She beamed.

But, of course, I had never quite found the time to even crack it open.

Now, almost three years later, just finding the stupid book turned out to be a major project. I went through every bookcase in the house. I used a flashlight to search through the top layer of book boxes in the basement, battling cobwebs and risking the distinct possibility of confronting a mouse or something even scarier. Finally, I turned to my last resort: a cramped closet under the kitchen stairs leading to our loft bedroom. It was a tiny room carefully packed with Dave's stuff, from fishing rods, tackle boxes, and tool kits to beer signs, wildlife prints, and old family photo albums. But on the back wall was a metal shelving unit haphazardly crammed with my things, college papers and outdated home-decorating magazines and old gardening books recommending chemicals that had long ago been banned in Boston and everywhere else in the civilized world.

I had to pull some of Dave's boxes out to get at my mess. The dust was thick; having nosed his way in to investigate, my helper Woody started sneezing up a storm.

"Gesundheit," I said, rummaging through the stacks on the top shelf, uncomfortably aware that only a few days earlier such a sneezing fit would have sent me racing to my home-vet books for advice. "We're going to figure out where your grandma is going, if I can just find this dumb book. Any ideas?"

Of course, I knew he couldn't read; we loved this basset for his extraordinary beauty and houndly bouquet, not his brains. But he *had* been quite the book-hound as a youngster, and I liked to tell people the near-truth that he specialized in chewing up volumes from Lilian Jackson Braun's *The Cat Who . . .* series.

But he naturally couldn't find a specific book for me.

He gazed up at me mournfully, wagged the tip of his tail, and turned his attention to the bottom shelf. And naturally, there the little book stood, wedged upright between stacks of crossword-puzzle and logic-problem magazines.

"You're a genius, Wood."

He leaped about gaily as I shoved the boxes back in the closet, rousing the cocker and lab pup from their naps. I like to think his enthusiasm was a response to my praise—I'm sure no one had ever called him a genius in all his thirteen years—but more likely he thought finishing this task meant they could all go outside for a good sniff.

✣

WHILE WOODY, BEAV, and Shadow disappeared into the garden, I sat down at the kitchen table again and opened the book that would supposedly make everything clear.

Dave was still stretched out in his recliner, reading or pretending to. I was glad that he wasn't one of those togetherness freaks determined that we should share every experience. This was my mom's journey, and mine, and sharing was impossible.

And so I began reading my first book on Christianity.

✣

IF YOU'D ASKED my girlfriends about the chances of my becoming a Christian, most would've laughed in your face. Especially if you'd asked my golfing girlfriends.

For most of the 1990s, these three women and I spent the last weekend in February golfing and partying it up at resorts near towns like Fort Myers, Fort Lauderdale, Biloxi, and Albuquerque.

It was during one of our Fort Myers gigs that the subject of religion had come up.

Our resorts were nothing fancy, the fairways we played were usually parched and patchy, and we weren't exactly scratch golfers. I was probably the most consistently abysmal; I did well to break 120.

We were on the 12th hole. I, having shot a pathetic sixty-eight on the front nine, picked a handful of sparse grass and tossed it into the air as I'd seen the pros do on TV.

The girls howled.

"If you ever get religious on me," said the one I'd known longest, "I'm never going to speak to you again!"

"I don't think you have to worry about that," I said, chortling. "No chance! Nada! *Nyet!*"

"Can't you just see it?" she said. "Kitty with a statue of the Virgin Mary in her front yard?"

"And a rosary in each pocket!" said girl #2.

"And a Bible under her arm!" said the third gleefully.

"Could it be . . . Satan?" someone intoned nasally, aping Dana Carvey's Church Lady character on *Saturday Night Live*.

I laughed until my mascara ran.

⁂

I WASN'T LAUGHING that awful night in May of 2000. I was frantically looking for hope in a book I wouldn't have been caught dead with just a short time ago.

It didn't look too promising. C.S. Lewis opened *Mere Christianity* with a section entitled, "Right and Wrong as a Clue to the Meaning of the Universe." I'd been looking for something along the lines of "Proof Positive that God Exists and Your Mother Is Headed Straight for Heaven." But it was all I had, so I plunged ahead.

It was slow going. Not that it wasn't readable, but some of the concepts were difficult for someone who'd daydreamed her way through Philosophy 101. Lewis was making a philosophical case for the existence of an all-powerful Creator and for the deity of Jesus Christ, and I didn't trust myself enough in this realm to know whether his ideas reflected truth. But he was sparking a ray of hope in my heart; I kept reading.

⁂

OVER THE COURSE of the next few days, I read the first two parts of *Mere Christianity* three times—the second and third to make sure Lewis wasn't just messing with my mind. In the end, I'd become fairly well convinced that, indeed, his line of reasoning *could* be true.

Late one Saturday afternoon that June, I shared this finding with my dear old chum and once-upon-a-time roommate JoAnn. We were sitting on Dave's and my deck, sipping wine coolers and munching potato chips while our husbands talked football.

"So it looks like what you've always believed is true after all," I said, wishing that we'd talked about this whole thing years earlier.

"How so?" She was the first to admit she didn't really know much about her faith, just that she had always been sure of God's presence and love.

"It seems that there's proof that God really exists," I said, "and cares about us and about what we do."

"Yes?" She drew out the word, letting it slide up an octave, a polite way of saying, wordlessly, "What's your point?"

I lit a cigarette and sat back in my chair, one of those plastic-webbed, metal-framed models that were so popular in the '90s.

"Well," I said, "according to this book, there is a strict moral law that tells us how we ought to behave. Every culture has one, and—get this—they're all exactly the same. So it's a universal law."

"Okay," JoAnn said politely, lifting her bottle to her husband, Ben, to indicate we were both ready for another. She'd known me long enough to understand that she was probably in for a lecture.

"Okay, so this moral law isn't man-made, Lewis says," I continued. "No man *would* have made it up, because it goes against our nature. We don't *want* to be generous, courageous, and humble; we *want* to be stingy, safe, and known far and wide as the best, right?"

She grinned. These were goals we could both identify with.

"And yet when we don't follow the universal law, when we instead do what we feel like doing, we feel guilty."

"That's true," JoAnn said thoughtfully. I could tell she was interested because she'd tipped her head a few degrees clockwise.

"Okay, now, here's the kicker," I said triumphantly. "This law's only possible origin is a larger-than-man Power who's directing the universe. In other words, God!"

"That really does make sense," she said, accepting our drinks from Ben with an affectionate smile. "I *knew* there was a reason I believed in Him! So what else did Lewis say?"

I strained to remember the order he had followed to make his case; even then, my memory was starting to go into the partial retirement so many brains sink into as we pass age fifty.

The word *contradiction* streaked across my mind.

"Oh, yeah," I said. "He said that there are a bunch of different ways of viewing or describing this God—something like that. But these ideas contradict each other. So even if there are elements of truth in all of them, there can be only one view that is 100 percent true."

"Can't argue with that," said JoAnn. "What else?"

I racked my brain. *Evil* skidded through.

"Okay, this is next," I said. "Only two views face all the facts of this world, including its obvious evil. The first is called 'dualism' or something like that. It says there are two *equal* powers behind everything—one good, and one evil."

JoAnn donned her "now you're pushing it" smile.

"I can't help it—that's what Lewis said, and he was some hotshot professor at Oxford. He couldn't have been too weird."

"Go on," she said, reaching for the chips, as I stubbed out my cigarette.

"So, he said that these powers cannot be equal, because of the fact that we recognize 'good.'"

"Which means we see one power as superior to the other."

"Right. Okay, so dualism is out. Then he said that the only other view that acknowledges both good and evil is Christianity, which says we live in a good world that's gone bad—a world created by a good God but ruled for the time being by an evil, fallen angel named Satan. So by default, Christianity is correct."

JoAnn tilted her head even more and raised her eyebrows.

"What?" I said.

"Nothing, really, except—well, I just wondered about Judaism. And maybe Islam. Don't they recognize both good and evil? Not that I'm arguing against Christianity. It's just that this doesn't seem like a very good argument."

I was stumped; what did I know? A couple years later, after I'd learned more about theology, I would remember this conversation and realize that she was correct on both counts. But by that time, I'd found a ton of quantifiable evidence for Christianity, and could appreciate the fact that Lewis had at least narrowed the field to a few religions with this argument. In the meantime, my theological ignorance was protecting me from needless confusion.

"You got me," I told JoAnn. "Okay, then try this—Lewis's explanation for why Christianity stands apart from all the rest. He said . . ." I hesitated, letting my brain buffer the information it had so painstakingly absorbed. But the hard drive in my head was grinding fruitlessly. "Let me read it to you—it's just a couple paragraphs."

We didn't get to it for a while. As soon as I stood up, Dave decided to scrape down the grill in preparation for cooking up some steaks, which, of course, got The Beaver, Woody, and Shadow so excited that I had to feed them, as well as the cats, while JoAnn tended to her famous potato salad and set the table. And then we had to eat and clean up. So it was nearly 8:00 before I remembered my earlier mission, and they were getting ready to go home.

When I reminded her of the paragraphs I'd wanted to read to her, JoAnn said she had time to listen.

"Okay, check this out," I said, opening *Mere Christianity* to a dog-eared page in part two. We were standing in the kitchen, and Ben was by now hovering, so I decided to just hit the highlights.

"Lewis says, 'Among these Jews there suddenly turns up a man who goes about talking as if He was God. . . . He told people that their sins were forgiven, and never waited to consult all the other people whom their sins had undoubtedly injured. . . . This makes sense only if He really was the God whose laws are broken and whose love is wounded in every sin.'"

I looked at her expectantly.

"Makes sense," she said, nodding. "Cool."

"Okay, you're going to love this," I said, turning the page to the next series of triple-starred paragraphs. "Lewis says, 'I am trying here to prevent anyone saying the really foolish thing that people often say about Him: I'm ready to accept Jesus as a great moral teacher, but I don't accept His claim to be God.'"

I glanced at her to make sure she was paying attention. Her head was tipped in "I'm listening" mode.

"Then he says, 'A man who was merely a man and said the sort of things Jesus said would not be a great moral teacher. He would either be a lunatic—on a level with the man who says he is a poached egg—or else he would be the Devil of Hell. You must make your choice. . . You can shut Him up for a fool, you can spit at Him and kill Him as a demon; or you can fall at His feet and call Him Lord and God.'"

I looked at her again, this time through teary eyes; for some reason the thought of falling at the feet of this Jesus made me feel like crying. Her eyes looked a little bright too.

"And then he finishes it this way: 'But let us not come with any patronizing nonsense about His being a great human teacher. He has not left that open to us. He did not intend to.' There, that's it."

"Wow—that's great," she said. "Definitely worth pondering."

⁂

JoAnn and Ben left then, and Dave headed into the living room with his book. But I stayed there at the kitchen counter and reread this last paragraph of Lewis's another ten times or so before deciding that, yes indeed, Christianity was beginning to look a little like it might possibly contain—or maybe even *be*—truth.

Assuming, of course, that we could be sure Jesus had actually said and done all the things Lewis claimed he'd said and done.

Assuming, in fact, that He had really existed at all. We were talking about events that supposedly took place a couple thousand years ago, after all; what if this was all myth?

Still, Lewis seemed to believe it, and his credentials were impeccable.

On the other hand, there'd been that potential problem JoAnn had detected in his dualism argument. How could I be sure he hadn't overlooked even more critical facts?

Then there was this other little matter I had discovered in part two, one that I had been too embarrassed to share with JoAnn: the issue of believing in Satan as a literal being. Even if Lewis *was* an Oxford don and a friend of people like J. R. R. Tolkein and T. S. Eliot, he had to be a little *off* to believe in a literal Satan, didn't he? And he said he wasn't talking about a cute little fellow in a red suit, but the embodiment of everything evil, the enemy, the father of lies, the fallen angel who would be God, whose primary goal is keeping us as far as possible from the kingdom of God—a horrid creature who had been given temporary run of the world and had working for him thousands and thousands of his fellow fallen angels, all determined to make us follow *their* master rather than *the* Master.

I just had to smirk at this idea. It struck me as ridiculous, a super-intellectual grown man, believing in an actual devil; visions of *SNL*'s Church Lady danced through my head once again.

But then I decided to shelve this particular issue for the moment. After all, I was beginning to look at a lot of things in a new light, and it was at least possible that Lewis was correct on this score too.

CHAPTER 9

Let not your heart be troubled:
Searching for a mother's peace

8:30 p.m., May 30, 2000

I was cruising along through *Mere Christianity*, nodding in agreement, or at least in understanding, as my eyes scurried over line after line, when I heard the laughter of some kids who lived a few houses away.

It was getting dark out. It would've been just about this time, forty years ago, that my little friends and I would've been racing to get in one more game of hide-and-seek or Statue, knowing that our mothers would be calling us in at any moment.

More laughter, this time accompanied by barking. The sound broke my heart: poor kids, so innocent, so unaware of the heartache that awaited them a day or year or half century from now.

I turned my attention back to Lewis, hoping that I was safe in interpreting his logic as truth. It was becoming apparent that I'd done that with Betty Friedan and had made a big mistake in doing so. I didn't want to waste the next twenty-five years believing in something incapable of protecting me from another dark night of the soul.

EVEN WITH THE logic of *Mere Christianity* under my belt, I was still miles away from being 100 percent certain that Christianity was fact. Maybe 50 percent certain, with another five or ten percentage points thrown in because I wanted to believe that it, or something like it, could be true. I was like a meteorologist trying to read a Doppler radar image of the soul, vacillating between forecasts of sunshine and clouds, wishing that I could just come down on one side of the question and be done with it.

I just didn't seem to be able to do that.

So as the summer of 2000 unfolded, I read more Lewis, breezing through titles from *A Grief Observed* to *The Joyful Christian* to *The Weight of Glory*. I stumbled across and into a warm and love-filled church with knock-your-socks-off worship music and started taking notes during the sermons. I bought a Bible with study notes in the easy-to-read New Living Translation and began thinking of myself as potentially heaven-bound. And for a few hours or sometimes even days at a time, I would be at peace.

But I felt like a cancer patient who'd been declared disease-free: I kept searching for signs that the good news wasn't really so good, that someone had made a mistake, that truth wasn't quite as simple as all that. I let the doubts slither in to nibble away at the certainties that Lewis was so neatly inserting into my mental database. I was no expert in logic, after all; maybe I was missing some obvious fallacy that would bring his whole house of cards crashing down the moment it became apparent.

In a new panic I would set off on yet another search of atheist Web sites for the evidence that would once and for all prove Christianity untrue, so I could rest at last, however miserably. Then I would look for Christianity's response to each objection, in the process surfing scores of pro-Jesus Web sites. I spent entire days this way, racing down all sorts of rabbit trails and chasing red herrings until every last hint of a fatal error was resolved—invariably, in Christianity's favor.

When I was in the midst of one of these frenzies, a review of the double- and triple-starred sections of *Mere Christianity* would help somewhat (by this time I'd underlined practically every word, and scrawled stars and notes in the margins on almost every page, so I had to rely on the doubles and triples for quick reference).

But C. S. Lewis wasn't enough to give me the lasting assurance I hungered for. Nor were my pastor's sermons or my early forays into the Bible. Besides, I had major questions that no one was answering, including the one that pierced me early on: *How do we know Jesus really existed and really said those things?*

By September 2000, I had plenty more:

How could a loving God allow all the suffering in this world (and, so some said, in the next world, too, in an eternal hell)?

How could He be so arrogant as to demand that everyone worship Him, forsaking all other gods?

What about all the good Buddhists, Hindus, and Muslims out there?

What about all the people who'd never heard of Him—were they going to hell through no fault of their own?

Still, I'd already taken a major step from one critical standpoint: I was willing to set aside these objections for the moment. I was past the point of caring about what I thought would be "fair" or what would make me happy.

I was on the trail of truth, no matter where it might lead.

※

I WAS SURE of one thing that May night as my mom lay dying: some people never really get over the loss of their mothers.

I'd always sort of had that feeling about her, in fact. It wasn't just that she spoke of her own mother with such respect and love—almost reverence—even though they'd been parted by death in 1948, when my mother was in her mid-thirties.

Nor was it the theme of some of the poems she collected in fat ring binders, poems she had clipped from magazines and copied out of books and even written herself, like this one:

My Mother's Hands

When I was only twenty-one
My hands were slim and fine;
And all the world and I well knew
None were so soft as mine.
I looked with scorn at Mother's hands
That were no longer fair.
I didn't know that love for me
Had etched the wrinkles there.
But when my mother's hands were still
Forever, ever more,
I saw such beauty through my tears
As I'd not known before.
Now that I tend my own hearth fire,
I pray, when my work's done,
My hands will look like Mother's did
When I was twenty-one.

—Ethel Boehm Foth

By the time I was a kid, my mother certainly was not openly mourning her mother's death. But in 1964, during her first health crisis, I came to understand how deep a daughter's love can run.

Then in her early fifties, she'd been sick in bed with the flu, and maybe the problem was caused by the medications she had taken for that. Or maybe it was the result of a recent tumble she'd taken when standing on the kitchen sink to clean pea soup off the ceiling. (In my opinion, pressure cookers should be banned.) The doctors never did figure out what had happened to afflict her so suddenly at this relatively advanced age; indeed, the problem that started that winter night so long ago would plague her intermittently for decades, forever dumbfounding teams of world-class physicians.

Here's what happened.

My dad had just brought me home from a Green Bay Bobcat ice-hockey game. Ecstatic over another Bobcat victory, I had told her all about the game, kissed her good night, and gone to my room to get ready for bed, when I heard strange sounds coming from their room: deep, guttural sounds that sent chills down my spine. I dashed up the hall and found her on the floor, jerking and foaming at the mouth and making these horrible sounds. My dad was kneeling next to her, trying to take her in his arms, saying over and over again in anguish, "What's wrong, my sweetheart, what's wrong?"

Horrified, I told myself that they were for some mysterious reason play-acting, pretending there was something wrong with Mom.

"I'm calling an ambulance," I said, sure that this threat would put an end to their little charade.

But they ignored me.

"Right now," I said.

She rose to her knees, shoved my dad aside with superhuman strength, and crawled to the nearest window. It was closed—it was winter and this was north-central Wisconsin—but she was clawing at the sash as if there were monsters chasing her.

In total panic, I raced down the stairs and called the operator, begging her to send an ambulance immediately, hoping to hear my dad laughing, saying, "Don't call—we were just teasing you!"

But he didn't. I waited about thirty seconds and called the operator a second time to find out what was taking so long.

Later, we learned that she'd been having a grand-mal seizure. No one knew why, which made it difficult to treat the underlying problem, but the doctors at the nearby hospital somehow managed to stop the attack, at least temporarily. But she remained unresponsive, so they checked her into a room for observation.

There must not have been ICUs in those days, because we ended up having to supply people to sit up with her every night at the hospital until she finally came out of this state. Dad kept watch some nights, and Mom's best friend took a shift or two, and my sister Andy and I spent at least one sleepless night there together.

She had at least one more seizure that I witnessed during this hospitalization, before they released her and sent her to UW Hospitals in Madison to get checked out by a big-time neurologist. As we all piled on top of her in a vain attempt to stop her body from jerking—just the opposite of what is recommended today—she began crying out the first understandable word she'd said since this whole thing had begun.

She wasn't asking for my dad, or for me, or for anyone else we could summon to her side.

She was crying, "Mama! Mama!" again and again, apparently looking for comfort that only one human being could ever provide.

❧

NOW, MORE THAN a quarter century later, with my own mother getting ready to leave me forever, I remembered that episode.

And I knew just how she felt.

CHAPTER 10

A reason for the hope that is in you:
Looking to the Minister of Defense

9:00 p.m., May 30, 2000

*T*he phone remained silent. I could forgive our friends and family members for not calling—they knew what was going on and undoubtedly didn't want to tie up the line. Or maybe they didn't know what to say to me; I could understand that too. But it seemed that even the telemarketers had abandoned me. I almost wished that someone would call to try to sell me lawn services or aluminum siding, just so I could say, "Sorry, but my mother is dying, and I don't want to tie up the phone."

Dave was still sitting in our little living room, reading another book—some massive hardcover, maybe a Stephen King. The dogs were slumbering at his feet. I didn't interrupt him; I had nothing new to report, and I certainly wasn't anywhere near ready to share my initial impressions of *Mere Christianity* with him.

Restless, I wandered from bookcase to bookcase in search of something else I could concentrate on reading, something a little lighter than Lewis. But I didn't see a single candidate until I got to the Packer room—another spare bedroom, this one crammed not with office equipment but with Green Bay Packer memorabilia, a big TV, and green leather furniture—and noticed Reggie White's autobiography, *In the Trenches*, sitting on the bookshelf between a Lombardi biography and one of Fritz Shurmur's books on coaching defense.

I thumbed through it, trying to recall my first read-through back in 1997. I didn't remember much about it.

Thinking Reggie might have more to say to me at this point in my life, I took it back to my spot at the kitchen table.

IT WAS IMPOSSIBLE to grow up in Green Bay in the '50s and '60s without knowing at least a little about football. At least it was impossible in our household. My dad had been a Packer fan long before Lambeau Field was built, in the days when the Pack played at City Stadium. In fact, he was one of the original stockholders who, by buying a couple shares of valueless stock, helped build Lambeau in the late '50s. He also bought five season tickets that first year at Lambeau—one for himself, one for my mother, and one for each of his three girls. (If you're a football fan, I invite you to eat your heart out: they were in the 18th row on the 40-yard-line behind the Packers' bench.)

Trouble was, Andy was the only one who was really interested in going to games with Dad. Carrie, the eldest, had left home to marry in 1957; I think her ticket must have been a symbol of his hope that she would change her mind and come home. My mother was less than thrilled about attending games once the temperature dipped below fifty degrees; in those days, women got all gussied up whenever they went out, wearing stockings and high heels and cute hats and elegant gloves, and were usually shivering by the end of the first quarter.

That left my dad and me and Andy. Sibling rivalry being what it is, spending an afternoon at a football game with her was the last thing I wanted to do. And so I'd stay home with Mom and Granny while she and Dad trekked off to Lambeau with family friends to witness the beginning, and later the collapse, of Vince Lombardi's dynasty.

Still, during the long, cold Wisconsin winters, we often played a football board game that required an understanding of first downs and field goals, safeties and sacks. So when I finally deigned to show real interest in football in the early 1990s, and Dave and I started going to games, I wasn't as lost as most new fans might have been.

It didn't take me long to become obsessed with football. I have spent my life consumed by pastimes, from boys and horses to gardening and golf; in the 1990s, pro football reigned in my heart. I began watching every televised game, NFC and AFC alike. I knew who coached every team, and won five dollars in a friendly bet because I could name the Steelers' cute young coach (Bill Cowher). Dave and I taped every Packer game, and I studied the wins during the off-season. At football parties, while the rest of the women hung out in the kitchen to talk about girl stuff, I'd be the lone woman watching the game with the guys, making wise comments like, "The corner was expecting safety help" in the wake of long touchdown passes. And, as the Packers improved under coach Mike Holmgren, I even began reading books about football strategy.

In truth, it was this obsession as much as my mom's faith that would eventually point me to Christianity.

That's because, in 1993, the Packers lured Reggie White away from the Philadelphia Eagles—the *Reverend* Reggie White, the Minister of Defense, the all-pro defensive end and the heart and soul of the Packers through the '98 season. He was an awesome player—the kind of player who could take over a game almost single-handedly, the kind of player whose very presence on our roster attracted other great players, like the Dolphins' Keith Jackson, the Seahawks' Eugene Robinson, the Oilers' Sean Jones, and the Bills' Don Beebe.

At first, I just found it curious that Reggie capped every game—win or lose—by leading players from both teams in down-on-your-knees prayer at midfield. After a season or two, I found this practice very cool; it was so politically incorrect, after all. I watched and admired those who prayed with Reggie. And I found it neat that, instead of making nasty comments about their mothers or sisters or wives, Reggie would growl "Jesus is coming" at opposing offensive linemen.

But my big Reggie moment—the moment I'll never, ever forget—didn't happen until Sunday, January 12, 1997. Dave and I were at Lambeau Field for the NFC championship game between the Packers and the Carolina Panthers. It was cold and windy—a typical Wisconsin winter day—but few of us fans cared. With a win, the Packers would go to their first Super Bowl in nearly thirty years.

I don't know when it happened—whether it was during halftime or during a commercial time-out late in the game—but at some point, the Packers' front office fired up the Jumbotron for something other than a replay. There, materializing in front of my eyes, was a much-larger-than-life Reggie White. I think he was wearing street clothes, and I think he was standing before a stormy background of some kind—others have said that I'm wrong about that, that it was some kind of summer scene. Maybe so, but I remember dark, swirling clouds and lightning.

Anyway, there was Reggie, singing a haunting tune:

Amazing grace! How sweet the sound . . .

I gave him my full attention.

That saved a wretch like me!

Although those who challenge my visual memory of the occasion also claim that the sixty thousand other people in the stadium sang right along with him, I don't remember it that way. In fact, all those people just seemed to vanish. It was just Reggie and me, all alone.

I once was lost, but now am found;

Was blind, but now I see.

Reggie and me and the Holy Spirit, to be more accurate. Although I didn't know it at the time.

Surely I had heard that song before, somewhere along the line. It is, after all, one of the most popular hymns in the English language—a hymn written, as it turns out, by slave-trader-turned-abolitionist John Newton, in 1779—and surely we'd sung it at my parents' Congregational church. But it seemed new to me that day. And it took my breath away, for a few moments at least.

Then it was over. The game resumed, we cheered, and the Packers rolled to an easy 30–13 victory over the Panthers to advance to the Super Bowl (which we also won, 35–21, thanks in no small part to a heroic performance by Reggie White, who had a record-setting three sacks in the second half).

After helping to return the Lombardi Trophy to Green Bay and the Title to Titletown, Reggie addressed Packer fans everywhere. "I wanted to make sure to honor God," he said. "A lot of people don't like that. But I wanted to make sure people knew God had His hand on this team."

If that was true, then God enjoyed a lot of victories that season, it would seem; the Packers won all but three games. But as far as I'm concerned, He posted His most impressive win back at Lambeau during the NFC championship game, when He used Reggie White to make this hard-as-a-rock forty-four-year-old heart sit up and take notice of Him at last.

※

AT FIRST, MY 1997 Reggie moment seemed like nothing more than a pleasant memory. I continued living the way I always had—shacking up with Dave, working long hours to earn as much as possible while further solidifying my self-esteem and my reputation as a very fine copywriter, re-outlining the great American novel that would ensure my immortality, socking some of my money away in a retirement account while spending the rest on more Packer stuff, more clothes, more rose bushes and rare perennials, more golf outings and warm-climate vacations.

The only difference I noticed, at first, was in my attitude toward some long-held beliefs. And even then, I didn't attribute the change to anything that had happened at Lambeau Field.

Abortion was a prominent example. As a staunch libertarian who couldn't stomach being told what to do or what not to do, I'd been pro-choice for as long as I could remember. My thinking had gone something like this: Death is not a problem for the dead, but for those who are left behind to grieve. Therefore an abortion is potentially sad only for the aborter, and since she doesn't want the kid, there's nothing sad about it. "If men could get pregnant, abortion would be a sacrament" was one of my favorite sayings, right up there with the one about the fish and the bicycle.

But now my thinking on this subject was changing—most notably in my reading of the *Conservative Chronicle*. Before Reggie, I'd always skipped columns opposing abortion, viewing them as blatant attempts to undercut a woman's inalienable right to life, liberty, and the pursuit of child-free happiness. Now, however, I began to read even those pieces. Instead of making me angry, they were beginning to make sense; human life at any stage was beginning to seem almost sacred, I suppose, although the word made me feel uncomfortable.

All of which left me feeling confused at first . . . and, eventually, solidly against all abortion. I didn't admit this to anyone. Although there was no way I could be certain, having never heard of it happening before, I was pretty sure that such a defection would be considered high treason among those whose opinions mattered most.

As it turned out, I was right. When the real "Jane Roe," Norma

McCorvey, changed her mind and said that abortion was morally wrong, she wasn't exactly treated as a hero by the news media.

⁂

THEN THERE WAS the subject of marriage. For years, I'd been checking the tax tables each April to see if Dave and I would be better off financially if we were to marry. The answer was always a resounding "No!" Case closed.

But quite suddenly, in 1998, my thinking on this subject began to change: getting married had suddenly become a moral imperative for me. Dave didn't have a problem with the idea. So in February of 1999 (after a week of being so nervous and fearful that I was quite sure I would upchuck on the judge), we went to the Waukesha County courthouse and took the vows.

I don't remember much about the ceremony, except that the judge was a woman and that I wore a brand new Packer-green dress that I'd bought on sale at J. C. Penney's for just $39.98. I also recall signing the marriage certificate afterwards; I remember writing my own name and Dave looking so aghast, that I added a hyphen and his last name to my signature because we'd just gotten married and I didn't want him to feel bad. And I remember going straight to the nursing home when we were done to show Mom my ring, which consisted of the diamonds from her wedding ring displayed in a new setting.

She was very happy about it all, but she seemed to be in the minority. My friends were shocked; some seemed horrified.

"Why in the world did you do it?" one after another asked incredulously.

"I don't know," I answered honestly, time and time again.

"I can't believe it!"

"Me neither," I would agree, worrying especially about the mingling of our finances under Wisconsin's Marital Property Act, and how many people of both genders I'd known who'd been ruined by that stupid law. "I really don't know why we did it. I guess it seemed like a good idea at the time." And I would laugh nervously.

After a while, I began developing some theories about the whole thing. The best explanation I could come up with was that the Clinton scandals had divided our nation into moral and amoral camps, and I wanted to make it clear that we were in the former.

"Really?" my girlfriends would say upon hearing this idea. "That's really . . . odd."

Eventuallly, I would realize that it was an act of obedience to a law I didn't yet acknowledge—a law that was written in my heart, just as it's been written in the hearts of every other human being who has ever lived. But I was months away from understanding that.

Either way, I managed to put a feminist spin on it. Several days after Dave and I were married, I went on our honeymoon with my golfing girlfriends, leaving him at home. It was the girl's annual mini-vacation, and that was the year we'd flown to Biloxi. When we were through golfing and eating and partying, the girls headed back to Wisconsin, and Dave flew down to meet me for the rest of the week. We golfed and gambled and drove to Brett Favre's hometown of Kiln, Mississippi, to have a few beers at the Broke Spoke, a dumpy bar owned by a friend of Brett's.

I was very proud of these little heresies, this further proof that I was not like *other* brides. I made sure that everyone who heard about the incredible fact of our marriage also heard about the equally surprising facts of our liberated honeymoon.

CHAPTER 11

A new creation:
Turbulent times for an atheist sympathizer

9:30 p.m., May 30, 2000

In the center of *In the Trenches* were sixteen glossy pages of black-and-white photos of Reggie White, his beautiful family, his teammates, and his friends. Many of the shots featured that famous Reggie smile—a joyful expression, and supremely peaceful, and not one bit arrogant. It was impossible not to smile back, remembering what he'd done for the entire state of Wisconsin, bringing the Title back to Titletown after an absence of nearly thirty years. Not to mention what he'd done for my opinion of my mother's faith.

But that wasn't my purpose in taking another look at this book of his. I wanted some of his peace. And I figured this was as good a place as any to look for it.

THERE WERE SOME other changes that followed Reggie's amazing song at the 1997 NFC championship game. Prayer, for instance. I went from occasionally wishing on stars to feeling a need to pray just in case God really did exist. Not having a clue how to make a proper prayer—perhaps not even realizing that such a thing existed—each night I simply started saying, in secret silence, the two prayers I remembered from my childhood.

The first was easy:

> *Dear Jesus in heaven, look down from above,*
> *And fill my little heart with love.*
> *Bless me every single day,*
> *Keep me good and sweet always,*
> *Amen.*

When I said this prayer, I always pictured myself back in my bedroom in our house on Quincy Street. There was a photograph-quality picture on the wall between the twin beds, a picture of Jesus—a brown-haired, bearded white man in a white robe, seated on a bench in a lush garden, showing the palm of one hand to a little girl and a little boy. The memory made me feel very peaceful.

The other prayer I said was a little trickier, because my German Granny had taught it to me when I was just a kid, and I never knew what it meant:

> *Ich bin klein,*
> *Mein herz ist rein,*
> *Soll niemand darin wohnen,*
> *Als Jesus allein.*

I had studied German for a while back in the '70s, when Mom and I traveled to Europe together, so this time around I *did* know what I was saying:

> *I am little,*
> *My heart is pure,*
> *No one shall live in it*
> *Except Jesus alone.*

Which seemed a bit nonsensical at the time; surely God or Jesus, whichever one was in charge, would want *everyone* living in our hearts, wouldn't He? I suspected it was a translation issue. But I had no one to ask, and in truth, no desire to admit that I was praying to a probably nonexistent God. So I kept it in my two-prayer "just in case" repertoire, leaving it intact, figuring that if there were both an error *and* a God, He would understand my position.

※

THE OTHER ODD thing was that, as the millennium drew to a close, my ambitions started slipping away. I cared less and less about making lots of money and having prestigious companies on my client list. Writing the great American novel no longer interested me. I still enjoyed digging in the loamy soil of my garden, but had apparently reached my limit on the number of books I cared to read about horticulture, as well as the number of beds I cared to dig, fill, and maintain; and that, in turn, meant shrugging off dreams of a garden grand enough to be featured in a slick gardening magazine.

Just as strange, I found myself in more and more conversations about spiritual topics, for the first time with people who actually believed in a higher power.

In the past, my discussions had been with any number of like-minded girlfriends, who would agree with me wholeheartedly when I'd say, in a confidential tone, "I don't know *what* I believe."

"Me neither," the girlfriend would say, sometimes adding something along the lines of, "But Buddhism is really a beautiful philosophy, don't you think?"

"Yes, I do," I would respond, knowing absolutely nothing about it. "And I've always liked the Hindu people."

We would talk as if our conclusions had been the product of intense thought, and as if thought alone should be the only mental activity needed to arrive at the ultimate truth—the Hercule Poirot "little gray cell" school of theology.

But now I was starting to speak the *G* word with people who actually acknowledged and embraced God almighty.

Some of our talks were pretty stressful—no doubt as much for my victim du jour as for me. I invariably brought the subject up, listened to my companion's opinions a little, and then became irate.

Such talks would usually play out something like this:

> **Me:** So you're telling me that people who do all these nice things for other people and for charities are *not* going to heaven.
>
> **Her:** I don't know that—only God knows that.
>
> **Me:** Whereas you *are* going to heaven. Even though you never lift a finger for anyone.
>
> **Her:** That has nothing to do with it. It has to do with our faith in—
>
> **Me:** So in other words, it's a something-for-nothing scheme. The less you do for others, the more "in" you are with God.
>
> **Her:** No, that's not—
>
> **Me (feeling quite murderous by then):** And that doesn't *offend* you?

It did not occur to me that, if this faith-before-good-works idea *did* turn out to be true, my taking offense at it would not have had any impact on its accuracy. I liked to think that the reason I rejected it was some innate ability to discern fact from fiction; more likely, it was just my generally contrary disposition combined with a sincere desire to keep this God of theirs at a safe distance.

MY CONVERSATIONS WITH my mother on the things of God—most of them conducted over the phone as day melted into night—were more positive experiences.

Mom: I can't make you believe anything. But I want you to know that the Lord Jesus is incredibly important to me, and I wish you would have at least a little faith. ("A little faith" turned out to be a biblically significant quantity, I later learned. She was a clever woman, that mother of mine.)

Me: That's nice, and if it's true for you, good deal. It's just that it's not true for me. I believe that I'll come back in my next life as a well-loved family dog, if I want to.

Mom: Mmmmm. Well, that does sound wonderful, but I think heaven will probably be the best place to go. And your father will be there, you know.

Me: Oh, right. Well, then, maybe I'll go there instead. After all, I'm a good person; I do a lot of nice things for other people, so I shouldn't have any trouble getting in.

Mom never tried to set me straight on what the Bible said about heaven's entrance requirements, which, as it turned out, have nothing to do with being a good person. In fact, she went along with me on some of my ideas, almost playfully. But I knew my vision of the afterlife wasn't changing hers. And as far as I could tell, these little mother-daughter talks didn't seem to be changing me, either.

UNTIL REGGIE, I'D been careful to keep my mother's attitude toward the God of the Bible from creeping into my thoughts. But I had to admit to being curious about her apparent assurance that her next stop would be His heaven. I sometimes envied her assurance. I remember wishing more than once that I could be gullible enough to believe the same heavenly myths that she did.

But sooner or later even her cautious talk of God would make me uncomfortable. It reminded me of a letter she'd written me shortly after my father died in 1970. She had never sent it to me, had instead stuck it in an envelope with my name on it and tossed it in the kitchen "junk" drawer where I couldn't miss it.

It was all about God.

"There's nothing more important I could wish for you than the kind of faith I have, and your father had," she'd written. "Nothing else matters."

It was a painful memory, intertwined as it was with my dad's death. I refused to dwell on it.

Instead, I would shift the focus to whatever was currently substituting as my religion. In the '90s, it was horticulture, and my favorite garden writer, Allen Lacy, had made a perfect case for the transcendent importance of our shared passion:

> I do believe that there is such a thing as a gardener's eye and that it is a gift of what Christians call grace—a gift that comes from outside, that is apart from one's own intentions, and that can never be entirely fathomed. Gardening is, in other words, something religious. And its religion involves a point in time, a moment of conversion that separates things into before and after. . . . One was not

a gardener. . . . Then the gift comes, and one knows that one had been living in darkness, but that now there is suddenly a new world to see, a world whose beauties and wonders many lifetimes would not be sufficient to encompass.[1]

I can remember reading that passage to Mom one day in my kitchen, barely able to suppress my tears of joy over its beauty and power. Although I didn't say it, my thoughts were running something like this: *My* religion—which is what it is, since Allen Lacy has said so—is so beautiful and life-affirming that it brings tears to one's eyes. Whereas *your* religion is mean-spirited, discriminatory, and altogether unfair. Besides, I have soil, a shovel, and a credit card good at any nursery in town; you have this imaginary friend named God.

Confused as I was in those days, I was quite sure that I was the winner in this little match-up.

CHAPTER 12

Behold, now is the day:
Okay, you've got my attention

9:45 p.m., May 30, 2000

I surprised myself by yawning. True, I hadn't been sleeping well lately, but this night of all nights, how could I even think about sleep?

Still, an escape into unconsciousness sounded mighty inviting. I climbed the stairs to the loft and crawled into our queen-sized platform bed, still fully dressed. My Siamese, Sam, was sleeping on Dave's pillow; I grabbed him and hugged him close, bumping his purr into high gear. Himalayan Max popped up out of nowhere and joined us in a group hug.

I scrunched my eyes shut and tried to fall asleep, telling myself it would just be a short nap at most.

It didn't work. I kept thinking about that last rites gig, about those ominous phrases being uttered over my mother's slumbering form. I was instantly as wide awake as if I'd been pounding coffee all night.

I left the cats snuggled up together and headed back downstairs.

ONLY GOD KNOWS why, but in the mid-1990s, I started thinking now and then about giving church a whirl. I even attended a couple of services at a nearby non-denominational megachurch, almost daring Him to show Himself to me.

The first time I went because of a deal I'd made with this hypothetical God. It was fall, and the Packers were in Texas, facing another humiliating defeat by the hated Dallas Cowboys. "I'll give You a chance to prove Your existence," I'd told Him the night before the big game. "I'll go to church tomorrow morning. All I ask in return is a Packer victory in the afternoon."

I held up my end of the bargain by attending a jam-packed Sunday-morning service at this megachurch. In some ways, the service was a trip down Memory Lane. I hadn't picked up a hymn book or tried to sight-read music since I was a kid taking piano lessons, and it gave me a bittersweet longing for my childhood. In other ways, the service was horrifying: an Asian man got up and spoke about how missionaries from this church had "saved" him from Buddhism. *The arrogance of these Christians*, I thought. Implying that their way was the *only* way and that people needed rescuing from other religions!

Feeling persecuted on behalf of Buddhists everywhere, I headed home to watch the Packers lose to the Cowboys.

For some reason, I went back to this church a second time. I honestly can't remember my motivation that time, and as it turned out, it was hardly worth putting on pantyhose. (I may not have believed in their God, but I sure as shootin' wasn't going to walk into His house in pants, the way some of the women had last time I was there.) There was a lot of talk about a change in the pastoral guard. It was pretty boring, and I figured that would be the end of my church-going career.

I THOUGHT OF my visits to this megachurch as my mother lay dying. In those days I'd been looking for just a little magic from this alleged God, like a few more victories in the Packers' "W" column. Now I was looking for something much bigger: if not a cure for my mother—and I wasn't sure that's what we needed, given how miserable life really was becoming for her—then total assurance that she was going to heaven and that I could one day meet her there.

That was asking way too much of any book by a mere mortal, it turned out. Still, as I skimmed through Reggie's book, focusing this time on the sections devoted not to football but to his faith, I found that he had some surprising things to say.

For instance, he said a lot of people questioned how he could supposedly love God and be involved in such a violent sport. "In order to be a Christian," he wrote, "living after the example of Christ, you have to be aggressive, just as Jesus was aggressive. He wasn't timid or weak; He was tough and aggressive, more tough and aggressive than anyone who ever played the game of football."[1]

Huh? Reggie said the teacher or prophet or Son of God who allowed Himself to be hung on a cross was *tough*?

That's what he said, all right, adding, "In the original Greek language of the Bible, the word that's translated 'meekness' doesn't mean weakness, it means *controlled aggression.*"

I liked that. I rolled the words around in my head.

Then, in telling the story of a fellow NFL player and friend of his who'd died in a car accident at age twenty-seven, Reggie said, "God alone knows the state of Jerome's heart when he died. No one has the right or the power to judge his relationship with the Lord."[2]

No one has the right to judge? Not even Christians, Reggie? I thought that was very strange. It seemed to me that most Christians were supposed to be horribly judgmental. Wasn't that why sane people hated most of them?

Then I got to the part that stopped me—Reggie's comment that, if there was a lesson to be learned from his friend's death, it was this: "Jerome thought he had all the time in the world. . . . We should never take chances with eternity. We should never wait until some future time to get right with God. We should get right with Him today and stay right with Him today, while we have time, while we have life."[3]

I hadn't paid any attention to that passage when I first read *In the Trenches*. But that night in 2000, it seemed like the most important thing I'd ever read in my whole life.

If, of course, any of this business about God was true.

The day after Christmas 2004, not long after he had stepped out of the public spotlight to study Hebrew and thereby improve his understanding of the Bible, Reggie White surprised everyone by dying. The cause was a cardiac arrhythmia caused by sarcoidosis, a systemic inflammatory disease he'd had for years. He had just turned forty-three. He left behind a beautiful family, thousands of fans, and no doubt more than a few converts.

That day, after Dave had delivered the news about Reggie's death, I spent a lot of time thinking about what his life had meant to me personally. I thought about him singing "Amazing Grace" that magnificent day in 1997, for a moment, at least, transporting me to another realm. I thought about how, in retrospect, hearing him sing that song seems to have been a turning point in my life.

And I remembered what Reggie had written in his book about the importance of getting right with God. The great Reggie White had done just that as a young man, and had apparently never looked back.

I may not have agreed with him that night in 2000, as my mother's life slipped away. But I was apparently ready to listen.

"We should never take chances with eternity."

CHAPTER 13

What is truth?
Your guess is as good as mine

10:00 p.m., May 30, 2000

The dogs were down for the count, the cats were still in bed, and my husband was watching the news and reading the same heavyweight book he'd been working on the last time I checked on him. I picked up the kitchen phone to make sure there was a dial tone, then checked voice mail to make sure that no one had somehow slipped past both the ring and the message-waiting alarm.

No messages.

Pulling on my Packer jacket once again, I stepped out the back door for some fresh air. I think my initial idea was to do a little fervent wishing upon a star, but once outside, that seemed too Jiminy Cricketish for the circumstances.

I stood with my hands jammed into my pockets against the familiar chill of a spring night in Wisconsin and tried to distract myself with thoughts of summer gardening. The deck looked pretty sad for the end of May. We normally started a riotous display of annuals early in the month, protecting them with old sheets if a late frost threatened. But I hadn't even bothered to clean the pots yet; they sat in their appointed spots, dirty and filled with last year's dead foliage, waiting for attention I didn't feel like giving them.

My Daytimer said it was late May, and any other year I would've been so horrified by this untidiness that I would have been out there sprucing things up until midnight.

But not this year.

Not this night.

Dave had done much of the heavy clean-up of the garden a few weeks earlier, and I'd even spent enough time out there to cut my mother some fresh flowers, mostly daffodils and tulips. Just a few days earlier, I had gathered a pail full of glossy green pachysandra and purple Woodstock hyacinths and arranged them for her in a lovely antique green and white bowl that had been her grandmother's. She had been so delighted when I put it on her hospital-style overbed table, but was, sadly, near tears that evening, when she called to tell me that she'd knocked the whole arrangement over.

"I am such a klutz," she said, her voice heavy with sorrow, "and I'm so so so sorry. I don't even know how it happened, but I smashed that beautiful old bowl into a hundred pieces, and it's beyond repair. Will you ever be able to forgive me?"

Now, three days later, I was supremely grateful that I hadn't been angry and hurtful. My moods had never been predictable, depending largely upon the day's circumstances; if my afternoon had been especially frustrating, I might have taken it out on her, become surly about my flower-arranging efforts having gone to waste.

It was probably a sign of how worried I was about her that I responded kindly.

"It's just a bowl," I said sincerely, thinking that I'd trade a million such bowls for the restoration of her health. A zillion. "Please don't even think about it. I've got more hyacinths budding out; I'll make you another arrangement."

She hadn't been totally relieved. We talked for quite a while about other things, about how my workload seemed to be skyrocketing again, how she hoped to get back to her Bingo games soon, and what we'd each had for dinner that night; but she kept bringing up the smashed bowl.

Mercifully, the morphine would soon wipe it out of her thoughts.

⁂

WHEN I WAS younger, "truth" was a personal concept meaning whatever made me happy; there were no absolutes of any kind. For instance, when I was in my early twenties, *my* truth said that recreational drugs, alcohol, and tobacco were perfectly safe. That a good sex life and a high-flying career were every woman's right. And that evolution had proven religion a crock, so let's eat, drink, and be merry, for one of these years we were all going to die!

Truth was, after all, completely subjective.

Not that I'd been born a relativist. I had once known certain things to be true—my Granny was the best, there were parts of the world where it never snowed, lying to Momma about sleeping over at Rosie's so that we could camp out in our backyard was very dumb, and starving children in China would be grateful for my rutabaga.

But somewhere along the line, I had fallen for the idea that *your* interpretation of truth was every bit as valid as mine.

How this happened, I'm not sure. It might have had something to do with studying Russian history in the '70s and doing a term paper on the Soviet definition of "Pravda," which means "truth." In the course of researching this subject, I learned that, to the Communists, truth was anything that was good for the Communist Party. To write my paper, I had to get to the point where this definition made some sense to me; maybe the mental gymnastics this exercise required had impaired my ability to recognize objective truth.

Or maybe it was the fallout from a 1974 analysis I did, for

another college paper, on the Big Three newsmagazines' treatment of the Thomas Eagleton affair in the 1972 presidential campaign.

"I don't know what's true anymore," I'd told a classmate I'll call Ginny on the way out of class the day we turned our papers in.

"Because Nixon won after all?" she asked, remembering that my paper had something to do with the McGovern campaign.

I shook my head. "Because I discovered that *U.S. News & World Report* is the most objective of the newsmagazines."

"Ha!" Ginny laughed delightedly; she was the first conservative kid I'd ever known, and I hadn't yet taken the Econ 101 class that would show me the error of my ways. *U.S. News* was her magazine of choice; *Time* was mine. "Let's go get a drink, and you can tell me all about it," she said.

We headed over to a dive on Oakland Avenue: one of my favorite bars, it featured a grungy atmosphere, largely disgusting clientele, and great prices.

"So tell me about it," she said after we'd seated ourselves in a booth with our drinks—a Lite beer for me, a rum and coke for her.

"You remember Eagleton, don't you? McGovern's VP candidate?" She grinned and nodded. "I remember."

"Right," I said, wondering how someone I liked so much could have been on the wrong side in the McGovern/Nixon race. "So you remember when it came out that Eagleton had been treated for depression?"

"Yes—with electroshock, I think. Pretty scary that McGovern would choose someone with that kind of past as his running mate."

"I don't know about that," I said. "But what *was* scary was that at first the news media were all over McGovern for saying he would stand by Eagleton—all of them, even *Time* and *Newsweek*. *U.S. News*, too, of course—that was to be expected."

"McGovern was practically a Communist," Ginny said in apparent defense of all three magazines.

"Separate issue," I said evenly, saving that argument for another time. "My point is that when McGovern caved in to their pressure and replaced Eagleton with Shriver, all of a sudden the press went nuts on him for dumping on the mentally ill! All of them, that is, except for *U.S. News & World Report*."

"They stuck to their guns?"

"Yes," I admitted, though it pained me to say so. "*U.S. News* said that McGovern had done the right thing."

"Objective reporting is alive and well somewhere," she said. "I'm glad to hear it."

"Objective reporting?" What a funny thing to say. "Of course it's alive and well. And it always will be. How can you doubt it?"

⁂

EXCEPT I'D BEEN horribly wrong about that; the *Time* and *Newsweek* flip-flops were just the opening salvos in the mainstream news media's all-out attack on objective truth.

"It is not enough to refrain from publishing fake news or to take ordinary care to avoid mistakes," said newspaper-publishing legend Joseph Pulitzer many years ago. "You've got to make everyone connected with the paper believe that accuracy is to a newspaper what virtue is to a woman."

I knew from first hand experience what had happened to a woman's virtue. By the 1990s, the same thing had apparently befallen American journalism—in the process, nurturing a subjective, devil-may-care attitude toward truth in stony hearts like mine.

"What *is* truth?" I remember thinking now and then in the tumultuous last decades of the twentieth century. Never having read the Bible, I didn't realize that I was quoting Pontius Pilate, the Roman governor of Judea in Jesus' day, the opportunist who had ordered Jesus' crucifixion even though he could find no fault with his victim.

I HAD BEEN shocked into at least temporary respect for the truth when I was in my late twenties and my bedroom-eyed boyfriend of four years moved to Cincinnati for a new job. We saw each other every few weeks and talked once or twice a week until suddenly, midsummer, he suggested we save our meager incomes for airfare rather than blowing it on phone bills. I agreed; long distance *was* pretty expensive in the early 1980s, and like most people, we wrote letters as easily as one fires off e-mails today.

But old habits die hard: a few days later I called him one last time to confirm the date of his next visit.

A woman answered the phone. A woman who was not his mother.

I gulped, then stoically introduced myself and asked for my boyfriend—let's call him Lyle. She was probably just the cleaning lady, I told myself.

"Oh, hi, Kitty," she said, her voice riding a wave of obvious delight. "He isn't here, but I'm so glad to finally talk to you. I've heard such great things about you!"

I was too stunned to respond.

"This is Laura," she offered, and when I remained silent, "Didn't Lyle tell you I was moving down here with him?"

"No, he didn't," I said. "Well, nice talking with you. Tell him I called, please."

I hung up, meditated for a moment on how I no longer needed to save my pennies for airfare, and called her back. Whereupon she and I had a long, wine-fueled talk, mutually painful until we'd both become loaded enough to find our situation comical.

In the process, we discovered that, for the last two years, handsome Lyle had been deceiving us both. We actually knew a great deal about each other, much of it true; but the untrue things were whoppers, like the part about how we were each nothing more to him than an old-girlfriend-turned-friend.

"So tell me about the night you tried to commit suicide," I said, well into my third glass of wine.

"What?"

I lit another cigarette, remembering the evening just last winter that Lyle had called to beg off our date, saying that his good buddy Laura had overdosed on tranquilizers, and he needed to get her to the hospital.

"No attempted suicide?"

"No. How about you? Did you really have an emergency appendectomy last summer?"

"Nope," I said. "Although I did tell him that my dad had almost died of a burst appendix before I was born."

We also figured out there had been plenty of warning signs that things were not quite as this boyfriend of ours had presented them.

"Did he avoid being seen in public with you?" Laura asked.

I had to think about that one for a moment. "Now that you mention it, yes—at least when we were on the East Side. If we went out at all, he liked to head down to the south side. You?"

"Northern suburbs."

We sighed.

"How could we have been so stupid?" Laura asked.

"He's a great liar," I said. "We can't blame ourselves."

But that wasn't quite true, I realized the next day, as I nursed a monster hangover and tried to decide whether or not my heart was officially broken. If either of us had really been interested in the truth, she would have long ago discovered her involvement in this unwitting ménage à trois. We had simply not been interested enough to investigate. It would have been inconvenient, it would have been distressing, and it would have forced us to give up something we both found irresistible—this attractive two-timer.

And so, as long as we had alternative explanations to cling to—however far-fetched they may have been—we chose to hang on to them for dear life.

But as Daniel Webster once said, "There is nothing so powerful as truth." And once it had forced itself on us, we no longer had any choice; it won out over every objection we could muster.

⁂

APPARENTLY I DIDN'T quite learn my lesson from the Lyle-and-Laura experience. I spent the next couple decades operating with a truth detector that worked only intermittently, when I really wanted it to. Which means I spent a fair share of my life being dead wrong.

The 1995 O. J. Simpson case was a good example. My interest in pro football was skyrocketing that year, as the Packers climbed into the ranks of the elite teams, and O. J. was a true NFL hero. I didn't *want* him to be guilty of murdering his ex-wife. So I eagerly embraced the contention that, unlike the bloodbath at the crime scene itself, there were only a few drops of blood in his Bronco. I agreed that those drops had undoubtedly been planted, perhaps by a corrupt or jealous policeman.

I clung to these notions, using them to screen the rest of the evidence. When it came time to look at the big picture, I donned my Agatha Christie lenses, absolutely certain that the solution could not be as obvious as it looked. I reasoned that no one could have been as *stupid* as O. J. would've had to have been to commit this terrible crime. I concluded that there was another killer on the loose—perhaps his son—and that O. J. had either been expertly framed or was sacrificing himself for his kid. I made no secret of my relief when the not-guilty verdict was delivered.

In February of 2000, lying on a beach in Jamaica with my anti-O. J. golfing girlfriends, oblivious to the cancer growing in my mother's belly, I read lead prosecutor Marcia Clark's book *Without a Doubt* and discovered that I had done quite a remarkable job of closing my eyes to an entire evidence-room full of indisputable facts.

When I sheepishly admitted my error to my girlfriends, they crowed.

"Ha!" said the one I knew best. "I told you so! I *told* you! Next time, maybe you'll listen to me!"

It was then that I decided never again to let my emotions and biases distort objective truth. It was a major departure for someone who had always been ruled by her feelings; Marcia Clark had done what multiple leakers and liars had failed to do.

※

PERHAPS NOT SO coincidentally, my resolve to search out the unvarnished truth would be tested just a few months later, as I began investigating my mother's faith.

Once again, I was being forced to consider the possibility that something I had long refused to believe might actually be true.

In the very early going, I kept stumbling over my virtual certainty that my mother's religion was ugly and prudish and intolerant; that it was arrogant beyond belief with its claims of absolute and exclusive truth; and that it starred a Creator who, if He existed, took great pleasure in giving His creatures good things like food and drink and money and sex and then telling them, "Hands off!"

These were among the reasons I had developed my own little theological system over the decades—one that could be adjusted whenever necessary to accommodate some fun idea put forth in a conversation or book or even a movie like the too-cool afterlife fantasy *What Dreams May Come*, with its resident-run, "they all lived happily ever after" portrayal of heaven.

Even though I was sort of leaning toward the existence of a God by the mid-1990s, my personal theology certainly didn't depend on such a being. Mine was a passive-tense theology: We *were put* here to reach our full potential as human beings. We *would be judged* based on our characters and good deeds. Those who *were allowed* into heaven (if it existed) would include just about everyone except Adolf Hitler and Christian fundamentalists.

If I didn't want to address the issue of who, if anyone, would do the putting, judging, and allowing, well, that was my business; it was my afterlife scenario, after all. And it was just as valid as anyone else's, because no one could possibly know for sure what happens to us after we die. No one.

DURING THE 1990s, I even toyed occasionally with the flip side of the "can't know" coin—the idea that absolute truth doesn't even exist, no matter what the ancient Greeks may have thought.

But then in early 2001 I read an interesting refutation of that idea. It went something like this:

To say that absolute truth doesn't exist is to make a statement of absolute truth.

If it's true, it's false.

And so it breaks the law of noncontradiction.

I thought about that long and hard and could find no way around it. Absolute truth was apparently alive and well in our twenty-first-century world and apparently always would be.

It was a very reassuring conclusion.

CHAPTER 14

They are without excuse:
Could their imaginary friend be real?

10:15 p.m., May 30, 2000

Apparently I was no longer much interested in gardening. Something was definitely wrong with me. I went back inside and pulled out the most recent of several neatly organized photo albums dedicated to my garden; maybe a peek at last summer's highlights would resurrect my passion for horticulture.

Here was my practically disease-proof White Meidiland shrub rose with its smallish but prolific and fully double blossoms, long my favorite; it would begin popping within a couple weeks. Here in its midsummer splendor was Malaysian Monarch, my most exotic daylily, an early-to-midseason bloomer with enormous rosy-purple petals of waxy substance and a stunning butter-yellow throat haloed in pale pink. And here, a shot of a Taboo rose, rare because this delicious black-red hybrid tea hardly ever put out more than three or four blossoms for me in an entire season, and when one opened, I was normally too excited to think to grab my camera.

But gardening seemed pretty foolish now, hardly the life-or-death pursuit I'd treated it as. Hardly worth all the watering and fertilizing and mulching. Not even worth the film I'd recorded it on.

I had hundreds of photos of my flowers. And maybe a few dozen of my mother.

It all seemed about as useless as the home-grown theology I'd been cultivating ever since my father died.

※

IN THE SUMMER of 2000, just months after Marcia Clark's book had destroyed my O. J. theory, I began putting that silly theology of mine—as well as my mother's faith—to the test.

At first my investigation was scattered. I didn't have a clue how to approach this enormous task, so I just kept reading whatever looked interesting. In addition to bulldozing my way through much of C. S. Lewis's fiction and nonfiction, I devoured a chaotic array of books from the library and bookstore of the church with the warm congregation and uplifting worship music. I began immersing myself in my new study Bible, a fat volume with overview essays, charts, and maps, as well as endless footnotes explaining what various verses mean to our lives today.

I read all these things and started to see my ideas as pretty weak—and pretty childish, based as they were on fantasy and wishful thinking. And I started to gain confidence that my mother's faith could, after all, be true, that there really might be a heaven and we might actually all be together again someday. Maybe I could even bank on it.

But I couldn't be 100 percent certain, could I?

And so I worried, intermittently but intensely, that it was all a myth some ancient leaders had cooked up to keep the masses in line. Or, as some of my fellow feminists would have said, a myth cooked up by men to keep their little women barefoot and pregnant and home.

Which meant that I had yet to set the whole question of atheism permanently aside. A distressing realization: I had toyed with its negative brand of absolutism for too many years already. And as someone had said, you can't prove a negative: Even if you know 99 percent of everything there is to know in the universe, how do you know that God isn't in that last 1 percent?

Besides, atheism no longer had any appeal for me. I figured that marrying Dave had put the kibosh on my last remaining need for a godless universe devoid of moral absolutes.

But at first, all I had to *prove* God's existence was C. S. Lewis's argument about our instinctive understanding of a universal moral law—what some people refer to as the "argument from conscience." It was a good argument, but I couldn't accept it as conclusive evidence.

I kept going around in circles.

Did science eliminate any need for a Creator?

Did near-death experiences render atheism obsolete?

Might all religions be true, in their own way?

Could it be that my home-grown philosophy was right after all?

And so I returned to square one.

It reminded me of my single days, when I would spend hours wondering whether some guy was telling me the truth, weighing and reweighing the evidence, agonizing over what to do about each of three or four possibilities. I still hadn't learned to think linearly, it seemed.

(Was my circular thinking evidence that Eastern thought was true, after all?)

And then, somewhere along the line, I read that, centuries earlier, the world's foremost philosophers had narrowed all these big questions down to the three *biggest* questions—the only ones that really matter:

1. Where did you come from?
2. What are you doing here?
3. Where are you going?

I had at least two answers: Science had solved #1 (from prehistoric chemical soup), and Betty had taken care of #2 (to become independently wealthy, protect my dignity, and promote the sisterhood).

So #3 was the only outstanding issue.

Where are you going?

I'd once sidestepped this question by telling myself that writing the great American novel would assure my immortality; it would buy me a place in the hearts and minds of the intellectual elite for centuries to come, even if it didn't reveal where *I* would be during this posthumous adulation.

But now my final destination had become enormously important, related as it was to the final destination of everyone I'd ever loved.

Especially my mom.

✄

"TRY," SAID THE professorial man on TV, "to imagine a new primary color. You can't."

I tried. He was right. It's impossible.

"We can't imagine anything that doesn't already exist," he said. "We can think of a pink elephant, for instance, but pink already exists, and elephants already exist."

I knew just what he was talking about. I had recently watched a few minutes of a special about *Star Wars* or some such movie. On the screen was a scene in a bar or restaurant featuring a bunch of strange-looking creatures. The voice-over was talking about how creative these characters were, but all I could see were dozens of existing or exaggerated animal parts mixed up in new ways; I couldn't see that there was anything truly original on display.

"We just can't do it," the professorial man said. He was white haired and balding and bearded, and his eyes were twinkling with amusement. "We cannot imagine anything that doesn't exist. Now, what does that tell us about the fact that we can imagine God? If He didn't exist, would we have ever thought of Him?"

Again, I couldn't quite see this as conclusive evidence for God. But it definitely pushed me another step or two in His direction.

⁂

I THOUGHT ABOUT all these things incessantly the summer and fall of 2000, tirelessly outlining my own ideas, as well as the ideas of an almost ridiculous range of authors. My hope was that these activities would put to rest, once and for all, the answer to question #3, *Where are you going?* Even if the answer turned out to be "nowhere," at least the issue would be settled, and I could escape from this whirlpool of "yeah, but" thoughts.

And then something happened to set me free.

The occasion was dinner with the golfing girlfriend I knew best. The location was the Thunder Bay Grille, just off the freeway west of town.

"So, anyway, I'm tired of waiting for you to figure it all out," she said out of the blue as we lingered over before-dinner drinks. "I bought a book."

"*You* bought a book on Christianity?" I was so astounded that I swallowed wrong and just barely avoided a coughing fit.

"Not on *Christianity*," she said, scrunching her lips as if she found the whole idea distasteful. "I don't even know if there's a God."

"Then . . . ?"

"It's a book about God. In fact, that's the name of it—*God the Evidence.*"

I discreetly tucked my notes back into my purse—lately I'd been spending hours outlining my findings in preparation for breaking bread with this girlfriend, hoping to convince her to come along with me on this spiritual journey. So far, I'd gotten nowhere with her, but maybe this book of hers would do the trick.

The next day, I went to Harry W. Schwartz's Brookfield store to pick up a copy for myself.

※

THE BOOK'S OFFICIAL name was *God the Evidence: The Reconciliation of Faith and Reason in a Postsecular World*. It was written by Patrick Glynn, associate director and scholar in residence at the George Washington University Institute for Communitarian Policy Studies. And while my girlfriend later admitted that she never did get around to reading it, I learned a great deal from this volume—enough to send me off on a whole new research track that would, in the end, turn my on-again, off-again faith into rock-solid assurance.

After visiting the bookstore that autumn morning, I headed home and raced through the work I absolutely had to finish that day—a cattle-industry case study and a slim-jim brochure on mammography marketing materials—and settled down at the kitchen table to see what Glynn had to say on the subject of God.

I was immediately entranced. He said that there's a growing problem for scientists who support the idea of random-chance origins for our universe—a problem called the *anthropic principle*. This principle, he explained, "says that all the seemingly arbitrary and unrelated constants in physics have one strange thing in common—these are precisely the values you need if you want to have a universe capable of producing life."[1]

Well, that was interesting, I thought, especially when I learned that these cosmic "coincidences" are too numerous for serious scientists to gloss over when they're brought up at scientific meetings—something which apparently happens fairly frequently these days. According to Glynn, they include things like the relationship between gravity and electromagnetism and the nuclear weak force. If any of these relationships had been tweaked just a bit, he said, there could be no life on earth.[2]

There was a ton of material, some of it pretty heavy stuff even for a late-blooming science geek like me, who'd had to learn enough about physics over the course of my career to write technical papers on subjects like NMR spectroscopy. And admittedly, there was no way I could know for sure that it was all true; I don't know if the nuclear weak force is really 10^{38} times the strength of gravity, or if gravity is really about 10^{39} times weaker than electromagnetism.

But Glynn made a persuasive case that these things *are* true. What's more, after finishing his book, it seemed like everywhere I turned I was running into confirming evidence or additional proof that, indeed, our world could not possibly have come about by accident.

Which meant it was beginning to look like there had been some sort of Creator after all.

※

IT TURNED OUT that the anthropic principle described by Patrick Glynn had begun surfacing in the 1960s, and that these other things had been discussed behind closed doors in the scientific community for years.

I wondered why I'd never heard any of these things before. They all seemed like subjects as newsworthy and important as anything else covered by our news media.

※

THIS LINE OF inquiry into our origins led me to several major surprises right off the bat, and I forced Dave to listen to every last detail.

"Okay, check it out," I said one Sunday afternoon when he was sitting in the huge green leather chair in our overstuffed Packer room, trying to watch some big golf tournament. "Are you listening?"

"Go ahead," he said. He gave me what was meant to be an encouraging glance, but he was clearly more interested in the hushed voices of the commentators than he was in yet another science lesson from me.

"Okay," I said, perching on the edge of the love seat, "First of all, did you know that most scientists agree that the universe is not eternal? That it had a beginning and presumably will have an end?"

"No, dear, I didn't know that."

I've always felt that the only thing better than knowing such interesting stuff is sharing it with someone who's still in the dark. Satisfied with his response, I continued. "Okay, here's the second thing: Did you know that when it comes to what *caused* that beginning, there are really only two choices? The universe was either created by an intelligent designer—in short, by God—or it is the product of time plus random chance."

"Really," he said. I noticed that Tiger Woods was on the tee box, so I waited until his drive had landed and Dave had shared a few oohs and ahs with the TV gallery.

"I have to admit," I said finally, when the camera had cut to some golfer in a sand trap, "that I resisted both of these principles for a while. The universe is *not* eternal? There are only *two* possibilities? How could this be? You know?"

"Yes, dear, I know," my husband said, sighing to underscore how patient he was being to put up with my chatter while Tiger was on the course.

"But in the end, I haven't found a shred of support for any other solution. So you can see why we have to accept these things as true. There *was* a beginning to this universe, and it was caused by either a God *or* time plus chance."

"Interesting," he said.

"Are you really listening?"

"Yes, dear."

Good deal. I decided to tell him about some of the other amazing truths I'd come across—jaw-dropping truths that had kept me from going off on all kinds of wild goose chases. I also decided to grease the skids with a little snack; I retreated to the kitchen to pour a bowl of Planters peanuts, the good, slightly greasy and perfectly salty kind.

"Did you know," I said, returning to his side and placing the bowl on the little table next to him, "that of all the world's major religions, only Judaism, Christianity, and Islam have *any* explanation for the origins of our universe? And that they agree it's what's covered in the book of Genesis?"

"Really," he said, popping a few peanuts into his mouth.

"That's the first book of the Bible," I said, to see if he was paying any attention to me.

"I know that, dear," he said, mildly exasperated now. But at least I knew he *was* listening, at least with one ear.

"Of course, some people say we came from aliens, but that's simply *moving* the problem, not really solving it." Tiger was putting, threatening to shut down the ear that had been trained on me. I raised my voice a little to keep it open. "Why, you ask? Because it doesn't explain how the aliens, and their worlds, came into being!"

"Watch some *Twilight Zone* reruns," he said, trying to be funny. "I'm sure Rod Serling knew the answer."

I sighed loudly. "I'm serious, Dave."

"Okay, I'm sorry," he said, turning in his chair so that he was actually facing me. "What else?"

"Well," I said, keenly aware that this undivided attention had coincided with a bevy of commercials. "There's this: Saying that everything came from a parallel universe that is not detectable, and never will be, is moving the problem clear out of the realm of reality. And perhaps sanity."

"We wouldn't want that," he said, smiling brightly.

"Of course not. And just as important, saying that modern science simply hasn't figured it out yet but will someday is your right—or one's right, I should say. But it's betting one's eternal future on something that may not happen in our lifetimes—may, in fact, never happen. It's a risk only a high-stakes gambler would want to take."

"And one wouldn't want that, either," said my husband, turning back to watch the golfer who wears the goofy clothes hitting a fairway shot. "One certainly wouldn't want that."

AS IT TURNED out, the Glynn book had unlocked some invisible floodgates for me. Suddenly I was confronted everywhere I turned with evidence that evolution couldn't possibly have occurred—which meant there had to have been an intelligent designer behind it all.

For one thing, evolution theory broke all kinds of natural laws that modern scientists claimed to agree on—laws that I had actually learned somewhere along the way and had conveniently forgotten. For example:

- Something cannot come from nothing, according to the law of cause and effect. Yet that's what the evolutionary big bang theory requires.
- Life only comes from life, according to the law of biogenesis—not from non-life. Yet evolution theory says that it was nonlife that jump-started life in some long-ago, faraway chemical soup.
- Nothing improves with time, according to the second law of thermodynamics. On the contrary: everything clearly deteriorates. Yet evolution theory requires just the opposite.

These facts alone couldn't prove anything definitively, I could see. After all, it was possible that such laws had been inoperable once upon a time, in a land far, far away.

But there was even more damaging evidence against evolution theory. Perhaps most important, I learned that nearly all of the evolutionary "proofs" I'd believed since childhood were not true.

This was a little difficult to take, at least at first. I'd read about the Scopes Monkey Trial and had seen the 1960 version of *Inherit the Wind*. From this film and from random letters-to-the-editor I'd come across over the years, I knew how blind fundamentalist Christians were to the things of science, and especially about origins.

So it was with some shock that I discovered that the major evolutionary "evidences" associated with the Scopes trial had been bogus. Fossil ape-man Piltdown man, for example, turned out to be a deliberate hoax; Java man, a miscombined collection of ape and human bones; Nebraska man, the result of a tooth left behind by an extinct pig; and Neanderthal man, an old, arthritic human.

I was also surprised to learn that supposedly vestigial organs like the appendix really are not vestigial—a term that implies something that's withering away over evolutionary generations because it's no longer needed. As one lecturer I saw on TV said, every organ in our bodies has function and is functional. True, we can live without our appendixes and tonsils and gall bladders, he said. We can also live without our arms and legs, eyes and ears; that doesn't make any of these body parts vestigial.

But perhaps most amazing to me was the realization that no transitional fossils have been discovered. I could dig up a dog bone and a cat bone from the same backyard (mine, for instance), and *say* they proved that dogs had evolved from cats; but saying so would not make it so. I could hire an artist to draw a half-dog, half-cat family, adding all kinds of exotic trees and other imaginary transitional beings, but not even getting the picture published in every textbook in the land would make my idea true.

Yet apparently this is exactly what paleontologists have done to try to make a case for one type of creature evolving into another. And I'd bought it, hook, line, and sinker, starting with those drawings of adorable equine ancestors, and being thoroughly convinced by human-ancestor depictions such as Sir Grafton Elliot Smith's famous 1922 portrait of Nebraska man and his family.

And yet they were all nothing more than figments of feverish evolutionary imaginations. They were, in short, not true. And let's see, the opposite of truth is—hmmm, that would be lies.

One by one, the evolutionary "facts" I'd taken for granted crumbled before my eyes. And like so many before me, I was left with evidence that pointed insistently toward an intelligent designer.

<hr />

I WAS HOOKED. I began spending every spare moment studying the origins debate. I read book after book, ranging from Henry Morris's *The Long War Against God* to Marvin Lubenow's *Bones of Contention*. I practically inhaled the creation-science lectures I came across on TV—especially those of Princeton-educated theologian Dr. John Whitcomb, who had, with Dr. Morris, launched the modern creation science movement in 1961 with the publication of *The Genesis Flood.*

It soon became clear that the age of the earth (and by extension, the universe) was central to this debate. If it's billions of years old, then evolution could possibly be true; so could creationism, although the Bible's account of origins would have to be shrugged off as unscientific mythology. But if earth is instead relatively young—say, ten thousand years or less—then evolution could not have taken place, and intelligent design would be the only plausible explanation for our origins.

When I started examining this issue, I assumed the old-earth scenario would emerge the clear winner. After all, scientists certainly had proof that the "millions and millions of years ago" statements peppering our textbooks were factual, didn't they?

But that's not what I found out. Instead, I kept coming across clues suggesting that the earth is, indeed, just thousands of years old, not billions.

For instance, in *The Collapse of Evolution*, author Scott Huse, PhD, summed up readily available proof that an earth billions of years old would exhibit:

- a much higher concentration of salt in the oceans than what exists today.
- much more atmospheric helium—the product of the radioactive decay of uranium and thorium; current levels would indicate ten thousand years of decay, Dr. Huse said, assuming a starting point of zero.
- no mountains, because even the Himalaya and Rocky Mountains would erode to sea level in just ten million years.
- a lot more sediment deposited in the Gulf of Mexico by the Mississippi River, since what's in the delta now has been calculated to have taken about four thousand years to deposit.
- no more petroleum or natural gas beneath the earth's cap rock, because the extremely high pressures containing both would have blown through the rock in ten thousand years max.[3]

And that was just the beginning. Dr. Huse's book also pointed out that commonly held assumptions about certain processes taking long ages may well be wrong. For instance, marine and vegetable matter can be converted into oil and gas in as little as twenty minutes under the proper temperature and pressure conditions, such as what might have occurred during a global flood; wood and other cellulosic material, in just a few hours. All of which may explain why everything from human skeletons to jewelry have been found embedded in coal.[4]

It seemed that open-minded scientists were drawing similar conclusions from other natural processes not only on earth but throughout the universe—including comet decay, star-cluster maintenance, and super-star energy consumption. And in *The Modern Creation Trilogy: Science & Creation,* volume 2, doctors Henry M. and John D. Morris made what seemed to me to be a very convincing case for a young earth by analyzing the strength of its magnetic field.

Measured for well over a century, the Morrises said, this magnetic field is decaying at a rate corresponding to a half-life of 1,400 years, which means that 1,400 years ago it was twice as strong as it is now. They said that if we were to extrapolate back just seven thousand years—5 times 1,400 years—the earth's magnetic field would have been thirty-two times stronger. "It could hardly ever have been much greater than that," they said, "as the earth's structure itself would have disintegrated with a much stronger field."[5]

The doctors Morris also showed that today's human population of about 6 billion was a lot more reflective of life measured in a few thousand years than a million years. They demonstrated mathematically that, if you start out with just one man and woman, a population of 6 billion would be reached after about four thousand years of exponential growth at a very conservative 0.5 percent annually; this, they said, would allow for famine, disease, and wars.[6]

Then there was the rather major problem of how inorganic matter came to life in the first place. Somewhere I'd read that scientists to this day do not know the difference between a dead dog and a live one, other than the obvious fact that one is dead and the other isn't. In other words, they don't know what life *is.* Nor could they explain how the first cells came to life without a creator making it happen. From Ray Comfort's cool little volume *Scientific Facts in the Bible,* I learned that Cambridge University astronomy professor Sir Fred

Hoyle said, "The likelihood of the formation of life from inanimate matter is one out of $10^{40,000}$. . . . It is big enough to bury Darwin and the whole theory of evolution."[7]

I was also surprised to find out that natural and human history appear to have begun abruptly just a few thousand years ago. For instance, the oldest tree in the world is a bristlecone pine that hasn't even reached its five thousandth birthday.[8] The earliest evidence of a written alphabet is estimated to be just four thousand years old.[9] And the oldest civilization in the world is thought to be less than six thousand years old."[10]

The more I learned, the more difficult it became to shrug these things off as coincidence.

Astounding as it seemed, it was beginning to look like, maybe, just possibly, the earth was *not* millions or billions of years old—that it might actually count its birthdays in the thousands.

If this turned out to be true, it would mean that evolution was impossible.

Which would in turn mean that the only other possibility is true: there is an intelligent designer behind the universe.

Which would mean that there is, in fact, a God.

I FOUND IT impossible to keep such discoveries to myself. When visiting with old friends whose news focused on promotions, divorces, affairs, and killings in the stock market, I'd respond to any "what's new?" directed my way with a report on some great article I'd just read—an article showing that those notorious "annual" rings in Greenland's ice cores weren't really "annual" at all, for instance, or a piece discussing the Genesis Flood implications of the world's polystrata trees.

Usually, my friends just laughed at me, which was fine; I couldn't expect everyone to be interested in these things. But once in a while a buddy with an interest in science would at least feign curiosity about what I had to say.

One example was a beautiful and brilliant ad-industry acquaintance I'll call Carla. The last time I saw her, when I was more than a year into my study, we were lunching at a charming country restaurant that would have qualified as a tearoom for Nancy Drew and her chums. She even looked the part, wearing a smart gray suit and creamy silk blouse. I, dressed in my favorite blue jeans and Packer sweatshirt, did not.

After a half hour or so of discussing the usual (Carla's job, Carla's tenuous marriage, and Carla's favorite hobby), she smoothed her perfect blonde pageboy and asked me what was new in my life. She seemed fascinated as I described all the young-earth evidences I'd been reading about.

"Ah, but you're forgetting something important," she said when I paused to take a bite out of my sandwich. "Radiometric dating. It proves that the universe is billions of years old—which means it makes all this other stuff you're talking about irrelevant."

Carla wasn't the first person to bring up this objection, but this time I was prepared for it. Although it's not the simplest issue, I had studied it until I understood it well enough to discuss it at least semi-intelligently.

"Really?" I said. "That's interesting. I mean, I've heard and read lots about radiometric dating in the last few months, but you're the first person I've come across who actually understands it. How do you figure it proves vast ages for the universe?"

"Well," said Carla, sipping her coffee and glancing at her watch, "I'm not sure exactly how it works. But it's well accepted by the scientific community."

"Ah," I said. "Can I share a little analogy that purports to show how unreliable it is? Maybe you can tell me where I'm going wrong."

"Sure, okay," she said, sitting bolt upright, ready to jump all over my error.

I shoved my plate aside and, grabbing a pen from my purse, drew a pail on my paper place mat and added a wavy line running side to side near its bottom.

"So, what we have here is a plain old five-gallon bucket containing a gallon of water," I said, pointing to the wavy line with my pen. "It's a leaky bucket, currently losing about a gallon a year. Okay?"

"Got it."

"So tell me, Carla, how long has our five-gallon bucket been sitting here?" I asked, adding a tree, a barn, and a sun to my sketch.

"The obvious answer would be, let's see—leaking a gallon a year, one gallon left, I guess we'd say it's been sitting there for four years. But that's not necessarily the right answer."

"Why not?" I asked, smiling at her encouragingly.

"Because we don't know how much water it contained originally," she said, returning my smile and leaning back in her chair.

"And?"

"And? Hmmm. Well, we're assuming that no water has evaporated."

"Right. What else?"

Carla leaned forward again, frowning a little.

I drew a black cloud over my sun.

"Of course," she said, almost gleefully. "We're assuming that it hasn't rained—that no water has been added to it in that time."

"Good. One more."

She squinted at my picture and shook her head. "I give up."

"We're assuming that the leak rate has been constant over time—that it has always leaked at a rate of a gallon a year, that the holes haven't become larger from vandalism, say, or smaller from mineral deposits."

Carla tilted her head and nodded. "Good point. But without any more data, of course, we have to make these assumptions, don't we?"

"Exactly," I said triumphantly. "Which is apparently what happens with radiometric dating."

She stared at me. "How do you figure?"

"Well, I may be wrong, but it's my understanding that there's no way to know what the original radioactivity levels were in the rocks being dated . . . that there's no way to know whether some radioactive material might have been lost to, for instance, rain and flooding . . . and that there's no way to know whether some radioactive elements might have been added by leeching from other rocks, or by daughter isotopes—"

"Okay, enough," Carla said. She wasn't smiling. "I don't know enough about this to respond, so you're wasting your time and mine."

"Okay," I said. "I was just going to add, 'so they have to make assumptions in each of these areas—'"

"Yes, I get it. And those assumptions can throw off the readings." She checked her watch again and stood up abruptly. "I've gotta get going," she said, taking a twenty out of her purse and tossing it on the table. "Lunch is on the agency. Take care, now."

She was gone before I had the chance to deliver the punch line: that this is probably why radiometric dating so often delivers erratic results, assigning vast ages to materials *known* to be young, and that evolutionists routinely discard dates that don't jive with their long-ages philosophy. As a result, it looks to us laymen like radiometric dating tells a mostly consistent story about an old, old earth.

Nor did I have a chance to thank Carla for lunch, and so far I haven't had another opportunity to do so in person. My e-mails to her go unanswered.

Not that it's a big deal. We were hardly close friends, and there'd never really been a business relationship of any importance between us.

But to this day it makes me sad that someone committed to the evolutionary idea refuses to entertain any criticism of her theory.

CHAPTER 15

The heavens declare:
How could I have missed all this?

10:30 p.m., May 30, 2000

I couldn't believe that no one had called. Not a soul. Not that I had actually *told* anyone that I was beyond comfort . . . but surely those who knew me best should have *known* that I would be a train wreck by now.

I made a mental list of everyone who'd failed me this horrid night and vowed to fail each of them just as soon as I had the chance. After all, Mom wouldn't be around to gently suggest that I'd be better off forgiving them, so I wouldn't even have to feel bad about plotting my revenge.

There was one good thing, anyway, I thought bitterly: no Mom, no battered conscience.

Feminism had taught me to say, "I don't respond to guilt." With my mother out of the picture, maybe I'd finally be able to live up to that hardheaded sentiment.

※

IT WAS A FRIDAY afternoon in late autumn 2003. A girlfriend I'll call Anne and I had played hooky to get in one more round of golf before the weather turned. We'd already lost several balls amid all the falling leaves, and if we got too close to the garbage containers, the bees swarmed us. But the course—Western Lakes, one of my favorites— wasn't all that busy, and we'd been allowed to go out alone. Besides, it was a heartbreakingly perfect Indian summer day; the warm, moist air bore just a hint of the chill that was to come, a hint that transported me back to childhood anticipation of Thanksgiving and Christmas and endless joy.

We were on the tenth tee box when Anne made a shocking statement.

"So you've come to the conclusion that there's a supreme being," she said.

"Why, yes, I have," I said. "An intelligent designer, aka God." I was blown away that this topic had been broached by a woman whose scientific education and life's work had left her hostile to anything smacking of the supernatural.

She busied herself with a few practice swings.

"There are only two explanations for our origins," I added, unable to bear her silence. "A god or time plus chance, as in evolution. I studied it, and I'm certain the answer is a god."

"Prove it."

Prove it? Atheist Anne was interested in hearing evidence for God? I was thrilled; I wanted nothing more than to tell her about the incredible truths I had discovered.

"You want the five-minute tour or an hour-long lecture?"

"Puh-leeze," she said, teeing up her ball. "I listened to enough lectures in school. Just give me the CliffsNotes version."

She hit her shot an impossible distance, maybe a couple hundred yards. Even though it had sailed a bit right on her, into the fringe, it would take me at least two shots to catch up.

"Five-minute version, coming right up," I said, teeing up my Golden Girl and hitting it about a hundred yards, straight down the middle. I used the moments of silence to quickly riffle through the "science" files in my head. By that time, I'd collected overwhelming proof against evolution theory, having listened to scores of lectures and read more than a dozen books on the subject. I could tell her with a fair amount of confidence about the origins implications of everything from genetics and geological formations to paleontology and sedimentology.

But Anne was a big-corporation manager who based her decisions on high-level information, not details; I needed to pick just a few of the points that would be most eye-popping to her.

Ah, here, filed under *M* not far from "magnificent."

"First, mutations," I said, climbing into the cart as she stomped on the accelerator. "Mutations that actually *add* to a creature's genetic information. Evolution can't function without them."

"True enough," she said.

"They don't exist. Name one."

"Come on, that's not my field. You should ask an expert. Hit your ball."

I climbed out of the cart and slapped it with my 7-wood, the only fairway wood I seemed to be able to hit more than fifteen feet. My Golden Girl formed a perfect little arc and landed another hundred yards closer to the green. It sat prettily in the middle of the fairway to the left of Anne's tee shot.

"Cart golf," I said, jumping back in. "I *did* ask an expert. I e-mailed the head of the federal government's human genome project and asked him for one example of a positive, additive genetic mutation."

"What did he say?"

"He didn't have an answer for me."

She used her 8-iron to loft her ball onto the green; amazingly, I achieved the same result with my trusty 7-wood.

"Did he answer you at all?"

"Immediately. He said people with sickle cell anemia don't tend to get malaria."

"Well, there you go."

"Not quite," I said. "It may be positive for the person with sickle cell anemia, of course, but it's not an *additive* mutation. It doesn't *add* anything to the DNA, which is what would be required if, for instance, a dinosaur were to sprout wing stubs on its species' way to becoming a bird."

She shrugged. "Then if that was the best this guy could do—well, he's probably just an administrator."

"MD and PhD. He's a chemist and a geneticist."

She shrugged again and headed for the green with her putter.

We finished out the hole (she with a par, me with a double-bogey) and headed to the next hole. A foursome was just teeing off, and from the first one's drive, it looked like we might have a long wait.

"Okay, I'll grant you, that makes some sense," Anne said, picking up the conversation where we'd left it at the tenth green. "Strike one against evolution. What else have you got?"

The second golfer had teed up by that time, buying me a few moments of silence to return to my mental file cabinet. "Irrefutable" was the word that popped into my head—and indeed, there was my answer right next to it, straight out of biochemist Michael Behe's book *Darwin's Black Box*.

"Irreducible complexity," I said as soon as the golfer had connected with her ball, sending it out a good twenty-five yards from the tee box. I had no idea if Dr. Behe's line of thought would impress Anne, but his book had blown me away. "The fact that biological systems are too complex to have been formed through bunches of tiny little modifications."

"Too complex? Or too complex for you and these authors you're reading?"

"Too complex period," I said, praying for the wisdom to capture this subject in a few sentences. Her question reflected evolutionists' portrayal of intelligent-design advocates as too dumb to understand, and too cowardly to even try. "The book I read on this was written by a biochemist, so I'd say he understood the subject pretty well."

"Geez, we're going to be here forever," Anne said, waving her gloved hand toward the tee box, where a golfer in bright aqua shorts had just completed her second total whiff of the ball.

"We could ask if they'd let us play through," I said, wishing they'd take notice of their pokiness and wave us through without being asked.

"That's okay. We're not in any hurry, are we?"

"Not me," I said, popping open the Diet Pepsi I'd picked up at the turn and taking a good swig. "So—irreducible complexity. Consider, if you will, the lowly mousetrap. Platform, hammer, spring, catch, and a holding bar."

She rolled her eyes at me and smiled wickedly. "You don't think it's odd that you know the parts of a mousetrap? You, who would do anything to avoid ever having to *touch* one?"

I had to laugh. "But reading about it isn't so bad. Anyway, it has these five parts. It can't function without all five of them."

She thought for a moment. "Right—I can see that."

"That makes it an irreducibly complex system. If it were a living system, it could not have evolved component by component. Without *all* of these interdependent parts in place, none of them would've functioned, and none would have survived the natural selection process. Make sense?"

Anne considered this for a few ticks and nodded. "Okay. I can buy that."

I took a deep breath. I'd always been afraid of Anne; she's one of these very frank people who thinks it's her duty to tell you if you're being an idiot, and I don't usually appreciate hearing that. Besides, I've never been articulate, and this aging brain of mine is beginning to betray me now and then—a potentially lethal combination for someone intent on making a mission-critical point, as we say in the ad biz.

But I could hardly quit now.

"Well, what this biochemist did," I said, "was show how human systems are irreducibly complex and so could not have evolved. He described a handful of them in some detail—blood coagulation, cell operation, and the immune system, for instance. He showed how these things could not have come about by gradual evolution of interdependent parts, and how they had to have been designed as complete systems from the start."

Anne was watching the fourth golfer tee off. It looked like she was lost in space. She wasn't, though; I knew she was thinking about what I'd said.

"Eyes," she said. "I've heard that argument applied to eyes. Something about some ancient fossil having incredibly complex eyes."

I tried not to show my surprise that she'd paid a lick of attention to this sort of information.

"I've read that too," I said. "Trilobites, maybe? Something like that, anyway. If evolutionists are to be believed, they were among the earliest creatures and went extinct hundreds of millions of years ago—yet they had these amazingly complex, multilensed eyes that let them see underwater without any distortion."

"Yes, I think that was it, and there's no evidence of precursors." She was putty in my hands, it seemed—except apparently she couldn't quite leave behind what she'd always been taught: "That they've found so far, at least."

It was finally time to tee off, and the slow foursome ahead of us stood back to let us play through. Whereupon we both duffed our drives, which led to friendly laughter and chatter all around as we worked our way down the fairway.

I decided to let the subject of origins ride for the duration. Like most of my friends, Anne already thought I'd gone off the deep end on this God thing, and I wanted to prove I was still a real person interested in the real world. We chatted about work and vacations, clothes and movies.

But she brought it up again as we approached the par 3 seventeenth hole.

"So you don't deny natural selection," she said out of the blue, surprising me again.

"Not at all," I said. Were we really having this conversation? "It happens; it's like a manufacturer's quality control system, except it occurs without man's intervention. It happens artificially too, which is why there are hundreds of breeds of dogs today. Certain genetic traits are kept; others are bred out."

"I thought creationists—that's what you are, right?—I thought creationists denied that sort of evolution fundamental." She parked the cart and marched over to the tee box.

"I'm pretty sure it predates Darwin," I said, smiling at the understatement. "In fact, the first book in the Bible—Genesis—records artificial selection in some sort of livestock."

She looked back at me, her eyebrows raised in surprise.

"Really, it does," I said, aware that I was in danger of drifting. "It's what they call 'microevolution.' Whereas when evolutionists say we evolved from slime, they're actually talking about macroevolution— that's what creationists deny. It's bait and switch—evolutionists use real-life examples to get you to agree to microevolution, then say it explains macroevolution. Pretty deceptive."

I refocused my thoughts on the main point of today's discussion: showing Anne there's good reason for believing that this universe is the work of an intelligent designer in general; I'd save the God-of-the-Bible evidence for another day.

"But the point is that natural selection describes the *survival* of the fittest," I said, grateful to whoever had come up with this easy-to-remember way of explaining a critical distinction. "It can't describe the *arrival* of the fittest. It isn't a *creative* process."

She teed off then, using an iron. Her ball landed about an inch from the hole, causing a group of grounds workers who'd gathered on the last fairway to erupt in cheers.

WHAT I'D SHARED with Anne was just the tip of the iceberg in the case against evolution theory's chance-plus-time idea—and therefore in the case *for* an intelligent designer.

I doubt that I'd convinced her of anything that day. Still, someone had obviously been planting seeds of belief in her heart, and maybe I'd watered them a little. And maybe they would one day germinate and grow into a faith that would crush her doubts just as surely as it had mine.

Reflecting on our conversation later that night, sitting at my kitchen table while Dave and the dogs snoozed in the living room, I longed for a day when Anne would be sitting firmly on the fence on this issue, needing only a good shove to fall onto the side of what I now knew was the truth.

I flipped through my Bible and pulled out a page of quotes I'd compiled in anticipation of such a day. They just might do the job.

My favorite was from evolutionist Richard Lewontin, who wrote in the January 9, 1997, issue of the *New York Review*:

> We take the side of science *in spite of* the patent absurdity of some of its constructs, *in spite of* its failure to fulfill many of its extravagant promises of health and life, *in spite of* the tolerance of the scientific community for unsubstantiated just-so stories, because we have a prior commitment, a commitment to materialism. It is not that the methods and institutions of science somehow compel us

to accept a material explanation of the phenomenal world, but, on the contrary, that we are forced by our *a priori* adherence to material causes to . . . produce material explanations, no matter how counterintuitive. . . . Moreover, that materialism is absolute, for we cannot allow a Divine Foot in the door.[1]

Running a close second in my heart was this quote from Aldous Huxley of *Brave New World* fame, whose grandfather, Thomas Huxley, had been one of the earliest and most ardent promoters of Darwin's theories:

> I had motives for not wanting the world to have a meaning; consequently assumed that it had none, and was able without any difficulty to find satisfying reasons for this assumption. . . . The philosopher who finds no meaning in the world is not concerned exclusively with a problem in pure metaphysics; he is also concerned to prove that there is no valid reason why he personally should not do as he wants to do. For myself . . . the philosophy of meaninglessness was essentially an instrument of liberation. . . . We objected to the morality because it interfered with our sexual freedom. . . .[2]

Anne wouldn't consider these quotes evidence, I knew. Nor did I, not really. I just found it incredibly interesting, not to mention heartbreaking, that these prominent opinion leaders shut God out for reasons other than the pursuit of truth—and then participated in foisting these teachings on entire generations of children.

⚶

THE FEMINISTS OF the '70s talked about moments of epiphany that they—we, actually—called the "click." They were moments when we realized that reality did not match the feminine ideal, supposedly.

But in practice it meant the increasingly frequent realization that we were in the presence of a male chauvinist pig or one of his drones.

Well, I'll tell you—a feminist *click* is nothing compared to the epiphanies that become practically a daily occurrence when the subject under investigation is Christianity.

Many of my clicks have come from a piece of scientific, historical, or cultural information. For instance, a few years ago I was lunching at a Chinese restaurant with some friends. We each had a "Chinese New Year" place mat, and while everyone else was busy looking for their birth years and those of their mates, I amused myself by looking at the animals chosen for the Chinese zodiac:

Dragon	Rabbit/cat	Dog
Rat	Goat	Pig
Ox	Monkey	Snake
Tiger	Rooster	Horse

I looked again at the first animal: Dragon.

My stomach flip-flopped, just as it had when Paul Newman and Julie Andrews saw the second bus following them in Alfred Hitchcock's *Torn Curtain*.

How is it, I wondered, that the ancient Chinese had chosen eleven real animals, and one mythological critter?

I remembered hearing, too, that all major cultures have dragon myths (not to mention "great flood" myths), and that ancient dragon images have been found all over the world, from Babylon and Egypt to China; they've been found drawn on Viking ships, shown in relief sculpture in Aztec temples, and carved into bones by Inuits. And when I thought about all the dragon drawings I'd seen over the course of five decades, they all blurred into just a few types of creatures.

But, of course, scientists have managed to explain these similarities away. Because, of course, the alternative is unthinkable: we couldn't possibly admit the possibility that these dragons had actually lived with man, that they were, in fact, dinosaurs (a word that wasn't invented until the nineteenth century), that—horrors!—maybe "millions and millions of years ago" was nothing more than the opening words of today's adult fairy tales.

Click.

⚘

RECENTLY MY HUSBAND told me about an analogy that I wish I'd come across at the beginning of my study of our origins.

It was a gloomy January morning and I'd just joined him at the kitchen table, grousing about yet another newspaper article that presented evolution as a proven fact.

"It was on some show earlier this week," Dave said. "This guy was saying that if you wanted to know how a personal computer *operates*, you could figure it out simply by examining the PC itself."

"That makes sense," I said tentatively, clueless about where he was headed with this.

"But he said that if you wanted to know how that same computer *originated*, examining it would be useless." He smiled triumphantly.

I looked at him blankly.

"I figured this would be a piece of cake for you," he said. "Apparently not."

I shrugged.

"Well, think about it," he said. "Knowing that a computer's printed circuit board handles certain functions isn't the same as knowing how that board got there in the first place. Same with knowing that the computer's 'intelligence' relies on various combinations of ones and zeros—that doesn't tell you a thing about how this one-and-zero system arose in the first place."

The analogy was beginning to make sense. I nodded encouragingly.

"The point is," Dave said, "to know anything about where this contraption *came* from, you have to look beyond the PC itself—in fact, you have to look to man as designer and builder. Only then will you have a chance of understanding how it came to be."

"And if that's true of something as relatively simple as a computer," I said, finally catching on to the premise, "why wouldn't we expect to do the same thing to figure out how the universe came into being? And life? Why would we restrict our answer to only what's *in* the universe?"

"Right. This guy said that's what evolutionists do, by limiting themselves to a naturalistic explanation for everything. They won't look beyond the material world to try to figure out how that world came to be."

"I've read that they have actually defined anything supernatural out of science," I said. "So that by their definition, if it's supernatural, it's not scientific."

He shook his head. "And to think we believed all of that garbage."

"Of course we did. Our teachers presented it as fact."

"Would we have believed it if they'd said printed circuit boards created themselves out of a bunch of chemicals?"

"Good point," I said, amazed that we could have overlooked such a fundamental error, one that could be exposed by a simple analogy. Another analogy I'd heard crept out of a corner of my mind. "Or that Mount Rushmore had been carved by wind and rain?"

WITHIN MONTHS OF cracking open Patrick Glynn's *God the Evidence* in the fall of 2000, science had convinced me that there had to be a God.

All I had to do was figure out exactly who He (or She) really was.

CHAPTER 16

No other gods:
Would the real One please stand up?

Still muttering to myself about all the alleged friends who hadn't called me, I suddenly remembered that I'd been outside earlier for close to fifteen minutes. It was possible that I'd missed a call *and* that the message light on the phone was broken!

Alas, the dial tone was steady. Still, voice mail had messed me up any number of times over the last few years. I dialed into our mailbox once again, just in case.

No messages.

I sat down at the table again, unable to think of a single thing I wanted to do except maybe crawl out of my skin.

It was the first time in my life that I actually understood that expression.

I racked my brain, trying to think of whom I could talk to, or what I could listen to, or watch, or read, that might help me find some peace amid this horror.

There was no one. There was nothing.

So this is it, I thought. This is what they mean when they say you come to the end of yourself. It's being utterly helpless, recognizing for the first time that there's nothing anywhere in this world that could make everything all right again.

No natural resources, anyway.

Which pretty much left me with nowhere to turn except the supernatural.

※

IT'S TRUE THAT I was putting the cart before the horse by joining a church in the summer of 2000, before I was even convinced of God's existence.

But I was hurting, and it was very comforting being around people who were 100 percent positive not only that He exists, but also that Jesus Christ *is* God almighty and that trusting in Him will assure you of a spot in heaven, no matter how checkered your past had been. That, they said, was the gospel—literally, the good news—and I liked the sound of it.

Still, I had to be equally certain in my own mind that these things were true, and all the emotion-packed singing in the world was not going to turn me into a true believer. For that, I needed verifiable facts.

My family was no help. They just believed. I could've asked a pastor, but it never occurred to me to do so.

And so this doubting Thomasina set out to determine exactly *whose* God was the real God. (If, of course, He existed at all.)

※

NOT SURE WHERE to begin, I just started picking up books that looked promising or simply interesting. That meant books by contemporary writers like Lee Strobel, Josh McDowell, and Max Lucado—writers representing a smorgasbord of styles and content, but all presenting a common doctrine with Jesus Christ solidly at its center.

I'd never noticed such books before. But suddenly I found them everywhere, even in secular bookstores that I'd frequented for years, like Half Price Books and Barnes & Noble. Much to my amazement, these stores had entire sections devoted to religion and spirituality. And there were thousands of additional volumes in the church library and at local Christian stores, and while the nearby megachurch auditorium had left me a bit cold, its bookstore did not, packed as it was with books on every spiritual subject imaginable.

Best of all, that first autumn, I stumbled upon a little Christian bookshop that was going out of business and had marked everything down by 75 percent. I walked out with armloads of books that I might never have come across in even a decent-sized church library, and certainly could not have afforded at cover prices.

I drove home that day with butterflies in my stomach, convinced that I'd found the book that would unlock the door to faith for me, wondering which one it might be.

⸙

AMONG MY 75 percent-off bargains was James Sire's *The Universe Next Door: A Basic Worldview Catalog*. It was this astounding book that gave me my first big-picture view of the world's major belief systems— including theism, deism, naturalism, nihilism, existentialism, Eastern pantheistic monism, New Age and postmodernism.

Naturally, I was familiar with some of this information; one could hardly make it through two years at a radical, liberal-arts college in the 1970s without being steeped in the writings of Jean-Paul Sartre and Albert Camus and the films of Ingmar Bergman. (At least, *I* couldn't have avoided these things, given the fact that the drug-free guy I was dating then was a philosophy major who was really into that sort of existentialist entertainment. But I wasn't alone. Seeing a

Bergman "film" and then dissecting it over a few beers was a standard date among Ripon intellectuals.)

Sire described these belief systems in enough detail to give his readers a grasp of each one's basic tenets. Perhaps even more important, he provided some very wise criteria with which to judge a worldview:

- Its inner intellectual coherence—i.e., the consistency of its essential elements.
- Its ability to account for the data of reality—for instance, to explain a phenomenon such as a man rising from the dead.
- Its ability to explain what it claims to explain. Sire wrote, "The crucial questions, then, to ask of a worldview are, How does it explain the fact that human beings think but think haltingly, love but hate too, are creative but also destructive, wise but often foolish and so forth? What explains our longing for truth or personal fulfillment? . . . These are, of course, huge questions. But that is what a worldview is for."[1]
- Its ability to deliver subjective satisfaction—something that he said *requires* it to be true. "[T]ruth is ultimately the only thing that will satisfy," he wrote. "But to determine the truth of a worldview, we are cast back on the first three characteristics above."[2]

Sire concluded his analysis by saying that the only worldview passing all these tests is Christian theism. And he made an excellent case that all the others—from deism, naturalism, and existentialism to Eastern pantheistic monism, New Age religions, and postmodernism—have fatal flaws.

I couldn't be sure that this fellow's criteria were the right ones; what did I know about it? But I couldn't see any problems with his approach. I know some people would argue that, as a Christian, he was biased; but I'll bet he would say that he had become a Christian *because* of his objective evaluation of the alternatives.

So, armed with books like this one, I was ready to begin making some sense out of the confusing array of alternatives.

I was acutely aware that most of the authors I was reading were Christian. But I simply couldn't find any comparable books by representatives of other worldviews, and certainly nothing that seemed to make a case for the truth of those worldviews.

Did that make my journey a self-fulfilling prophecy? Perhaps. But as my knowledge of subjects like ancient history, theology, and science grew, I read more widely and went out of my way to check out secular articles and programming on other religions.

In doing so, I never once heard that increasingly familiar "click" alerting me that I'd just had a brush with truth.

※

IT WAS RIGHT about that time, in the autumn of 2000, that I had a nice long talk with a writer friend I'll call Tim. He'd been a Christian for years, and no one was happier than he was when I traded in my *Horticulture* subscription for a good study Bible.

This luncheon of ours took place at The Harp, an Irish pub located on a nicely restored leg of the Milwaukee River. We sat out on the deck, overlooking the river, enjoying the sun with dozens of other chattering workers.

"So," he said after we'd ordered our sandwiches, "how's your investigation coming along? Still leaning toward our side, I hope?"

"Yes, definitely, although I'm still trying to keep an open mind." I was grateful that he didn't point out how shameless it looked, settling down with Christianity while keeping an eye out for something more appealing. "If there's something else out there that makes more sense, I want to get right on it and get right with *that* God—and then drag my loved ones along with me."

"No doubt you mean those who've gone on ahead of you, too,"

Tim said, chuckling at the idea of retroactive redemption. "You have to talk to my wife—she went through the same process years ago."

"Really? Hmmm—maybe she could save me some grief."

"Possibly, but I think this is something that you have to work through yourself. How are you going about researching this subject? Are you spending a lot of time on it?"

"Enough," I said. "At first, I just evaluated the big names in worldviews to see which ones I could cross off the list right away."

"Let me guess. Scientology? Shintoism?"

I laughed. "Among others."

I told him about the books and articles I'd been reading, and the Web sites I'd visited—from sites associated with religions to generic spots like www.beliefnet.com.

"I'm not making much progress, actually—I think Christianity's the answer, but I'm not 100 percent certain. I keep thinking I'm missing something. Got any suggestions?"

Tim thought a moment before answering. "How about this: doing Web searches for 'proof of blank,' where blank is the name of a specific religion. See if you can learn something that will get you unstuck."

I thought that was a great idea, and said so. In fact, although the rest of our lunch was fun, filled as it was with chatter about everything from business to politics to Christian doctrine, I couldn't wait to get home to pursue this new line of inquiry.

※

TIM'S IDEA TURNED out to be brilliant—especially in terms of revealing what some were willing to accept as "proof." For instance:

- Some said that their worldview was true because it was the ideal system for humankind. But I was looking for truth, not practicality or efficacy.

- Some said that their worldview was true because many of its adherents were healthy and wealthy, or because it had inspired great art or humanitarian efforts. This argument struck me as awfully weak, because as far as I could see, there were people of all faiths, and none at all, who would be considered healthy and wealthy, or great artists or humanitarians. So how could that be considered proof that a particular worldview was true?

- Some redefined the purpose of a worldview, saying that the intent of all religion is the happiness of the individual—and that the religion with the happiest adherents was therefore true. By the time I came across this idea, however, I knew that earthly happiness was not the goal of Christianity, which rendered this criterion meaningless.

- Some redefined the very concept of proof, saying, for instance, that if a religion has writings, this is proof that it's true. I kept looking further into this, figuring that there had to be some sort of qualification that had been lost in the translation. To date, I haven't found one, which makes this a truly bewildering proof statement.

This line of inquiry was getting me nowhere fast. Christianity aside, there just didn't seem to be any sort of truth claim that could be objectively evaluated. Do Hindus live longer than or outnumber the rest? Are Buddhists wealthier? Are Muslims happiest? Do New Agers contribute more to mankind?

And even if such things could be demonstrated, would any of them prove that the subjects had a lock on ultimate Truth?

Saying so wouldn't make it so, any more than O. J. proclaiming his innocence proved him innocent.

It seemed to me it would take real evidence to ascertain the truth. Blood evidence, perhaps. And I wasn't finding any amid the "proofs" for these exotic worldviews.

CHAPTER 17

**Let no one deceive you:
There's Christianity, and there's everything else**

11:00 p.m., May 30, 2000

The grandmother clock struck eleven, a count that always sent little stabs of fear into my heart, because it would now be silent until 6 a.m. It meant we were entering that lonely hour when good people were tucked safely in bed, gathering strength for a new day, and anyone still awake and alert would surely be exhausted come morning.

Which reminded me of the insomnia I'd suffered in grade school. Waking in the middle of the night and unable to fall back asleep, I would head downstairs for a glass of milk. Somehow my mother always heard me, even in our big old house. She would come down to the kitchen and make me hot milk and some special treat—usually Triscuit crackers, buttered Dairy State style and broiled until they were golden brown—and talk to me until I felt sleepy.

I looked: we were out of both milk and Triscuits.

I thought about those days and all the interesting talks she and I had at all times of the day and night—talks about horses and husbands, dads and dreams, hopes and happily-ever-afters. Which in turn reminded me of the discussions we'd had about reincarnation;

she had actually toyed with the idea briefly in the late 1960s, when we all read *Here and Hereafter* by "psychic" Ruth Montgomery.

My mother had ditched the idea after my father died, I was now happy to recall. I couldn't imagine anything more horrible than her being reincarnated as someone I would never meet. Maybe she'd felt the same way about Dad; maybe that's why she dropped it.

Still, it was a concept many people seemed to believe, my very smart family aside. I made a mental note to check it out once things had settled down again. I didn't want it to be true, but if it might be, I'd simply have to deal with it.

⚬

As THE YEAR 2000 melted away and I dug deeper into the "which God?" question, it became clear that I would actually have to learn something about each religion in order to evaluate its truth claims; the "proof of" exercise had been a bust, giving me nothing concrete to go on.

Even worse, I was discovering a bottomless pit of possibilities—there seemed to be literally *scores* of religions out there. Sure, many seemed to be permutations of major belief systems, but still, what if some weird offshoot of Asatru or Falun Gong turned out to be true? And what if I missed it?

Fortunately, before I'd driven myself crazy with such speculation, my friend Tim e-mailed me to suggest I begin by evaluating the big five—Buddhism, Hinduism, Islam, Judaism, and Christianity. Then, he said, if truth hadn't yet made itself known to me, I could wander down some less-traveled roads.

And so, using Sire's *The Universe Next Door* as my tour guide and supplementing it with lengthy Internet sessions and books by men like Dave Hunt and Dr. Walter Martin, I formalized my search for the one and only true God. Honestly, I *did* hope the whole thing would turn out to revolve around Jesus, for simplicity's sake. But I was nowhere near ready to concede the race to Him.

I started with Buddha (alias Siddhartha Gautama), the "Enlightened One," who founded Buddhism hundreds of years before the birth of Christ. Not that Buddha claimed to be God. In fact, it seems that Buddhism generally denies the very existence of a Creator. But Buddhists are apparently supposed to honor images of, and objects associated with, Buddha. And why not? He was the one who came up with *dharma*, or "saving truth," to help humankind overcome suffering and achieve nirvana; if *dharma* is truth, he no doubt deserves some adulation.

It turned out to be an intellectually challenging religion. For instance, I read that Zen Buddhism, the most common form in the West, says that the final reality is the Void—something that is neither nothing nor something. The individual, on the other hand, *is* something—the aggregate of previous individuals. A Zen Buddhist's goals include realizing that his roots are in nonbeing and emptying his mind of thought. When he dies, he disappears, and another person emerges from his body, feeling, mind, consciousness, and perception.

Or something like that.

It made no sense to me—no doubt because I am such a slave to Western thought. When I did my Google search for "Proof for Buddhism," what came up were essays explaining that Buddhism is true because it works, presumably by giving people peace. Which didn't make sense to me, either; how peaceful can you be, knowing that upon death you'll disappear?

But the biggest stumbling block for me was Buddhism's denial of a Creator. I had already been persuaded on that point, and so felt safe in moving on.

Next up was the Hindu universal spirit, Brahman (and the hundreds of thousands of gods that make up Brahman).

At first blush, it was tempting to just shrug off Hinduism because of its association with the caste system of social classes and un-touchables, not to mention the worship of cows, monkeys, and snakes, among other creatures. But I've known a number of Hindus over the years, and they're among the dearest people I've ever met—maybe for genetic or cultural reasons, or maybe because they so respect the law of karma and its impact on their future lives. They are also exceedingly smart and lots of fun to be around. So when I thought about this and then read that Hinduism had somewhere in the neighborhood of 800 million followers—all of them apparently striving for spiritual perfection to break the cycle of reincarnation and possibly to achieve god-hood themselves—I thought I'd better look into it.

Unfortunately, I found Hinduism as difficult to grasp as Buddhism. Take-aways, like these from Sire's book, which delivered the most comprehensible description I found, just didn't do it for me:

1. *Atman is Brahman; that is, the soul of each and every human being is the Soul of the cosmos.* . . . Each person is (to put it boldly but accurately in Eastern terms) God.
2. *Some things are more one than others.* . . . [W]hen one is one with the One, consciousness completely disappears and one merely is infinite-impersonal Being.
3. *Many (if not all) roads lead to the One.* . . . Almost all of these techniques . . . are methods of intellectually con-tentless meditation.[1]

I read the chapter containing these lines several times and scoured the Internet for even a shred of proof that these things were anything more than unsubstantiated ideas. All in vain: No clarity, no proof, just constant reminders that it was Hinduism that had popularized and perpetuated the horrific caste system.

It was while I was in the midst of this Hindu quagmire that I came across a Bible verse that seemed pertinent: "For God is not the author of confusion but of peace."[2] As it turned out, this passage was not addressing religions, but it seemed to me that any God worth His salt would be interested in, and capable of, helping His creatures understand something about Himself.

After giving it what I thought was a fair shot, I decided to set Hinduism aside too.

Was Islam's Allah the one true God? That was my next question. I started looking into Islam months before 9/11 sent America, however briefly, to its knees in fervent prayer.

I was not persuaded.

One reason was that, by this time, I'd noticed that most of these religions were based on the supposedly divine revelations received by one lone person. In the case of Islam, that person was a seventh-century Arab named Mohammed, whose writings allegedly contain the secrets to eternal life as revealed to him by Allah—"The God."

Mohammed claimed that his revelation built on Judaism and Christianity, meaning that Allah was the God of the (allegedly distorted) Bible, at last revealing the *real* truth about Himself to the world. But as I looked into this, I came across some credible reports that Allah was really an ancient pagan moon god whose wife was the sun goddess and whose daughters were the stars[3]—and no credible evidence of the alleged distortions in the Bible.

At any rate, since Mohammed was apparently alone when these revelations of his came down, it seemed apparent that he *could* have dreamt it all—including the idea that Allah holds the keys to eternity in paradise or hell, and that to make it into paradise, one's good deeds must outweigh the bad.

Keeping your personal scales tipped to the good side seems to be the major challenge in Islam. I later saw on TV two ex-Muslim brothers who said that, as Muslims, they had gone to bed every night, terrified that they had done more bad than good that day. They also said that the only exception to this rule was martyrdom achieved while waging jihad, or holy war; whether they're suicide bombers who blow themselves up on Israeli buses, or skyjackers who fly planes into tall American buildings, such friends of Allah die convinced that they will wake up in paradise.

I learned about Islam with growing distaste. Not that this proved it false; there's no law that says the truth has to be pleasant. But I needed something to hang my faith on. And I could find nothing even remotely persuasive on Islam.

Then there was the New Age movement, an umbrella term for a range of amorphous spiritual systems that all seem to emphasize the power, or even the alleged divinity, of the individual adherent.

Researching this movement was like listening to blind men describing different parts of an elephant. And along the way I learned that many of these parts contain elements of the occult, astrology, and Eastern mysticism, such as meditation, chanting, channeling of spirits, and a belief in reincarnation. It was adding up to a rat's nest of confusion.

As a result, assessing the truth of the New Age movement turned out to be next to impossible. I looked into various amalgamations of these ideas, checking out everything from the Human Potential Movement to cosmic humanism. I read with interest reports on psychic phenomena, "impossible" memories of previous lives, psychokinetic effects such as levitation, and Luciferian "white light" special effects.

I came across many such teachings in my research. Each set had been put forth by a lone soul who'd somehow tapped into the "truth." Each one contradicted the next one in key respects. And each one was completely unverifiable except for the occasional historical reference, often hopelessly inaccurate.

Was it possible that, hidden amid these claims, there was one that revealed Truth? I supposed so; after all, I had examined only a fraction of the ideas in the vast universe of New Age thought. But it would take many lifetimes to evaluate them all, and so far I was unconvinced that any of us have multiple lifetimes at our disposal.

In the meantime, I had come across some even more interesting ideas from the camp of biblical Christianity—ideas involving the career of Satan, his campaign to be worshipped as God, and his liberal use of deception, distortion and outright lies to achieve that goal.

Wasn't it possible that, if he really existed, he and his minions were behind all these New Age "revelations" and psychokinetic phenomena?

I thought so. And so I moved on, vowing to return and poke around some more if I struck out on all the other worldviews, too.

What about the Baha'i faith? This was another difficult one for me to evaluate objectively, because I know some very sweet and intelligent people who are devout followers of this religion. Still, I was on a search for truth, not friendship.

I learned up front that these nice people believe all religions teach the same truth: that God is unknowable, although His presence and works are evident; and that Adam, Jesus, and Mohammed are among the religion's important prophets, all succeeded by Baha'i founder Baha'ullah.

Although I did read further, it really wasn't necessary. This religion's opening premise was wrong: all religions do *not* teach the same truth. Buddhism says there is *no* God. Hindus say there are hundreds of thousands, and you can be one too. Muslims say there's one God who is impersonal and unapproachable. Some New Agers think *they're* God.

And Jesus? Well, He said *He* is God.

Somehow none of this sounded like the same truth to me.

※

THERE ARE, AS I said, scores of other religions out there, some interesting, some pretty wacky. In the early months of 2001, I started checking them out one by one.

For this little research project, I included religions that claim to be

Christian but are in reality Buddhist, Hindu, Islamic, or Gnostic in nature—Christian Science and Unity School, to name just a couple.

I included eminently progressive, "it doesn't matter what you believe as long as you're not a Christian fundamentalist" groups that seem to worship, above all and often exclusively, tolerance of everything except a plain reading of the Bible.

I included bizarre worldviews like Scientology, as well as explicitly evil paths, like Satanism.

And I included an array of religions devoted to worshipping the gods of nature, from Japan's native Shintoism to various expressions of Native American spirituality.

The only readily apparent common denominator among all these worldviews was the idea that whatever your view of heaven or paradise or nirvana, what gets you there is living the right kind of life.

Except for Christianity.

Christianity says that what gets you there is Jesus.

※

MY SEARCH POINTED me, again and again, toward biblical Christianity. Whatever the reason, it was easy to find solid and satisfying evidence of its truth—truth that applies to Judaism too, although the Jewish people are still waiting for the Messiah, having rejected Jesus Christ in spite of the hundreds of Messianic Hebrew Bible prophecies that He fulfilled to the tiniest detail.

Unlike the alternative worldviews I'd been assessing, Christianity appeared to be backed by astounding proofs. I found that books like Josh McDowell's *Evidence That Demands a Verdict* and *A Ready Defense* documented everything from the prophetic, archaeological, and historical accuracy of the Bible itself to the evidence for Jesus Christ's resurrection from the grave. These books and others like them blew up critics' most common challenges to the Bible's truthfulness, such as alleged contradictions. And they took on the accusations and innuendoes of the professional critics who make their livings ripping it apart—and won.

I underlined madly as I read, using pale yellow Post-It notes to flag particularly exciting passages, filling legal pad after legal pad with notes and outlines and lists of additional books and magazines and articles I'd have to get my hands on.

My truth detector was clicking like a Geiger counter at the mother lode of uranium deposits.

❧

I TOLD EVERYONE I knew, Christian or not, what I was learning.

"Get this," I said to JoAnn in 2001. She has been without question the most patient of my victims. "It's undeniable that the Bible was written by at least forty different people, over sixteen hundred years. And yet it hangs together to deliver a single coherent meganarrative, without contradiction or error—a meganarrative that recounts the world's past, present, and future."

"Wow, really?" she said. "Where'd you hear all that?"

"Everywhere!" I said, wishing immediately that I'd reserved this key piece of information until I'd had a chance to actually *study* the Bible thoroughly enough to come to an independent conclusion. "But you're right, I'll have to check it out myself."

I got right on it and reported back after finishing up my first complete read-through of the *Life Application Study Bible* in the New Living Translation.

"It's true!" I told JoAnn. "Totally coherent! Amazing!"

She responded politely and positively, although I'm quite sure she had forgotten the discussion that had launched this aspect of my investigation.

Considering the fact that I'm a copywriter by trade, called upon to communicate complex subjects to audiences from lay to professional, I don't do a very good job of explaining the significance of such explosive information. I know in my heart that it's big and it's conclusive but can't seem to convey my conclusions very convincingly.

Fortunately, there are plenty of articulate Christians out there who do it daily.

Author Dave Hunt, for one. He summed up this particular line of evidence perfectly:

> It would be difficult for a single author to avoid contradiction when dealing with such a lengthy period of detailed history involving so many individuals and nations and covering such a wide variety of subjects. But 40 different prophets writing with one voice over a period of many centuries? There can be only one explanation: divine inspiration![4]

Yes, indeedy. It was beginning to look a lot like the truth, the whole truth, and nothing but the truth, so help me God.

※

I HAD LET the idea of universal truth slither around my mind for years. But now that I was looking at the subject seriously, it became apparent that it was impossible for all religions to be true, or even for two of them to be true, because they contradicted each other. For instance, if one says God is merely a force, and the other says He's a grandfatherly fellow from outer space who has produced zillions of spirit babies, they can't both be correct.

In fact, by early spring of 2001, it had become clear to me that both viewpoints could be false, but both could not be true. When I compared the central tenets of Buddhism and Christianity, for example, there were only three possibilities:

1. Both are false.
2. Buddhism is true and Christianity is false.
3. Christianity is true and Buddhism is false.

It was equally clear that the same logic would apply in comparing the central beliefs of every other religion to Christianity's. The correct answer would always be 1, 2, or 3; never "both are true."

Which meant that if I became convinced that Christianity was true, any religion denying its major claims would automatically be false. If I were to believe beyond all doubt that Jesus is God, for instance, and some other religion denied it, then I could safely shrug off that religion's teachings.

I laid this entire case out for my still-skeptical friend Anne via e-mail. "What do you think?" I concluded, hoping she'd find my logic irrefutable.

"It makes sense," she replied. "So I guess this proves that not all religions can be true. I just hope for your sake that you don't suddenly discover that they're all false."

She was right, of course. Given the dearth of evidence I'd found for everything else, if I suddenly found credible evidence against Christianity, I would be left with nothing. As far as I'd come in my thinking, this was no longer an idea I would welcome.

But embrace it I would, if it turned out to be true. In the meantime, I wasn't going to lose sleep over it; the evidence was definitely pointing in the opposite direction.

THE MORE I studied, the more crystal clear the case for Christianity became—and the more frequently friends and acquaintances and even strangers tried to derail my budding faith by inviting me to become Buddhist or Baha'i, Mormon or Unitarian, a channeler of spirits from the Other Side or a plain old-garden-variety Jehovah's Witness.

One of my most ardent recruiters was an elderly Christian Scientist, one of my mother's acquaintances at the nursing home. "Please read *Science and Health* to me," she would plead, unable to hoist the book herself because she was paralyzed—no one knew quite why, since she refused to see a doctor. "Mrs. Eddy was a genius, and you will see the truth of what she wrote."

I complied but never found much truth in anything Mrs. Eddy said; I just couldn't buy her claim that we don't really exist physically and that pain is the result of errors in thinking.

Then there were the kind people who felt it their duty to inform me that Jesus was something other than what He said He was.

"To me, Jesus is an allegory," said an exceptionally pretty, nice, and intelligent artist of my acquaintance, when I told her at a professional meeting that I thought I was becoming a Christian.

"An allegory for what?" I asked.

She looked at me blankly, then took a good long swig of her cabernet. I sipped my Miller Lite, thinking of the headache I'd have tomorrow if I pounded a glass of red wine that way.

"Well," she said finally, licking her perfectly made-up lips, "He's an allegory for whatever you want Him to be."

I raised my eyebrows and waited.

"At the end of the day, all these religions are pretty much alike," she explained patiently, as if I were a seven-year-old. "They all promote the same ethical values, you see. Don't lie, cheat, steal, or fool around on your husband." She finished her wine and laughed. "Unless it's absolutely necessary! Did you ever see De Niro and Streep in *Falling in Love*? How could you resist *that*?"

Indeed, I had seen that movie years and years earlier, and had loved it, and was now tempted to let my mind wander down Hollywood's path toward just-can't-help-myself adultery. But my new truth detector was sounding a more irresistible alarm: all religions alike? No way!

I didn't offer these thoughts to this woman, however. I knew I was still skating on thin ice with this philosophy and logic stuff. Seeing that I wasn't biting on the De Niro/Streep bait, she wandered off to find someone interested in discussing the movie industry's take on romantic love.

※

OUR FRONT SLOPE was abloom in its 2001 crop of King Alfred and Mount Hood daffodils when I decided to close the case on non-Christian religions for lack of evidence. I would re-open it if any compelling new proofs came to light, I vowed, but in the meantime would turn my full attention to a painstaking investigation of biblical Christianity.

It wasn't long before I found myself up against an issue I'd been doggedly shrugging off: the claim that Jesus Christ had risen from the dead.

There were lots of Christians who seemed to treat this as a central and exclusive tenet of Christianity. The Bible itself seemed to do so.

But I had been singularly unimpressed with this claim, as well as with the evidences that various writers and speakers had amassed to prove that it was genuine history rather than legend.

That wasn't my problem, however. It wasn't that I doubted it had happened. It was that I doubted it was anything unique.

"Big deal," was my thought. "Like He would've been the first to rise from the dead."

Where I got the idea that resurrection was, if not a common occurrence, at least not terribly uncommon, I'm not sure. It might have been tied into my adolescent ideas about reincarnation. Maybe I'd read news reports alleging such occurrences. Or maybe it was simply my ignorance about what a miracle life is, a hangover from my once-solid belief in the time-chance drivers behind evolution; if a chemical soup can produce life under the right conditions, why couldn't other conditions bring a corpse back to life?

But here it was again, so I looked into it. And learned, to my surprise, that resurrection from true death really *is* extraordinary. There don't even seem to be many claims for it outside of the very few cases recorded in the Bible. Just as important, I learned that Jesus' resurrection has been vetted more thoroughly than any other fact of ancient history—by friend and foe alike.

I was one contrary truth-seeker, however. As soon as I began believing that this was a truly unique event in human history, and a well-documented one to boot, I began to doubt that it had really happened.

✂

IT TOOK A late-spring business trip to Minneapolis to open my eyes to the truth of Jesus' resurrection.

I had decided to drive rather than fly; at just over five hours, it was a horse apiece, and driving was considerably easier than flying. Besides, in a car I could smoke cigarettes to my heart's content.

My sister Carrie had lent me a bunch of audiotapes on C. S. Lewis for the drive, and I listened to them happily all the way up and for the first hour of my trip home a couple days later. But as I neared Menomonie, home of the University of Wisconsin–Stout, my current tape ended, and I couldn't quite reach the bag holding the rest.

Regretfully, I switched to the radio and searched around for something that sounded remotely spiritual.

And hit the jackpot almost immediately.

I don't know what station I'd found, or who the speakers were, but they were talking about proofs for Jesus' resurrection.

"It seems," said the first man—let's call him Bud, "that the eyewitness accounts that would become part of the New Testament were written within a few decades of Christ's death. True?"

"Definitely," said the second man, whom I'll call Edgar. "When these writings began circulating, there were still plenty of eyewitnesses around who could have sounded the alarm about any inaccuracies—just as there'd be an outcry if someone today claimed that aliens assassinated JFK. The risen Jesus had appeared to at least five hundred people, after all. And yet neither the Bible nor contemporary historians mention any challenges to what's written in Scripture about this particular event."

"No one would accuse those historians of being under the control of the Christians," Bud said.

"No, indeed," Edgar said. "The early Christians weren't winning popularity contests. They were being persecuted and executed."

"What about some of those alternate theories," Bud said, "those that say Christ didn't really die on the cross, that sort of thing?"

Edgar then launched into a discussion of death by crucifixion, going into gruesome detail as he laid out the evidence that Jesus had most assuredly died on the cross that day nearly two thousand years ago, and had been buried in a rich man's tomb.

I was beginning to lose interest. I'd read all of these things before, and convincing as they were, they hadn't erased my doubts. With even the wild shrubs draped in white blooms, the awakening countryside of northwestern Wisconsin was beautiful, and I let my mind wander. I thought about the projects I'd just picked up in Minneapolis, and the best approach to organizing all the information I was heading home with.

Suddenly peals of male laughter jarred me out of my mobile planning session. I turned my attention back to the radio, wondering what joke I'd missed.

They weren't about to tell me.

"Ah, yes, that was good," Bud said, his voice still bright with mirth. He cleared his throat. "But seriously, tell me what in your opinion is the single most important piece of evidence that Jesus did, indeed, die on that cross and rise again three days later."

"Hmmm, that's a good question," said Edgar. "Well, I guess for me it would have to be the behavior of His disciples. Right after his death, they were one dejected group. And then suddenly, something happened that turned them into the most joyful and energized people you could imagine. They went out as Jesus had instructed and began to preach the gospel all over the known world, in the process converting thousands of people to Christianity."

"Something happened."

"Yes. And as the years unfolded, all but one of them—the apostle John—died martyrs' deaths. And that's how we can know for sure that Jesus rose from the dead."

He'd lost me there. I didn't get it.

Apparently I wasn't the only one. "Explain that," said Bud.

I was listening intently now, but I was beginning to lose the radio signal—it must have been a Minneapolis station I'd been tuned into, and the static was increasing at an alarming rate.

I then did something I hadn't ever done before or since: to avoid losing another wisp of signal, I pulled off the highway and onto the shoulder, hoping that no state trooper would come along and interrupt Edgar's response. I didn't have to worry much about other travelers stopping to help; I hadn't seen another car in at least a half hour on this huge highway in the middle of nowhere.

"The thing is," Edgar was saying as I shifted into Park, "people die for what they know to be the truth. They will even die for what is actually a lie, as long as they *think* it's the truth.

"But no one dies for a lie."

My heart was pounding; he was right.

"If Jesus hadn't really been crucified, buried, and resurrected," Edgar said, "if He hadn't then appeared to them all, as well as to hundreds of others—if, in fact, His disciples had invented this fantastic fiction about Christ rising from the dead—then they all died for what they knew was a lie."

Silence, broken only by bits of static.

"And people simply do not die for what they know is a lie."

I found myself fighting back tears.

Because this fellow had brought me to the brink of an utterly life-changing conclusion: Jesus Christ had died.

And Jesus Christ is risen.

CHAPTER 18

Beware lest anyone cheat you: Separating scientific fact from science fiction

*A*ny other night, this would have been my last chance to get on the horn and call my mom if I hadn't done so already. She would've been settled in bed by now, face washed and teeth brushed, ready to call it a day, but letting worry about me keep her awake: *Where is she, and why hasn't she called me yet? She always calls me, every night, even when she's out of town. Could she have forgotten me?*

But of course, even if I dialed her number and let it ring for hours, she wouldn't be answering tonight.

Or would she? I wondered briefly what would happen if I dialed her number. If an aide or nurse would pick it up, or if Mom herself might answer. I picked up the phone and let my hand hover over the touch pad, ready to punch in her number. But then I thought about how she was probably alone by now, and how she might hear it ringing and ringing and be unable to answer and how horrifying that might be for her.

Instead, I opened another pack of smokes and popped open another Lite. It was tasting pretty sour by then, but I didn't know what else to do. My mother was dying; I could hardly drink soda, could I?

Still, I had to remain relatively clearheaded in case The Call came in. I continued sipping. My goal was to drink enough to keep the pain at bay, without becoming incoherent. So far, so good.

Or maybe not, because I was starting to wonder if I should call the south nurses' station, tell them to stop the stupid morphine and start the tube feeding. What if her cancer wasn't really all that advanced? What if this apparent strategy of knocking her out and letting her starve was killing her months or even years before her time?

I did not know what to do. I didn't even know who to talk to about it. Everyone seemed to think doing nothing but doping her up was the best thing for her.

And maybe it was. What did I know? She'd been pretty vocal of late about what seemed to me to be an idiotic approach to the subject of death. Maybe it really was time to let her go.

⁂

MY FIRST INKLING of my mother's new way of thinking about death came on the heels of a shocking phone call that came into my home office one morning in the late '90s. It was from the younger daughter of Arlene, one of my mother's few lifelong soul mates. It was horrible news, she said tearfully: her mom had died; would we please come to Madison for the funeral?

I was petrified: How could I possibly break this to my own mother? She would be devastated!

The news was too awful to deliver over the phone. I set aside my work and dragged myself over to the nursing home, trying desperately to think of the best way to tell her.

"Brace yourself" sounded about right; it had worked for Mr. Evans, after all, when he told me about my father. And then, quickly: "Arlene has died."

But it didn't play out at all the way I had envisioned.

I found my mother in her bathroom combing her hair, getting ready to head down to the dining room. She was surprised to see me—and a little frightened once she saw my expression.

"What's wrong?" she asked in that quick, quiet tone we use when we fear the worst.

Whereupon I knelt down next to her wheelchair and burst into tears, making it awfully difficult for me to give her the news about Arlene. But give it, I did.

Mom's reaction shocked me into silence.

"Oh, I'm so happy for her," she said, smiling and gazing dreamily at the ceiling. "Dear Arlene—home with George at last."

I was speechless.

I don't know if we sat there like this for five seconds or five minutes, but finally she noticed me.

"Oh, sweet Kitty," she said, touching my cheek with one soft hand, "you'll understand one day. At least I hope you will."

"Understand *what*?" I said crossly. "Your friend dies and you're *happy*? What is *wrong* with you?"

She sighed and shook her head. "There's not much left for us here—of course, there are our children and grandchildren, but you all have your own lives. I honestly can't wait –"

"Don't you dare say that!" I hissed. "I will not listen!" And I left, still in tears, not even willing to give this cruel mother of mine a ride to the dining room, waiting until our phone call later that night to apologize and make plans for taking her to Arlene's funeral.

Her attitude did not change in the months that followed, as the daughters of other old friends called me, one after another, to announce their own mothers' deaths. Invariably, they said they were calling me instead of my mother because they thought I should deliver the news myself, in person, to soften the blow.

I did not tell any of them that my mother would most likely greet the news with joy.

❧

I THOUGHT ABOUT these things that awful night, waiting for my mother to die.

I just didn't get it. She was the poetry buff; hadn't she ever read Dylan Thomas?

"Do not go gentle into that good night," he had written.

And "Rage, rage against the dying of the light."

Rage, Mom, rage!

And then I thought of how peaceful she'd looked when I left her a few hours ago, snoozing away, almost smiling.

Maybe she was finally getting the wish that I'd forbidden her to express in my presence.

❧

A YEAR LATER, as the last of my Mary Poppins tulips withered their way into horticultural history, I was busy investigating the possibility that Christianity is, from beginning to end, Truth—and that the Bible might be not only the inspired word of God, but also His inerrant revelation of Himself, of His will for us and of the entire history of man, from start to finish.

This leg of my investigation started with reading somewhere that the Bible alone among sacred books offers an explanation for the origins and operations of the universe—an explanation somewhat more plausible than the notion that our world has been eternally sitting on the back of an enormous turtle held aloft by a Ukrainian freedom fighter or dancing bear.

I'd come across a lot of biblical proofs already in my research. But now I started taking a much closer look at what was, for me, a major stumbling block: the scientific validity of the Bible. This seemed, from all I'd heard on the street, to be its weakest link.

And so I looked, and looked some more, and looked again. And was absolutely blown away by what I discovered.

※

IT WASN'T DIFFICULT to approach this study logically. I found gold mines of carefully organized information on these subjects everywhere I looked, from bookstores to Web sites, broadcast programs to blogs. Rather than wringing out an indication here and there of the Bible's scientific accuracy, my challenge became whittling down the evidences enough to form a coherent case in my own mind.

I started out looking at the shape-of-the-earth issue, since I had already been accused by more than one acquaintance of having become a Bible-thumping flat-earther. My question: Does the Bible really say the earth is flat, an idea that was supposedly pooh-poohed by the Greek sphere-promoter and mathematician Pythagoras five hundred years before Christ?

The answer: nope.

As it turns out, the biblical prophet Isaiah knew this truth a couple centuries before Pythagoras stumbled upon it. Writing around 700 BC, Isaiah said that God "sits above the circle of the earth."[1] Apparently the Hebrew word translated "circle" in our English Bibles can also mean a sphere. But even if he didn't mean that in this case, what shape does the earth take in all those photos shot from twentieth-century spacecraft?

Exactly: a circle.

Then there's the now-well-known fact that the earth is suspended in space, not supported by that gargantuan turtle or anything else as far as scientists have been able to determine. This must have been breaking news early in the second millennium BC, when the Bible's Job announced, "He hangs the earth on nothing."[2]

I thought about it: here was a guy who, some three thousand years ago, somehow knew that the earth was hanging out there in space, support-free. How could he have even imagined this? Why wouldn't he have simply assumed that the earth was endless?

There's also the notion that the sun has an orbit of its own, revealed originally by King David in Psalm 19:6: "[The sun's] rising is from one end of heaven, and its circuit to the other end; and there is nothing hidden from its heat." Secular scientists no doubt laughed this off over the centuries as they learned more and more about our universe. But the merriment must have ceased late in the twentieth century, when it was determined that the sun really *does* orbit through the Milky Way.

Oops.

Then there's the fact that no two stars are alike.[3] Considering that telescopes weren't even invented until the seventeenth century AD, it's intriguing that sixteen hundred years earlier, the apostle Paul had written in 1 Corinthians 15:41b, "One star differs from another star in glory."

I checked out the stars myself to see if their differences were at all apparent to the ordinary observer. Even allowing for some pollution out here in the Wisconsin countryside, it seemed impossible that Paul could have come to this conclusion simply by gazing up at the heavens.

I wondered if there was anyone but God Himself who could've known this in Paul's day.

Then this: the biblical prophet Jeremiah, born in the seventh century BC, wrote that "the host of heaven cannot be numbered," and put the stars on a par with the incalculable number of grains of sand in the sea.[4] And yet I've heard it said many times that the unaided eye can see no more than eight thousand or so stars on even the clearest nights.

Could Jeremiah have come up with this idea himself? I couldn't imagine how. Why would this thought have even occurred to him?

I learned, too, that the Bible contains some pretty impressive data about life on earth.

For instance, the New Testament book of Hebrews says, "By faith we understand that the worlds were framed by the word of God, so that the things which are seen were not made of things which are visible."[5]

That must have seemed like a very mysterious statement to the original readers of Hebrews (and no doubt to its author). After all, it was written before AD 70, more than 1,500 years before the first compound microscopes were developed to help man see structures invisible to the naked eye; 1,700 years before John Dalton began making the case that all matter was made of atoms, and 1,800-plus years before Einstein, in 1905, proved their existence.[6]

The Bible also describes the water cycle with details beyond the ken of ancient men.[7] And it talks about the springs of the sea and recesses of the deep,[8] as well as the mountains on the ocean floor[9]—features of the earth that were discovered by man only in recent centuries.

And on it went.

The Bible says in Genesis 1:25 that creatures reproduce after their kind, which is exactly what we all witness every day: dogs produce dogs, cats produce cats, and humans produce humans. There are practically infinite variations *within* kinds, which explains why no two people are identical and why we have so many different breeds of dogs and cats. But we never see one kind of animal producing another kind.

In Genesis 7, the Bible describes a global flood—a hydraulic catastrophe that remains the best explanation for the earth's geological formations and plentiful fossil graveyards,[10] the latter caused by rapid burial, and not gradual deposition.

The closer I looked, the more amazed I became.

There was all this "quality of life" advice the Bible gave the children of Israel—advice that even today sounds awfully up-to-date.

For instance, written in the fifteenth century BC, Exodus 23:11 says fields should be left fallow every seventh year—a practice, apparently unknown in the rest of the ancient world, that boosts their fertility.

In Judges 13:3–4, written in the tenth or eleventh century BC, the Bible advises women not to drink alcohol during pregnancy—something modern medicine didn't begin recommending until a few decades ago.

In Deuteronomy 23:12–13, the children of Israel were advised to bury their own waste outside of their camp—a practice that, many centuries later, apparently helped protect the Jewish people from the plagues that scourged much of the Western world.

And on it went.

To set the sons of Israel apart for God, circumcision was prescribed for all male infants on the eighth day after birth.[11] Medical science now tells us that this is the day on which our blood's ability to clot peaks, thanks to a complex interaction involving vitamin K. To get mothers and sons out of the hospital and off the books sooner, modern healthcare circumvents this natural timetable by injecting newborns with vitamin K prior to circumcision in the first days of life—in effect mimicking what would happen naturally, and confirming Scripture's wisdom for specifying day eight.

And there were more instructions such as these, more observations about the natural world, more indications that the authors of the Bible knew things that people of their day had no business knowing.

Not that any of these facts, taken alone, would have knocked my socks off; one or two or three instances could be dismissed as coincidence or lucky guesses.

But not dozens of them.

As I STUDIED these things during the summer of '01, an old hymn took up residence in my head. It was a long-forgotten hymn, one that represented what had to be some of my earliest memories.

It was "This Is My Father's World," written in 1901 by a New York pastor named Maltbie D. Babcock.

I remember singing this song as a little girl, sitting with my Sunday school classmates in front of the dark, Gothic sanctuary of Union Congregational Church in Green Bay. I probably wasn't the only one who felt a little thrill as soon as I recognized the melody the organist was playing, delighted that we were once again singing this beautiful song about my daddy: "This is my Father's world, and to my listening ears, all nature sings, and 'round me rings the music of the spheres."

And I'm sure I wasn't the only one who turned to look for my daddy. I remember it clearly, spotting him on the other side of the aisle, standing next to Momma and beaming back at me as I waved to him with my little, white-gloved hand and sang with great gusto: "This is my Father's world: I rest me in the thought of rocks and trees, of skies and seas; his hand the wonders wrought."

Now here I was, thirty years after his death, hearing the song over and over in my head, remembering him, and realizing that the hand we'd sung about hadn't been my daddy's after all.

⚘

THE BIBLICAL PROOFS I was finding did not go unchallenged. In fact, I found Web site after Web site attempting to rip them apart, claiming a coincidence here, a stretch there, and plenty of outright lies and ludicrous errors in between. The overall picture such sites were trying to paint of Bible believers was one of deception and despair.

I can't say that any of them made a very convincing case. They just weren't able to close the deal.

For instance, some critics pointed out that people knew the earth was round long before Columbus sailed the ocean blue. And that's true. However, it appears that the aforementioned prophet Isaiah may have been the first to know it; I could find no earlier references, anyway. And if this is so, then Isaiah had indeed revealed in Scripture something that no one else knew, something that he wasn't in a position to know himself: the fact that the earth is round.

Others dismissed this Isaiah passage entirely, pointing instead to a few biblical phrases that use language like "the four corners of the earth." This, they insisted, proved that the Bible teaches a flat earth.

I thought this was a decent charge until another commentator asked if modern meteorologists who talk about "sunrise" and "sunset" really think the sun rises and sets on us each day. Or are they simply using widely understood poetic language? And if the latter, why should this literary device be denied the writers of the Bible?

Good point.

After reading dozens of such protests, investigating their merit, and finding that they were based on red herrings or ignorance of Scripture or telling only half the story, the objections began to sound pretty desperate. Clearly, there was something going on here that the critics were refusing to admit.

Later, I realized that perhaps they were simply unable to see these things; the Bible *does* talk about people being blind to spiritual truth. In 2 Corinthians, for instance, the apostle Paul wrote this: "But their minds were blinded . . . even to this day, when Moses is read, a veil lies on their heart. Nevertheless when one turns to the Lord, the veil is taken away."[12]

Maybe we remain forever unable to see these truths unless we do what Paul suggests.

⁂

I RECENTLY CAME across a fabulous Web site by ex-atheist A. S. A. Jones, now a born-again Christian, who has written at length about her conversion and the logical case for Christ.

In an article entitled "Learning to Think Spiritually," she showed a stereogram, a piece of abstract art that looks like a bunch of squiggly designs in brown, white, gray, and black. But there's more here than meets the untrained eye, she pointed out: a 3D galloping horse is actually embedded in the image.

This horse remains invisible, however, to anyone who focuses his vision on the readily apparent plane of the picture or looks at it with only one eye. It can only be seen by those focusing both eyes on a plane *behind* this image, she explained.

There is a lesson to be learned here.

"Like many others," she wrote, referring to her atheist days, when she read the Bible only to tear it down, "I saw the gospel as a bunch of scribbles; I thought it was just a bunch of nonsense until my focus changed."

Describing the Bible as a spiritual stereogram, Jones wrote, "You need two aspects of the intellect to see the reality of God in its pages; you need to utilize both the logical and spiritual (or poetic) component of your thinking to see Him. If you use only one in the absence of the other, you will lose the effect. It's like covering one eye."

Jones pointed out that depth is key to seeing the truth in the Bible just as it is in stereograms. "I think the reason a lot of people aren't seeing its truth today," she said, "is that we have become a nation of shallow thinkers."[13]

I think A. S. A. Jones is brilliant. And I think she has it exactly right.

THERE WAS MORE—lots more than any of my friends wanted to hear about.

"You're nuts," said one.

"You're boring," said another.

"What is wrong with you?" asked a third. "If you want to go to church, fine—go! But why would you waste all this time?"

They just didn't get it. I had no intention of dabbling in this leap-of-faith business, not when eternity was on the line. I had to *know*.

As I continued exploring the Bible, I found myself asking, over and over again, "How could the writer have known this?" and "Who but God Himself could have told him that?" and "Is there any other possible explanation?"

When I answered "no" for about the fiftieth time, I was 95 percent of the way to certainty.

※

IT WAS THEN that an amazing thought occurred to me: just say it turned out to be true, that the Bible could be proven accurate in matters that can be objectively evaluated. Might it not be true in everything else it says—including its promises about eternity?

※

BY MID-SUMMER 2001 these clear indications of the Bible's divine origins had brought me within shouting distance of absolute faith. I can't explain why they made such a difference, except that perhaps the untruths I'd been taught had been major barriers to belief for me.

But now, the barriers were crumbling, giving me a glimpse of something that might be heaven.

My mother certainly believed in a heavenly future for herself. She even put it in writing.

I didn't know about this until 2005, when I finally summoned up enough courage to read her journal. It was one of those Meade composition books with rounded corners and pages lined in pale blue. Only about a third of the pages were filled in, but the book was stuffed with loose sheets; like any compulsive writer, she wrote whenever the spirit moved her, on whatever paper was handy. No doubt for every page that had made it into this book, there were dozens that had been lost along the way to a conscientious cleaning staff.

Her feelings about death were beginning to make sense.

"I do not understand," she'd written in a clear hand, obviously when she'd still been in fairly decent health, "why people feel that, because I do not fear death, it is a sign of despondency. To me it looks like the greatest adventure of them all."

There was that word again: adventure.

"I am tired of lugging this decaying body around. I can no longer plan a trip to Africa or China or Russia. But perhaps I may one day walk down strange and lovely streets with someone I love and stop at 10 a.m. for a glass of beer."

My heart stopped.

She'd been recalling one crisp October morning in the late '70s when she and I were walking the cobblestone streets of the old city in Salzburg, Austria. We were happy and healthy and ready for a day of exploring the wonders of this beautiful town, having just finished a delicious breakfast at our cheap but clean hotel near the train station. Although she wasn't a great fan of drinking herself, she did appreciate a good European beer now and then. And that happy morning, as a nearby clock struck ten, *she* suggested we stop for a beer. It had been a good memory for both of us; but it bowled me over that it had made it into her fantasies of heaven.

"Anybody, almost, can go to Europe," she wrote. "But I would like to venture into the great unknown. Is that so ridiculous? Will I see those whom I have 'loved and lost awhile' once more?

"I believe so."

CHAPTER 19

The future before it happens:
There's only one explanation

11:30 p.m., May 30, 2000

Ordinarily Dave would have turned in hours earlier; he was used to rising at 4 or 5 a.m. and being on the job at seven at the latest. So I wasn't surprised when he shuffled through the kitchen, pausing only to give me a silent hug, and trudged up the stairs to our loft bedroom. The dogs and cats followed him up.

But I wasn't quite ready to be left alone.

"What do you think will happen?" I asked him just before he reached the top step.

It was a dumb thing to ask, and I knew it, and he knew it, and he shook his head sadly at me and headed for bed.

That wasn't what I wanted. I wanted a good forecast, one of sunny skies and surprise cures. I wanted predictions, accurate predictions, of happily-ever-aftering.

※

IN RESEARCHING THE accuracy of the Bible the summer of 2001, I could hardly miss the many references to its historical accuracy. While it's not a history book, it is a book grounded in history, as many have pointed out. It's a book that purports to present the highlights of mankind's entire past, present, and future, from first day to last, and claims to answer those three big questions about where we came from, what we're doing here, and where we're going.

As far as the past goes, I learned that with every passing year, there's more archaeological evidence that the Bible is 100 percent historically accurate.

For instance, I've been fascinated by the story of David ever since I read about him in the Old Testament—David, the shepherd boy who slew Goliath, became king of Israel in 1010 BC, and wrote some of the most beautiful and poignant psalms in the Bible.

Over the years, some historians have apparently claimed that this was pure myth—that King David had never even existed. But then in the early 1990s archaeologists found the evidence they were looking for in three-thousand-year-old inscriptions from an ancient monument. "House of David," one read in Aramaic. More discoveries confirming David's life and rule have followed, fitting in neatly with the biblical accounts of that era.[1]

I rejoiced when I read these things: King David, whom God Himself had called a man after His own heart,[2] had really lived. No Arthurian-caliber legends here!

Another story that was long the object of secularist scoffing is the biblical account of the battle of Jericho, fought by Moses' successor, Joshua, centuries before King David assumed his throne. Although, "fought" may not be quite the right word, for Joshua and his men took the city by doing just as God said: marching around its walls once a day for six days, and then seven times on the seventh day, with a contingent of priests blowing rams' horns. Finally, the priests gave one long blast on the horns, Joshua's people added a mighty shout, and the walls collapsed. Or so goes the story, recounted in Joshua 6.

Foolishness, right? And yet, British archaeologist Professor John Garstang discovered something very strange when he studied the ruins of Jericho. It was apparent that the walls had fallen outward, making it easy for attackers to climb over the ruins and into the city.

"Why is this so unusual?" asked Dr. D. James Kennedy in his wonderful book *Why I Believe*. "Because walls do not fall outward. Ordinarily they fall inward, but in this case the walls were made by some superior power to fall outward, as the Bible says."[3]

It wasn't long before the Bible's historical accuracy began to look like an open-and-shut case. Modern archaeology has, it seems, uncovered a wealth of proof for the people, places, and events of the Bible. Serious historians no longer question the existence of Ur, Abraham's hometown, or of the Hittite empire. They no longer doubt the failed attempt of Assyria's King Sennacherib to capture Jerusalem in 701 BC. They no longer deny that the gospels of Matthew, Mark, Luke, and John were written in the first century,[4] or that Pontius Pilate was prefect of Judea when Jesus was crucified.[5]

"It may be stated categorically that no archaeological discovery has ever controverted a biblical reference," said Nelson Glueck, the famous Jewish archaeologist. Instead, he said, the Bible displays an "almost incredibly accurate historical memory . . . and particularly so when it is fortified by archaeological fact."[6]

That was good enough for me. But did it prove that this book was actually the inspired and inerrant Word of God?

Of course it didn't. Alan Bullock's *Hitler: A Study in Tyranny* and Isaac Deutscher's *Stalin: A Political Biography* are considered in some circles outstanding histories of important eras and people, but no one would suggest that they were inspired or inerrant.

I was not quite home free.

꙳

It was in July 2001 that I really took notice of Isaiah 42:9, which quotes God as saying, "Everything I prophesied has come true, and now I will prophesy again. I will tell you the future before it happens."[7]

The verse reminded me of all the references I'd noticed recently to the Bible's prophetic accuracy—noticed, but not investigated, being wrapped up in evaluating all these other aspects of its truth. But in light of what Isaiah had recorded, I decided to take a closer look.

I learned, first of all, that the Bible is alone among sacred books in containing detailed predictions—prophecies that were delivered not just years but often centuries before they were fulfilled.

In the end, I had to admit that, if true, this would be pretty conclusive evidence that the Bible actually *is* the Word of God.

And so I once again shifted the focus of my studies to find out if this, too, would turn out to be true.

꙳

To be honest, when I first came across this idea of fulfilled prophecy, my reaction was pretty much, "So what?" Lots of people had predicted the future, with great success, I thought—people ranging from Jeane Dixon to Nostradamus. Big deal.

But now that I was looking into it, I decided to first check on how accurate folks like Jeane and Nostradamus really had been.

The answer: not very.

When I was a kid, Jeane Dixon was all the rage, and I suppose she must have gotten some things right. But it turned out that she got an awful lot wrong, too, including warning that World War III would begin in 1958. Somewhere I read that she and her fellow psychics didn't even get 50 percent of their predictions right, according to those who track such things.

The sixteenth-century mystic Nostradamus turned out to be different but not much better, as far as I could tell. His predictions took the form of vague and unsettling quatrains that are today torn apart and reassembled in vain attempts to make them look authentically prophetic.

⁂

STILL, I DID not approach this subject with a totally open mind. Maybe I just couldn't get past the "psychic" comparisons. Or maybe I sensed that I was nearing the end of my journey and wanted to postpone coming to a conclusion that might mean explosive changes in my life.

But I did plunge ahead, sitting in my home office night after night, reference books scattered all over my massive desk, Internet connection up and running.

Here, in a nutshell, is what I learned on this critical topic.

The Bible contains roughly twenty-five hundred prophecies, depending on how you count them. They are, believers say, unlike anything we hear from modern "prophets": they're detailed, specific, and 100 percent accurate so far, with roughly 80 percent already fulfilled; the rest, referring to the last days, have yet to play out.

As I discovered early on and with very little digging—the information was all right there, waiting to be evaluated by whoever cared to look—these prophecies covered a wide array of topics, from the destruction of Jerusalem (which came true in AD 70) to the growth throughout history of the church, in spite of often-crushing opposition (undeniable).

The ones I found especially compelling concerned the scattering and restoration of the nation of Israel. I don't know why these passages in particular appealed to me. Maybe it was because I had seen and loved (but completely missed the point of) the Paul Newman movie *Exodus* when I was a kid, or was later totally into *The Diary of Anne Frank* and studying the Holocaust that was a prelude to Israel's restoration. Or maybe it was the fact that, as the Bible seems to make clear, the children of Israel are God's chosen people, the apple of His eye; if He's vitally interested in this nation, shouldn't we be too?

Whatever the reason, I was fascinated to learn that the predictions about the nation of Israel started about thirty-five hundred years ago in Genesis, the very first book of the Bible. Here, Moses made predictions that must have been puzzling in his day (and for centuries thereafter), but which have undeniably come true over the centuries: he quoted God telling Jacob that his descendents would one day be "spread abroad to the west and the east, to the north and the south," and would be brought back safely to Israel: "Behold, I am with you and will keep you wherever you go, and will bring you back to this land."[8]

It turned out that this promise of scattering and restoration appears again and again in the Bible. And what happened? In AD 70, the Jewish people—Jacob's descendents—were forced by Rome to flee their homeland, and were eventually spread all over the earth. Then, on May 14, 1948, the nation of Israel was born once again, in the same land that Abraham and Jacob had walked thousands of years earlier.

Just as the Bible predicted.

I also learned about prophecies revealing the details of Israel's rebirth. In the seventh century BC, for example, the prophet Isaiah predicted that it would be restored in a single day, after which the birth pains would begin.

And what happened? The very day that the Jewish people declared their independence, just as UN-mandated British control of the land ended, the U.S. recognized Israel's sovereignty. And within hours, the nations of Egypt, Jordan, Syria, Lebanon, Iraq, and Saudi Arabia attacked.[9]

Just as the Bible predicted.

Equally impressive, Scripture told the children of Israel that they'd one day be powerful far beyond their numbers: "You will chase your enemies, and they shall fall by the sword before you. Five of you shall chase a hundred, and a hundred of you shall put ten thousand to flight."[10]

I looked it up: When 20 million Arabs attacked the new nation of Israel, it took less than one million Jews to turn back this onslaught. Similar results against overwhelming odds have been achieved ever since.[11]

Just as the Bible predicted.

But the children of Israel were not promised an easy time of it, I learned. Enemies would occupy their land, the Old Testament predicted; passages in Leviticus 26 and Deuteronomy 28 warned that they would be persecuted in many nations—but would survive.

Reading this, I thought about what had happened to the Jewish people over the centuries—not only before Christ, but ever since. It seems that the persecution has skyrocketed in recent centuries, even in supposedly civilized nations. Among those officially setting their bloodthirsty sights on the Jewish people were nations like Germany and the Soviet Union, which set new standards for horror and brutality. And even today, more and more nations are turning their backs on Israel in the name of peace.

Just as the Bible predicted.

❧

AFTER THESE DISCOVERIES, I was not too surprised to learn that there are also more than 450 Old Testament prophecies of the coming

Messiah, or Savior—and that every last one was fulfilled to the letter by Jesus. Like those concerning the nation of Israel, all these prophecies were written long before Jesus' birth, as the 1947 discovery of the Dead Sea Scrolls confirmed.

Peter Stoner, professor emeritus of Science at Westmont College, calculated the chances of one person fulfilling just forty eight of these prophecies at 10^{157}—a number beyond our comprehension.[12] Some scientists have calculated that there are only 10^{79} electrons, protons and neutrons in the entire universe.[13]

And Jesus fulfilled not just the forty-eight prophecies covered in these calculations, but more than 450.

Perversely, I searched my memory bank for a prophecy Jesus could have deliberately fulfilled. I didn't have to look long: one prediction said He would ride into Jerusalem on a colt—which is what He did on what would become known as Palm Sunday. It seemed to me that He had total control over His mode of transportation into the city; how could this be considered prophetic?

That was probably a legitimate question. But no sooner had I congratulated myself for thinking of it, than I learned that most of the Messianic prophecies in the Old Testament involve events that were completely beyond Jesus' control—including His birth in Bethlehem (Micah 5:2, eighth century BC), His betrayal by a friend (Psalm 41:9, tenth century BC) in exchange for thirty pieces of silver (Zechariah 11:12–13, sixth century BC), the piercing of His hands and feet (Psalm 22:16, tenth century BC), and soldiers casting lots for His clothes (Psalm 22:18).

Oh.

I asked myself the only logical question: How in the world could all these Old Testament prophets have known that these events would one day come to pass? Could anyone have made such precise and accurate predictions without the help of a supernatural being who exists outside of earthly time?

I just couldn't see how.

IF 80 PERCENT of the Bible's prophecies have already come true, that leaves 20 percent still awaiting fulfillment. And that's where it really gets interesting, because, as it turns out, the remaining five hundred or so prophecies concern "end times."

As in *the end of life as we know it.*

And as I started taking a look at them just weeks before 9/11/01, it was easy to see that they're already starting to come true.

Take, for instance, Daniel 12:4, which says, "But you, Daniel, shut up the words, and seal the book until the time of the end; many shall run to and fro, and knowledge shall increase."

"Run to and fro"? *My, oh my,* I thought upon reading this passage, *What a great description of modern business culture.* And not just in terms of the nonstop travel schedules that so many keep these days; running "to and fro" seems to fit the job descriptions of most corporate employees today. Not to mention our personal schedules: I tried to think of anyone I knew who wasn't grappling with an out-of-control To Do list, and came up empty.

"Knowledge shall increase"? I'd read various guesstimates as to how fast information is piling up in this, the twenty-first century, but now took some time to explore the question on the Internet. The estimates still varied, but it's not uncommon for experts to say that the information transmitted globally via Internet is doubling each year[14]—or that the volume of corporate information doubles every eighteen months.[15]

Another interesting end-times prediction concerns Jerusalem's importance to the world. Zechariah 12:3 says, "And it shall happen in that day that I will make Jerusalem a very heavy stone for all peoples." I think it's safe to say that Jerusalem has become a huge problem for the international community, and is probably the only such city in the world. Yet Zechariah was writing in the sixth century BC.

And then there are the signs that Jesus told His disciples about, recorded in Matthew 24.

"Many will come in My name, saying, 'I am the Christ,' and will deceive many," He said in verse 5. This has happened here and there throughout Christian history, but in recent years it's become almost commonplace—thanks in no small part to religions that teach us we can all become Christ in our own right if we just do this or that.

"And you will hear of wars and rumors of wars," Jesus said in verses 6 and 7, and "nation will rise against nation, and kingdom against kingdom. And there will be famines, pestilences, and earthquakes in various places."

We take all these things for granted today, but they were apparently not so common two thousand years ago. As the late Henry Morris, PhD, wrote in 1995, "Worldwide, at least one war has been going on in eleven out of twelve years since the time of Christ. At the present time, there are estimated to be at least forty wars—small or large, civil or international—going on in the world."[16]

※

INTRIGUED, I STARTED doing more extensive Internet searches for "biblical prophecy," and came across an astonishing subcategory of last-days prediction: those that could not have been fulfilled in the past but have suddenly become entirely feasible.

For instance, referring to two end-times prophets who will torment the world with their prophesying, Revelation 11:9 says, "Then those from the peoples, tribes, tongues, and nations"—in other words, the entire world—"will see their dead bodies three-and-a-half days . . ."

Until television and satellites arrived on the scene, this verse would have sounded absurd. Now it makes total sense.

A couple chapters later, Revelation 13:16–17 warns that "[the false prophet] causes all, both small and great, rich and poor, free and slave, to receive a mark on their right hand or on their foreheads, and that no one may buy or sell except one who has the mark or the name of the beast, or the number of his name."

Another mysterious passage—except for anyone following current advances in microchip technology. Though I'm sure purveyors of this technology are disappointed that their products haven't yet taken the entire Western world by storm, people *are* beginning to accept implants bearing their medical data—and, more pertinent to these verses, their credit card information. All of which means that the technology is now in place to allow this prophecy to be fulfilled.

And that's just the beginning of what looks like an end-times-prophecy juggernaut.

My heart was beating faster than usual as I read about these things late one night, after every other creature in the house had gone to bed. So it was just as well that I came across some Internet commentator urging everyone to stay calm. The Bible gives no timetable for how quickly the prophesied events will unfold, he pointed out; it could be years, decades, or centuries.

Well, except for one possible hint that Jesus gave, recorded in Matthew 24:34, when He said, "Assuredly, I say to you, this generation will by no means pass away till all these things take place." He'd been talking about the beginning of the "sorrows" of the last days. Some scholars believe that He was referring to events of the twentieth century, such as World War II.

No one can be certain, however. As Jesus said a couple verses later, "But of that day and hour no one knows, not even the angels of heaven, but My Father only."

THERE IS NO shortage of scoffers out there today (hmm—just as the apostle Peter predicted in 2 Peter 3:3, when he said "Scoffers will come in the last days"). For instance, some say the Old Testament prophet Daniel missed the boat because his prophecies didn't precisely match what happened five hundred years later, in the first century AD.

Well, duh—even I could see the mistake: Daniel wasn't talking about the first century. He was talking about events that have yet to take place twenty-five hundred years after he lived.

When will they play out?

God only knows. But it's clear that we are wise to pay attention to the world around us and to be wary of what we hear presented as truth.

In the summer of 2006, for instance, the History Channel ran a program—I think it might have been "Digging for the Truth"—that made prominent mention of the Dead Sea Scrolls.

I was glued to the TV. The History Channel is sometimes surprisingly objective in talking about the Bible, and I thought maybe the host would explore how the Dead Sea Scrolls proved the flawless integrity of the Old Testament.

No such luck.

Interviewing some expert on the subject, the host asked something like, "So, is there any mention of Jesus in the Scrolls?"

"No," said the expert.

The host seemed surprised; he asked once again. And the expert again denied any mention of Jesus.

As I remember it, they stood there shaking their heads, as if this somehow shot huge holes in the foundation of Christianity.

I kept waiting for one of them to say, "But then again, the Scrolls were completed at least a hundred years before Jesus was born, so of course they wouldn't mention Him."

Or, "Why, yes, Jesus was foretold in many places in the Old Testament—which is what the Dead Sea Scrolls represent. If we look in the book of Isaiah, for instance . . ."

But they just stood there, letting this alleged omission hang there, as if it somehow represented evidence extremely damaging to Christianity.

That, at least, is the impression I would have had if I hadn't known better. And they gave that impression without telling a single overt lie.

Did this really happen? I wonder now, as I write about it. It almost seems too outrageous to be real. Maybe I'm losing my mind.

Or maybe I'm not.

We used to talk about TV being a vast wasteland. But I don't think that's quite true anymore. I think it's becoming dangerous to children and other living things.

⁂

ARE CURRENT CONDITIONS indeed the fulfillment of end-times biblical prophecy? Beats me. What do I know?

But prophecies that have already been fulfilled are another matter. This isn't fuzzy wuzzy Nostradamus stuff. This isn't Jean Dixon predicting the next president. This is the real deal. And as a result of my investigations into biblical prophecy, I am now fully persuaded that the Bible could not have been written without divine intervention. I am convinced that it is, in fact, the Word of God.

No wonder my parents' generation had such confidence in its teachings. They'd seen the nation of Israel resurrected with their own eyes, and at least some of them understood the significance of this unprecedented event.

As I reflected on all these things over Labor Day Weekend 2001, a certainty I hadn't known since early childhood began to settle in my heart. And with it an amazing feeling that I couldn't quite put my finger on . . . but it seemed like it might actually be what they call *peace*.

And so it was that I became, finally and forever, a joyous, Bible-thumping and born-again follower of Jesus Christ, the Son of God and God the Son.

CHAPTER 20

The spirit of wisdom:
What matters is what's true

11:45 p.m., May 30, 2000

Sick to death of beer, and still wide-awake and sober after hours of cautious imbibing, I fished a bottle of wine out of the back of the fridge. It was one of those giant bottles of Zinfandel, half-full or half-empty, depending on your point of view. It must have been in there for quite a while, because I couldn't recall what had happened to the first half of it. I poured myself a tumbler full and sipped. It tasted just fine to me, a connoisseur of wines sold in cardboard boxes. Apparently the cheap stuff ages well too.

So had my Mom, I thought, digging a bag of Cheetos out of the cupboard beneath the microwave.

At least I could be sure of one thing, I thought, standing at the sink, munching, and guzzling. If there was a heaven, my mother was headed for it, because she had always been a good person. A great person. A truly wonderful person, in fact! She'd have it made in the shade when she reached those pearly gates.

※

It took me a long time to figure out that it isn't quite that simple—that being a good person isn't what gets you into heaven, if the Bible is to be believed. A year into my studies, I could have spoken for an hour on various aspects of the evidence for Christianity. But I couldn't have summarized its central thesis—the gospel of Jesus Christ—if someone had put a gun to my head.

The trouble was, even though I was studying the Bible intently by this time, my extrabiblical reading was all over the place. In my ignorance, I'd even added some books on the occult to my growing library—books that masqueraded as Christian resources but promoted practices that I would later discover were anything but heaven-sent.

I'm embarrassed to admit that it took four years and a summer class to straighten it all out in my mind. Good thing it's getting to the destination that's important . . . not how long it takes us to get there.

※

The class that helped me to see the forest for the trees was on evangelism—the science and art of bringing people to Christ. Held at the independent Baptist church I'd joined just months before, it was taught by a pastor named Dan, who had an incredible knack for making complex theological concepts understandable even to us late bloomers.

It was Pastor Dan who showed our small but eager class what the Bible says, in a nutshell, about how a person gets to heaven. To wit:

1. Eternal life is God's free gift to us; we cannot earn it and do not deserve it. The Bible tells us, "For by grace you have been saved through faith, and that not of yourselves; it is the gift of God, not of works, lest anyone should boast."[1]

In other words, we can spend our lives knocking ourselves out on

God's behalf, but that's not what opens the gates of heaven to us. A gift is no longer a gift if the recipient pays for part of it.

2. We are all sinners. "For all have sinned and fall short of the glory of God," the Bible says in Romans 3:23.

The word *sin* has become taboo in our culture; use it, and people immediately think you're a prude who's obsessed with other people's sex lives. That's certainly what I'd always thought, anyway; sin was doing anything pleasurable.

But as I'd learned over the past few years, this isn't at all the case.

What "sin" means biblically is breaking God's law, summed up in the Ten Commandments. It is waving a clenched fist in His face. Stealing, murder, and telling lies are all sins—hardly acts that only a prude would be against. But so are some things that many would see as no big deal—using God's name as a cuss word, for instance, or lusting after someone or coveting another person's possessions or being disrespectful to your parents. Even being angry without cause is a sin, according to Jesus Himself—a sin tantamount to murder. And breaking the first commandment—placing anything at all before God, including money, career, even our loved ones—is idolatry, a very serious offense against the God who gave us life.

I had at first balked at these things. But then I pictured myself debating with God, telling Him that He was wrong to call such-and-such a sin; it wasn't an argument I could win, seeing as how it's His universe, and He gets to set whatever rules He wants.

I thought about how the Bible says He will forgive us: "If we confess our sins, He is faithful and just to forgive us our sins and to cleanse us from all unrighteousness."[2] And I thought about something I heard a preacher saying, that God doesn't just forgive; He forgets, wiping our slates clean of confessed transgressions. I finally decided that this was more than fair.

Besides, the more I pondered His commandments, the more I came to understand that obeying them is truly in our best interest. I couldn't think of a single case when, in the long run, I'd been better off for having violated them. Not one.

And it's not like sin is a once-in-a-while kind of transgression in my life. Even if I became a super-saint who managed to sin just a few times a day—for instance, failing to put God first, just thrice daily— I would rack up more than one thousand sins a year. And I'd spent my whole life as a world-class, 10,000-transgressions-per-hour sinner.

3. God is perfectly merciful—and perfectly just. Because "God is love,"[3] and is merciful beyond our imaginations, He doesn't *want* to punish us any more than a traffic-court judge would want to punish his own daughter, even if she showed up in court with 100,000 traffic tickets on her record.

But that judge would be corrupt if he let his daughter go without making her pay her fine. And God is not corrupt; He is perfectly just, "by no means clearing the guilty," according to Exodus 34:7. The Bible says that when we die, we will be judged, and assessed a penalty for our sins. It also tells us that the penalty is steep: "For the wages of sin is death."[4] In a word, hell.

I imagined myself standing before the Creator of the universe, guilty of 100,000 transgressions—or, more likely, 100 trillion, to the nth power. Each one, carrying the death sentence.

Clearly, this was a sin debt I could never begin to pay.

4. Jesus Christ suffered and died to pay for our sins. Fortunately, God knew we would be sinful creatures before He even created the universe. And, inexplicably, He loved us enough to provide us with a way out of our dilemma.

That way was the "incarnation"—God the Son coming to earth to pay the penalty for our sins in full. Jesus did this by suffering and dying on the cross nearly two thousand years ago, many centuries after the prophet Isaiah had offered this Old Testament prediction: "All we like sheep have gone astray; we have turned, every one, to his own way; and the LORD has laid on Him the iniquity of us all."[5]

Finally, I understood the one verse I'd heard often enough to recognize even before I cracked open my Bible the first time: "For God so loved the world that He gave His only begotten Son, that whoever believes in Him should not perish but have everlasting life."[6]

5. Faith is what opens the gates to heaven. This means we have two options that will determine where we spend eternity.

First, we can place our faith in our own self-righteousness. In this scenario, we stand before God on Judgment Day and offer Him everything we've done in our lives as a payment for our most likely countless sins. Our message is something along the lines of, "Well, Lord, I volunteered at a hospital twice a week for thirty-five years, I made many sacrifices for my family, I never killed a single soul, I went to church whenever I possibly could, and I've really tried to be a good person."

Alternatively, we can place our faith in the work of Jesus Christ. In which case we stand before God and say, "Jesus paid it all"—a privilege open to anyone who trusts in Jesus alone for eternal life.

This faith in Christ—what's called "saving faith"—means a lot more than intellectual acknowledgement of His existence. It also means more than fleeting temporal faith, which causes us to toss prayers up now and then when someone we love is sick or we really *really* want that new job. Saving faith requires belief so solid that we willingly make Jesus both Savior and Lord of our lives. Belief so solid that we repent of our sins. Belief so solid that we confess Him before others as our Lord.

So these are our choices.

Follow the latter course, repenting and trusting in Jesus, and enter judgment clothed in His righteousness, every last sin paid for on the cross.

Or follow the first course, and be judged by our own works, good and bad. I suppose the hope is that the good of our lives will outweigh the bad. The trouble is, God uses His definition of "bad," not ours. What's more, there's nothing in Scripture to suggest that good deeds cancel out sin—nothing. Instead, the Bible says things like, "For whoever shall keep the whole law, and yet stumble in one point, he is guilty of all."[7]

Let's see: let Jesus pay for our sins, or do it ourselves.

Seems like a no-brainer, doesn't it?

※

IT WAS DURING our third or fourth evangelism class, as I recall, that Pastor Dan provided the little demonstration that would finally make all of this clear.

"Here's an illustration that some people have found helpful," he said, sticking his right hand out at waist level, palm up, as if he were carrying an invisible waiter's tray. "This hand," he said, "represents me."

He retrieved a notebook from the table in the front of our little classroom and showed it to us. "This represents the book of my life, describing every sin I've ever committed." He placed it on his upraised palm.

"This," he said, raising his left hand over his head, "represents God. I think you can see what He sees when He looks at me."

"The book of your life," said one of my classmates. "Your sins."

"You got it," said Pastor Dan. He lowered his left hand to shoulder level. "But when Jesus went to the cross, He did so bearing all my sins." He transferred the notebook to His left hand and beamed at us.

I glanced around to find that everyone was watching him closely, as if he was describing something as complex as the physics behind magnetic resonance imaging. I suppose in a way, this subject is far more complex, and nearly impossible for the human mind to grasp: our sinless God suffering and dying to pay the penalty for sins He never committed.

Pastor Dan slid the notebook back to its spot on the table and returned his hands to the waiter and God positions.

"Now you can see that the situation has changed," he said. "Because Jesus paid for my sins on the cross, when God looks at *me*, He doesn't see those sins at all. He sees, in fact, perfect righteousness—the righteousness of Christ."

We all nodded, smiling. Yes, that was it. So simple. So life changing.

A line from the Crystal Lewis song "Seasons Change" popped into my head, for the first time making total sense to me: "I look at God and see what I want to be. He looks at me and sees His Son."

Except that it turns out the last word is *own*. But I really prefer my misunderstanding of the line.

⁂

ONCE I HAD accepted the notion that God, as our Creator, is of course the One who defines sin . . . and once I began realizing that what He calls sin is actually dangerous for us physically, emotionally, and spiritually . . . I started looking back at my own sin-spattered life with shame and, in some cases, revulsion. I had been living for my own happiness, comfort, pleasure, self-esteem, and glory. I had left a lot of pain in my wake. And I had, in the process, been thumbing my nose at the Lord and all the good things He'd ever given me, starting with the most loving parents and Granny a child could ever want.

Finally, I understood the concept of grace, defined by many as unmerited favor. Finally, I understood why God's grace is so amazing that it has transformed countless lives. And finally, I understood what it means to repent—to feel true sorrow over your past transgressions, and to deliberately turn 180 degrees from these sins to follow Him.

I also had a new appreciation for the grand old hymns I'd been getting to know again after a three-decade separation. I was now transfixed by lyrics such as these, written by a nineteenth-century businessman who had lost first his fortune and then, in a shipwreck on the Atlantic, his four daughters:

> My sin, oh the bliss of this glorious thought!
> My sin, not in part but the whole,
> Is nailed to the cross and I bear it no more,
> Praise the Lord, praise the Lord, oh my soul![8]

The old me would have sneered at this fool of a man—first for refusing to shake his fist at his imaginary God, second for believing in this cross myth, and finally for praising the Lord who, if He really existed and was really all-powerful, had allowed all these awful things to happen to the man.

The new me thought, *Yes.* This *is what it's all about.*

※

MY FRIENDS KEPT talking about my new "religion." But either I was explaining it inadequately or they were missing the point, because religion wasn't at all what I'd found.

As Hal Lindsey wrote in his riveting 1970 book, *The Late Great Planet Earth*:

> Christianity is not a religion. Religion is the process of man trying to achieve goodness, perfection, and acceptance with God by his own efforts. Christianity, on the other hand, is God taking the initiative and reaching for man. Christianity is God saying that man cannot reach Him except through the one path He has provided—through the acceptance of His Son, Jesus Christ.[9]

The first time I stumbled across a Christian snub of the word *religion*, I'd gone running to my online Bible to look it up, and was surprised to find that Scripture doesn't usually cast the word in a flattering light. In fact, Jesus apparently wasn't too impressed by the trappings of religion.

Now, thanks to a summer class, it made perfect sense: Christianity is about what God did, not about what *we* do.

⁂

THESE DAYS I think what surprises me most is that I lived for forty-seven years without understanding one simple principle:

It doesn't matter what I believe. What matters is truth.

We can perform good works all day, every day, for the rest of our lives.

We can meditate the years away, contemplating the oneness of all.

We can bust our brains trying to believe that matter is all an illusion and we don't really exist at all.

We can worship our beasts of choice till the cows come home.

But unless our thinking is based on truth, all such efforts are useless at best—or, quite possibly, spiritual suicide.

CHAPTER 21

The truth will set you free:
One woman's liberation

Midnight, May 31, 2000

Still wide awake, I started working a logic problem from the book I'd unearthed hours earlier. This was more like it: a mental workout heavy enough to keep my mind off my mother.

Until I started thinking about how we'd both loved puzzles of all kinds, from mysteries to logic problems to jigsaw puzzles. It was not a good memory that night, so I tried to concentrate on the problem at hand. It was a tough one, revolving around knitting, crocheting, and needlepoint projects, and five women whose names were so similar that I was having trouble keeping them straight.

Halfway through it, I began nodding off. I dragged myself upstairs, crawled into bed, and promptly fell asleep.

MOST WINTERS, DAVE and I do a jigsaw puzzle or two. We're particularly fond of mystery puzzles, those that come in fancy packages complete with a mini-mystery, solvable only by completing the picture puzzle so that you can see the clues missing from the narrative. Or maybe I'm particularly fond of them, and he puts up with them.

It occurred to me during the '06 NFL Playoffs that these puzzles might solve more than a fictional crime. They might actually serve as an analogy for solving the mysteries of life. They might, in fact, help us answer the "where did I come from, what am I doing here, and where am I going?" questions that we should all be asking ourselves while we're still capable of seeking the answers.

My studies have taught me that our answers to these questions invariably hinge on the preconceptions, biases, and knowledge that make up our worldviews.

We all have such a mind-set, whether we acknowledge it or not. Your worldview may be "I don't know, and no one else can know either," or "I couldn't care less." Or it may be Christian, Buddhist, Hindu, Muslim, New Age, secular, or even, sad to say, satanic.

Some people say one's worldview is like the lenses in a pair of eyeglasses. It's an apt analogy: how we interpret data in the world around us depends on how we see the data in the first place.

Lately, however, the jigsaw puzzle analogy keeps popping up as a fitting way of looking at these things. It's a tired comparison for anyone who's ever worked in advertising; way too many clients think it's terribly original to show a nearly finished puzzle with the missing pieces bearing the names of their products or services. But it turns out to be an excellent analogy for worldviews.

❦

"HOW 'BOUT STARTING that puzzle?" I asked Dave one Saturday morning in January of 2006, as I got ready to run some errands. "At least get started on the frame?"

"Mmmmph," said my aging and aching husband, who had just crammed the upper half of his body into the cabinet under the bathroom sink in yet another heroic battle against an apparently permanent clog. It would have been a painful task even for a young fellow, and I admired his persistence.

As it turned out, he didn't start the puzzle that morning. But as I drove down the gray streets toward the stores that at least add some color to our bleak winter landscape, the image of that jigsaw frame kept dancing around in my mind. At first I thought it was just wishful thinking, because for some reason it's the part of puzzle-making I like the least; perhaps I was hoping I'd come home to find that Dave had already completed it.

But later, as he and I sat and watched an AFC divisional playoff game between the Broncos and the Patriots (a game of little interest to us, since the Packers had weeks earlier been eliminated from playoff contention), I picked up my knitting and found that the puzzle frame was still hanging around in the back of my mind.

Get lost, I thought to the image. *Maybe we'll get you started next weekend.*

It grinned at me like the Cheshire cat—no doubt because I'd seen Disney's *Alice in Wonderland* again just before Christmas.

"Okay," I told the image. "What are you trying to tell me?"

As the pieces tumbled into place, it became obvious: a finished puzzle represents truth. And the frame, that all-important first step in puzzle solving, represents one's worldview.

I wish I could say that this was an original idea, but I'm quite sure it wasn't. Although, to my shame, I can't say specifically which of the authors I'd read over the previous five-plus years had used the jigsaw analogy, I know that more than one had done so.

But thanks to these writers, whoever they may be, as the Broncos were whipping the Patriots, I saw my jigsaw frame as a worldview.

The finished puzzle winked at me, Lewis Carroll and Walt Disney conspiring to entertain me into thoughts deeper than defensive strategies and the knit-one-row, purl-one-row scheme of my sweater in progress.

What if we could see the truth in a jigsaw puzzle—a puzzle so enormous and elaborate that it couldn't be completed in this life, but one that anyone with any sense is compelled to work on?

Well then, we would start out just as I wanted Dave to begin our mystery puzzle: by identifying and positioning the corners, each having two straight edges, as well as the pieces making up the frame's four "legs"—those having a single straight edge.

These pieces would share certain characteristics, making them trustworthy as contributors to the worldview of Truth. There would be none based solely on speculation or emotion or fantasy; all would be verifiable. There would be no missing pieces, and no pieces that merely came *close* to fitting. In the end, they would all have to fall into place perfectly, without the need for force or distortion. And there could be no edge pieces left over, to be discarded because they just didn't fit into the framework.

I liked this idea. My fingers flying fast and furious as I knitted my sweater, I tried the idea out on various worldviews.

For instance, I figured that if we chose the frame of biblical Christianity, we might find that the corner pieces are Jesus Christ's resurrection, a young earth having undergone a catastrophic hydraulic event, the Bible's unfailing historical accuracy, and thousands of detailed prophecies fulfilled. And we might find that the rest of the frame is composed of associated evidences, everything from archaeological findings at Jericho and Sodom to modern science's discovery that the sun does indeed have its own orbit, just as Psalm 19 revealed thousands of years ago.

From what I'd learned over the last five-plus years, was there any piece that would fit only when forced, or one that would have to be discarded because of incompatibility with the biblical framework? I couldn't think of one, not even from all the atheist stuff I'd read.

Dave woke me from my reverie with a disgusted groan. I focused on the TV again: Denver had apparently scored again, putting the game out of the Patriots' reach. Not that it mattered, of course, but because Denver had defeated the Packers in Super Bowl XXXII, whereas we beat the Patriots in Super Bowl XXXI, we would've been slightly happier with a Patriots victory in this game.

"Oh well," he said, returning to his paperback thriller.

"Oh well," I agreed, returning to my phantom jigsaw puzzle.

I tested the framework of evolution-powered naturalism and immediately ran into a problem with what would have to be a corner piece: positive, additive genetic mutation, the mechanism evolution relied on for transforming creatures from one kind into another. This sort of mutation is necessary to this worldview—and yet the evidence says it doesn't happen: instead of adding information to a creature's DNA, genetic mutations almost invariably distort or destroy existing information.

I tried substituting another corner piece: TBD, as in To Be Determined. "Scientists just haven't figured it out yet," an advocate of this framework would say. "But they will someday."

But TBD was speculation—way too shaky a premise to serve in a worldview framework, let alone as a corner piece. And that meant we were left with another gaping hole in our frame.

I took a spin with what I knew about pantheistic religions, and again found myself without decent corner pieces. "Because it works" just doesn't cut it when "it" involves entirely subjective criteria.

I tried the "everyone's right" philosophy of one world religion and noticed immediately the two-sided "Jesus was nothing more than a great teacher" piece. That ruled out this framework; I'd determined long ago, with the help of writers like C. S. Lewis and Lee Strobel, that this idea had no legs.

"Go Steelers," Dave said.

The Patriots had just been intercepted, ending any chance of a miracle comeback.

"Or Colts," I added. We were torn. We liked Bill Cowher and his

Steelers a lot. But we've always liked Tony Dungy a lot, too, and he and Cowher would be facing off the next day.

"Or Colts," Dave agreed.

It struck me that for years I'd been willing to use any Jesus-free worldview frame, even if it provided little to work with; maybe that's why I figured no one could answer these big-picture questions. I was grateful that I was no longer stuck in that no-man's-land, because now my puzzle was coming along very nicely.

It won't be finished this side of heaven; we can't even imagine what the finished picture will look like. But there's only one spot for each piece—and every time I put one into place, I get another glimpse of eternity.

✂

EVERYTHING'S DIFFERENT WHEN you frame your life picture in the biblical worldview. Suddenly it all makes sense. Just about every piece of information, experience, and idea in the box of your life fits into this frame. As long as they're thoroughly vetted, there's no need to force these pieces, or trim them back, or throw them away.

Sure, there are some pieces that don't seem to fit at first. You set them aside—throw them back in with the other loose pieces, perhaps those with the same colors—until you've got enough to work up a new section. Or until you notice that they fit somewhere else.

That happens to me constantly now, especially when I'm reading the Bible. I will go over a New Testament passage for the fourth time and suddenly realize, like a bolt out of the blue, that it answers some pesky question I had back in Genesis. Or I'll do a word-by-word study of a verse that has captured my attention, and suddenly a little-noticed preposition will bring the whole thing to life for me.

There are some other amazing things about the biblical-world-view frame too.

For one thing, it seems to repel fear. The Bible reportedly says "fear not," in various ways, 365 times—once for every day of the year, if whoever counted these mentions is correct. When I take the time to view a troubling circumstance through the biblical framework, fear flees. I have no more anxiety about going broke. I no longer step on the imaginary brake on the passenger side of the car. I have, it seems, no fear of dying—or at least such a dramatic reduction in that fundamental fear that situations which once sent me into a panic barely ruffle me now.

It's almost like He's turned me into an entirely new creature.

※

IN JOHN 8:36, Jesus is quoted as saying, "Therefore if the Son makes you free, you shall be free indeed."

It was in early 2002 that I had my first real experience of that freedom.

I still smoked as much as humanly possible—three packs a day, more often than not. I still drank a lot too; it was not unheard-of for me to put away a six-pack of beer or a bottle of wine in a single evening. But I didn't see this as a problem: early on I had overheard a pastor telling another new Christian who smoked, "We expect you to be in prayer about it." No problem—I could handle that. And in fact, I often mentioned to the Lord that anytime He wanted me to quit these little habits of mine, He should just say the word.

I guess I never expected Him to take me up on it.

Not that I actually heard Him *say* anything about it to me. But in mid-February of that year, in the midst of prayer, I suddenly knew with dead certainty that it was time to lose both cigarettes and liquor.

Even more amazing, I complied. Cold turkey. After thirty-plus years of chain smoking and beer guzzling, I became a teetotaling nonsmoker overnight.

What's nearly as remarkable, to me at least, is that my taste for alcohol vanished instantly. Upon occasion someone has given me a cocktail by mistake. Deep in conversation, I have taken a sip, and have had to literally spit it out—the taste is foul to me now.

This is real freedom, in my book—the God-powered freedom to turn one's back on even deep-seated behaviors in order to glorify Him instead of oneself. In my case, that meant being sober, as the apostles Paul and Peter repeatedly advised, and taking seriously Paul's admonition that the Christian's body is the temple of the Holy Spirit.

There are those who would deny that giving up a pleasure could be called *freedom*. But the "do what thou willst" freedom they prefer leads to enslavement. Just ask someone who's addicted to alcohol or drugs or gambling or exercise or gluttony or sex or self-importance or any of a thousand other out-of-control pleasures; if they're being honest, they will not describe their ability to pursue their poisons of choice as freedom.

"Freedom is slavery," George Orwell said in his book *1984*. Perhaps he was merely summarizing the propaganda he imagined would drive the totalitarian societies of the future. But it seems to me there's a lot of truth to this slogan for a "free" society, even if Orwell didn't realize it.

✼

As soon as the truth started coming into focus for me toward the end of 2000, I began wondering how in the world I could have made such massive miscalculations about everything of lasting importance. Why hadn't I seen any of this years earlier?

It was not long after Christmas of that year—my first spent voluntarily celebrating the birth of Jesus in a Christian church—when I discovered at least one reason for my relentless spiritual blindness over the decades. That was when I returned once again to the dwindling stack of 75 percent-off books I'd scored some weeks earlier, and came up with a dated-looking paperback entitled *What Is Secular Humanism?*

"Beats me," I said softly, confronted with yet another concept I'd apparently overlooked in my quest for a good time. I flipped through the slim volume and almost instantly came across a full-page picture of my once-upon-a-time hero, Betty Friedan. I looked further and found pictures of others worthy of twentieth-century admiration— B. F. Skinner, Karl Marx, Jean-Paul Sartre, Elvis Presley, Mick Jagger, Thomas Jefferson, JFK, Sigmund Freud, and Charles Darwin, among others.

"Curiouser and curiouser," as my old friend Alice in Wonderland had said.

I glanced at the table of contents and, seeing titles like "The Secularization of the West" and "The Cult of Self-Worship," decided this was the perfect book for a cold winter night. I took it into the Packer room and snuggled up on the leather love seat beneath a blanket of green and gold fleece. Cats Max and Sam joined me, purring, turning the scene into my own personal slice of heaven.

Published in 1982, *What Is Secular Humanism?* turned out to be the work of a Princeton-educated St. Louis University history professor named James Hitchcock—an academic with a surprisingly readable style and, wonder of wonders, a present-tense perspective that turned the years of my youth into history!

As it turned out, there wasn't a simple answer to the title question. Dr. Hitchcock spent the entire book explaining the roots, application, and implications of what is, in effect if not always in intent, an atheistic worldview. According to the author, secular humanism says that "man, for better or for worse, is on his own in the universe. He marks the highest point to which nature has yet evolved." Someone who is secular, he added, is "completely timebound, totally a child of his age, a creature of history, with no vision of eternity."[1]

As his book unfolded, Dr. Hitchcock demonstrated how the

Human Manifesto II, a document signed in 1973 by such American thought-leaders as Isaac Asimov, Andrei Sakharov, Skinner, and (surprise!) Betty herself, demonstrated a new level of intolerance for faith in God. He then traced the history of this worldview from ancient Greece through the French Revolution and showed how it had been molded into modern form by thinkers like Freud, Marx, and Hitler's hero, Friedrich "Superman" Nietzsche. (So much for humanism equaling kindness or respect for humankind.)

Nietzsche was, in fact, at the forefront of a very prevalent form of twentieth-century humanism, according to Dr. Hitchcock. Nietzsche saw that "once God had been denied, man could achieve true freedom only by denying all moral constraints on himself and inventing his own morality. The human will alone became sovereign."[2]

Hmm. That sounded kind of like what I'd believed all those years. Maybe I hadn't actually denied God, not completely and not so much recently, but I'd at least tried to keep Him tucked away in a deep corner of a rarely opened mental closet.

Reading about this idea now was giving me the creeps. It was especially disturbing to find out that this worldview had been refined and promoted by someone Hitler looked up to.

Besides, I thought I'd been somewhat original in thinking that freedom meant being able to do what I wanted, when I wanted, with whomever I wanted. I'd even thought myself somewhat innovative to equate freedom with earning tons of money and pursuing both hedonism and literary accomplishments that would ensure me of immortality.

But maybe the Nietzsche connection explained why, whenever I took a step toward achieving such goals, I felt closer to despair than satisfaction. For some reason happiness was always waiting just around the next bend, in the next plant-hunting expedition or vacation, or in some financial windfall that would ensure lifelong security, or in some sort of achievement that would make people generations from now stand in awe of my brilliance.

As I read on, the clicks starting going off in my head. Dr. Hitchcock was exposing the truth behind much of what I'd supposed to be my highly original thinking. And what I was seeing was pretty ugly: a culture enslaved to the tyranny of self, with "what's in it for me?" being the most important question one could ask about any situation or creed.

Weren't people always like this? I thought desperately, looking for an excuse for having abandoned myself to this worldview.

Apparently not. The good professor was relentless, describing "a frank and unembarrassed selfishness which has not been respectable in the Western world since the days of Rome."[3]

Respectable? Well, I guess it is: our schools even offer courses in self-esteem—courses designed to help us become more adept in our self-centeredness. (A recent Google search for "improving self-esteem" yielded 7,430,000 results; "improving holiness" produced just 947,000.)

Like any good feminist, I'd spent most of my adult life thinking about *my* happiness, *my* goals, *my* work, *my* desires, *my* self-esteem. I took my emotional temperature several times a day (I am feeling 80 percent happy right now, or 65 percent sad, or 99 percent bored, or 35 percent optimistic); my moods were subject to the slightest change in circumstances, and for some reason I felt I had to stay on top of them. Maybe because my emotional health was simply the most fascinating subject I could think of.

But now, as he brought these horrifying realities to my mind, Dr. Hitchcock was also giving me an inkling that maybe I wasn't entirely responsible for keeping myself in this all-me-all-the-time frame of mind. Maybe it was at least in part because of people like Freud, Marx, and Nietzsche that I had fallen into this trap representing the opposite of freedom—a trap that I would later come to see as part of the post-Fall condition of "natural man," described in such excruciating detail throughout the Bible.

What's more, Dr. Hitchcock's book made it clear that I wasn't alone. My thinking was typical of many who'd come of age in the 1960s under the "if it feels good, do it" banner . . . or in the 1970s, as members of the "Me" generation.

Noting that we'd been "a generation which had always gotten what it wanted," he wrote that young people of this era "had a low tolerance for frustration, and their rebellion was a collective demand that their parents' generation alleviate their frustration." It didn't take long for this frustration to extend from the political to "things which were essentially self-indulgent and self-gratifying . . . put forth as 'rights.'"[4]

In his discussion of the cult of self-worship, Dr. Hitchcock said that many in my generation were operating under a chilling new principle: "'Whatever or whoever tries to tell me what to do is oppressing me. Any law, any institution, any figure of authority which I have not created myself is my enemy, an unjust oppressor of my liberty.'"[5]

For some reason the Roberta Flack song "Killing Me Softly" started popping into my head after a twenty-five-year hiatus: "I felt all flushed with fever, embarrassed by the crowd, I felt he found my letters and read each one out loud."

And naturally my generation's dislike of authority had turned the God of the Bible into the ultimate oppressor, always trying to ruin our good times by putting our parents on our case or, occasionally, making us feel guilty about some of our worst excesses.

When *Time* magazine famously asked, "Is God dead?" in April 1966, at least some young people certainly hoped He was; if I'd thought about it, I probably would have been among them.

🔉

NOT EVERYONE WAS impressed with the fact that I'd quit smoking cold turkey. In fact, most of my friends shrugged it off with a "big deal." Others said it was all in my mind: because I *believed* God was helping me quit, I was able to *act* like He was helping me.

Okay, I'll agree: these things are possible.

But not this: the retreat of my anger, for many years my constant companion, hovering just below the surface, waiting to attack. I'm sure any number of people could vouch for this.

Here's the truth: it has virtually disappeared.

When my computer goes berserk in the midst of a major deadline.

When a driver cuts me off.

When someone close to me bashes my beliefs or character or motives.

When I learn about some costly new government program designed to help people who don't need any help.

When a client tears apart my work.

These things used to make me crazy. I never threw my CPU through a window, but I frequently felt like it. I never told those who offended me to go to hell, but I often wanted to. I never told a client off, but instead I complained mightily to whomever would listen, preferably another writer who would understand that client's utter stupidity.

All that relentless rage, gone. Without a single psychiatric intervention, tranquilizer, or antidepressant. Vanished, practically overnight, without any effort on my part at all.

Later, I would read in Philippians 4 about "the peace of God, which surpasses all understanding."

It was like that: peace that I hadn't felt since I was a little kid, before I knew the heartbreaks and fears and humiliations that can happen in this world. The sort of peace you feel when you know someone much bigger than you is in total control, loves you to pieces, and will take care of you always.

The simmering fury is gone. And anyone who thinks that is no big deal simply doesn't have a clue.

WHEN THE OLD me behaved badly, I liked to blame anyone and anything other than myself. And I have to admit that it's tempting now to try to blame feminism for my anger in the years before my mother got sick.

There is perhaps some justification for this. As Nancy Pearcey noted in her outstanding book *Total Truth*, "From the beginning, feminism was marked by considerable anger and envy—not toward individual men so much as toward the fact of the opportunities available to men in the public sphere."[6]

But it wasn't just the feminism. Being a libertarian contributed to the problem too. By definition, I had long rejected virtually all authority and resented anyone telling me what to do. That was one of the reasons that, before Jesus, I hadn't even considered quitting my three-pack-a-day habit; who were *they* to tell me I shouldn't smoke? Which, of course, paved the way for my feeling persecuted by the antismoking Nazis of the world—persecuted and ready to blow up.

And blow up I did. Once during a mid-'90s luncheon with a militantly pure-of-lung friend, I let a bit of my smoke drift in her direction, and she fanned the offending plume away from her nose. She hadn't said a word, but the wave of her hand was enough for me. In my fury, I let loose with the worst insult I could think of: "Oh, and I suppose you like Bill Clinton too!"

She looked at me as if I'd lost my mind—and indeed I had for the moment it took me to spit out this *non sequitur*.

Then there was an incident in the Detroit airport, circa 1995, when our flight from the Bahamas got diverted because of snow and we were trapped out on a runway for several extra smoke-free hours. The customs official who finally welcomed us into the terminal didn't appreciate my lighting up the moment I walked through the door, nor did he appreciate the words I hurled at him when he asked me—really, quite politely, I have to admit—to put my cigarette out.

Fortunately, my pure-of-lung lunchmate forgave me, and I didn't end up in a federal prison over the near scuffle with the customs official. But some of my eruptions no doubt *did* have long-term consequences, especially when they were directed at my mother.

Perhaps the worst incident of all occurred on Christmas Eve 1999, before she got sick. I was taking her back to the nursing home after a day and evening of presents and feasting at our house with both my sisters and their families.

My mother had been all smiles, all day long. And then, alone with me in my rusting Chevy Blazer, barreling up nearly deserted Barker Road, she sighed.

"I hate having to go back to the old ladies' home," she said. "I have that awful aide tonight, the one who's so rough with me, and—"

"I can't believe you!" I snapped, outraged, sure that she was not-so-subtly hinting that she would like to come live with us. "You're sweetness and light, until you're alone with me—and then all you can do is complain!"

I don't know that I've ever seen her look so sad.

"I'm sorry," she said quietly. "It's just that you're the only one I can talk to about these things."

"Well, I can't do anything about it," I said, already feeling guilty. I knew I'd need a good hour or two to think this one through until I found a way to justify my outburst. "Anyway, if you would just be nicer to this aide, maybe she'd be nicer to you."

As it turned out, I never was able to justify what I'd said to her that night. I wept over it more than once, and to this day cringe whenever I remember it. It's symbol of all the pain I had caused her over our lives together, of all the times I'd trashed the wonderful life the Lord had given me.

And yet, amazing God, he has seen my contrite heart and forgiven me even for this. And much, much more. As Isaac Watts wrote in his 1707 hymn "Alas, and Did My Savior Bleed?":

Was it for crimes that I had done
He groaned up on the tree?
Amazing pity! grace unknown!
And love beyond degree!

꙳

TO CREATE A coherent picture from jigsaw-puzzle pieces, you have to have all the pieces in hand. Or most of them, anyway; we have learned that it *is* possible to complete a puzzle even after the cats have fed the dogs a half dozen or so.

Trouble is, when it comes to biblical Christianity, you aren't going to get most of the pieces unless you search them out. Jesus has been banned from our public institutions, and the news media are largely silent on any topic that might paint the Bible in a positive light.

Dr. Hitchcock's book got me to thinking about news coverage of topics related to faith—especially, since it's sort of my thing these days, the play given to pronouncements by evolutionists. And here's the truth: every few weeks, I see a prominent story on some new evolutionary discovery that promises to be the missing link. At the same time, pronouncements about vast ages—the old "millions and millions of years" bit—are presented as fact, with nary an attribution to provide even a hint of opinion being mixed in.

I grumble to Dave about this regularly over the morning newspaper.

"Listen to this," I usually begin, forcing him to bear witness to yet another unattributed paragraph or two.

He normally just sips his coffee and nods and buries himself further in the section he's reading, no doubt hoping I'll be quiet. Neither of us likes to be read to, especially not from a story we'll soon have the opportunity to read ourselves, or one we've already taken a pass on. But I usually toss such concerns aside when I'm hot on the trail of yet another evolutionary fairy tale.

"What kills me," I then say, "is that when they finally figure out this isn't what they thought it was, we won't see any follow-up stories to let us know we've been misled by these clowns. And the clowns themselves don't care; by that time they'll have used this alleged discovery to get themselves fat new grants."

"Terrible," Dave typically agrees, wise enough to let me run with it.

"And in the meantime," I continue, "the public is left with the impression that evolution is fact."

"They should really all be shot, just as soon as possible."

He doesn't mean this, of course. But it always makes me laugh, putting an end to my complaint.

But it doesn't put an end to this problem of the news media presenting these tales as fact. Even when the claims are highly controversial—for example, there's no small debate raging about whether Lucy was a human relative or simply an extinct chimp—conventional news channels rarely bother to point it out.

This would be somewhat tolerable if news relating to Christianity received the same treatment: Unquestioning publicity, with no follow-up if things turn out to be not quite as they seemed at first blush.

But as long as I've been watching, I haven't seen that happen, not once.

For instance, the 2002 discovery of an ossuary that might have contained the bones of Jesus' brother James was reported on amidst repeated charges of fraud. Whether or not it was genuine didn't matter; readers were left with the impression that biblical artifacts should be viewed with suspicion that is rarely leveled against evolutionary claims.

Or consider the 2006 discovery of a four-hundred-plus-foot object in the mountains of Iran, more than thirteen thousand feet above sea level. Its finders believe it might be the remains of Noah's Ark. They had it tested by a Houston lab—one that the Smithsonian itself uses—and supposedly learned that it is indeed made of petrified wood, complete with fossilized sea critters buried inside.

I have no idea if this discovery will turn out to be anything more than a false alarm. But what's really interesting about it to me is the lack of interest it has generated in the news media. For weeks after the initial announcement, which I came across via a Christian news service, I searched the Internet diligently to see how the nation's big news organizations handled the story.

Surprise: most ignored it.

Why is that? A few bones can be declared evidence that we evolved from slime, and the newspapers are all over it; an archaeological finding may prove the story of the Genesis Flood true, and it's greeted with a big yawn.

There's definitely something wrong here.

CHAPTER 22

In my Father's house:
The ultimate wake-up call

3:15 a.m., May 31, 2000

I woke up to find myself almost leaping out of bed, in a state of terror unlike anything I'd ever experienced.

I listened: I was surrounded by a symphony of peaceful canine, feline, and husbandly snoring.

My heart was pounding too wildly to even attempt going back to sleep. I grabbed my robe and headed back down to my spot at the kitchen table.

I knew the phone would be ringing soon.

And it did, at 3:35 a.m.

I answered it, knowing full well what I was going to hear.

It was Carolyn at the nursing home.

"Ethel has passed away," she said, matter-of-factly.

"She did," I said, unable to think of anything else to say.

"I've called the doctor, and the time of death was 3:25."

"Oh," I said.

"I'll call the funeral home now," she said.

"Okay," I added.

"Are you all right?" she asked, sounding a little more concerned.

"Sure," I said, hanging up.

I comforted myself with the fact that Carolyn had been dead wrong about the time of death; it was definitely 3:15. I didn't have much else to work with at that point.

CHAPTER 23

Absent from the body:
The only itinerary we need

10:00 a.m., May 31, 2000

B y 5 a.m. I had e-mailed my friends and clients with my sad news. I waited until seven to call my sisters; there was nothing they could do about it now, anyway.

They said the same stupid thing I had upon hearing the news that Mom had died: "She did"—a question in the form of a statement.

And so we did what had to be done. Within a few hours, Dave and Carrie and I were at the nursing home, cleaning out Mom's room, even though the staff had said there was absolutely no hurry. Our reaction—to get right to it, without wasting a moment—is apparently not uncommon. You need to do *something*. Otherwise, you risk being alone with your grief.

Dave went to U-Haul and bought a stack of boxes and a couple of huge cardboard wardrobes, and we filled them and then packed them all in his truck and unloaded everything in our garage so I could go through it all and wash the things that we'd give to Goodwill and divide up the keepsakes among us girls.

In the afternoon, Carrie and I went to the funeral home to finalize the details of the funeral.

We were ushered through a great hushed hall, treading plush carpeting past romantic paintings and oversized French provincial armoires, into an equally lavish conference room in tasteful crushed strawberry. Nothing morbid here.

A young woman in a navy suit and stylish black-framed glasses greeted us with a sad smile and gentle handshake. She invited us to sit down and produced a file with quite a bit of paperwork in it already.

"This won't be too difficult," she said. "Your mother made the major decisions herself several years ago."

This was not a surprise. I'd been with her that afternoon, sitting in a little day room at the nursing home with a handsome young man with the equally handsome name of Giovanni, watching in horror as she selected her casket and cremation urn and told Giovanni where her plot was, with my dad's and her parents' in an old cemetery in Wausau, her hometown. It was both painful and surrealistic for me, but she had paged through the casket and urn catalogues with great enthusiasm, as if she were planning a cruise.

But now, sitting in this conference room at the funeral home, I was grateful beyond measure that she had taken care of decisions that would surely have been a source of further anguish for us.

"We'd like to hold the funeral at our church," Carrie said to the young woman, "St. Peter's in North Lake."

I tuned out while she provided the address and directions; what difference did it make now? I thought about how my mother's body was lying right here, in this very building, and how they'd said when I called this morning that we could see it if we wanted to, and how horrified I'd been at the thought of that. I wondered if it was wrong to not want to see her lifeless body, and if I should tell this young woman that I'd changed my mind, I would see it after all. I thought about how Scarlett O'Hara had spent a long time—hours, apparently—with her mother's body when she finally made it back to Tara upon fleeing Atlanta, with Melanie and her new baby in the . . .

"Is that okay, Kit?" Carrie was asking gently. "Saturday? That would give people time to come in from out of town."

"Sure," I said. What difference did it make? I wasn't going to let any of my friends come to it except my two oldest and closest girlfriends. This was not a party. Why were we even doing this?

"Now, about the time," the young woman said to Carrie.

I returned to my reverie, in a bit of a panic now, because apparently this meeting was coming to a close, and if I was going to do the Scarlett O'Hara thing, I'd have to make a decision soon.

But I couldn't decide, and so, in not deciding, I decided no.

We knocked the death notice out in about five minutes flat. Carrie didn't seem too concerned about what it said, and the phrase I'd read here and there—"born to eternal life"—sounded nice and upbeat to me, so we used that.

What difference did any of it make?

❧

DECADES AGO, NEWSPAPERS like my hometown *Green Bay Press-Gazette* regularly published items about residents' personal lives—including their travel plans. Now, I read the local death notices daily, and I feel like I'm reading the same sort of small-town gossip. The main difference is that these people are off to eternity instead of Paris or San Francisco, and won't be returning at all.

If the Bible is true, each one is headed straight for one of two eternal destinations: heaven or hell.

So, okay, maybe the Bible is simply incorrect. Maybe all the evidence I'd found supporting it is wrong, or coincidental, or just wishful thinking that somehow became reality thanks to a fluke of nature.

But reading the obituaries underscores what a risk we take if we do not consider these possibilities.

I read these notices and wonder how many spent less time planning their final journeys than they did planning their educations and careers and vacations and retirements.

Of course, it's difficult to tell these things from a death notice; very often, the notices say more about the survivors than they do about the dearly departed. For instance, I might read something like this about a fellow named Joe Blow:

> At the age of 57 years, Joe passed away peacefully, surrounded by those he loved. Survived by his children, his loving partner, Lee, and many friends. Funeral July 15th at the funeral home. Visitation 4:30 to 6:30; service at 6:30. "Joe was taken before his time. He remains with us in spirit each day."

Hmmm. An apparently secular service at a funeral home, a reference to a partner rather than a spouse, and a spirit still hanging around—all of which might indicate that Joe Blow was a secular soul with an interest in the occult. But there might be more to this story. Maybe Joe and his wife, Lee, moved here from Dallas shortly before he fell ill and hadn't had time to find a church. Maybe Lee was so devastated, she let the kids handle the arrangements, and they, being heathens, didn't know that Joe would have preferred a Christian service, so that they might hear the gospel themselves.

Lots of possibilities.

Where is Joe's spirit now, I wonder? Dwelling in the eternal misery described in Luke 16? Or exploring one of the Father's mansions that Jesus mentioned in John 14:2, living in depths of love and heights of joy that we can't even imagine?

Or is there some as-yet unimagined solution to this great puzzle of our lives—a solution that will somehow manage to explain away all those pesky evidences of the Bible's cover-to-cover trustworthiness?

"IF MY CHOICES are heaven or hell," said a colleague I'll call Morgan, "I'll take hell any day. Who wants to spend eternity with a bunch of holier-than-thou Christians? Oops, sorry."

No she wasn't. This was the fourth time in the last year I'd run into her at a business function, and the third time she'd let me know that she really has no use for Christians. Her apology could be sincere only if she had really forgotten my faith *again*, which was not likely: Morgan is a brilliant account executive.

"But you have to understand, all my friends will be in hell, having a good time with Satan," she said, smoothing her shoulder-length hair and smiling sweetly at me. "I'd rather party with them forever and ever than spend five minutes with a single Goody Two-Shoes."

We were sitting at the bar of an expensive restaurant west of Milwaukee, waiting for the program to get underway. I stirred my diet Pepsi with a straw while she sipped her wine.

She was baiting me, I knew, but I couldn't let her comment pass.

"The trouble is," I said, "according to the Bible, Satan isn't going to be in charge there, and it's going to be just the opposite of a good time. In fact, if Scripture is correct, hell is a place of eternal punishment, of gnashing teeth, where the worm never dies."

"*If* it's correct," Morgan said, rolling her eyes. "Oh, look, they're waving at us. They must be ready to get started."

She slid off her bar stool and trotted off toward the dining room, leaving me sitting alone to consider what I *should* have said. As usual, she'd brought up the subject—this time, with "Do you think heaven will be fun?"—only to shrug off the Christian viewpoint. As if her ideas were more valid than the Bible's proclamations.

I sighed as I followed in her wake, well aware that I had once thought precisely the same thing. And not all that long ago.

CHAPTER 24

You must be born again:
Getting positioned for eternity

9:00 p.m., June 2, 2000

I'd spent two solid days trying to produce a little brochure about my mother to hand out at her funeral—trying, first because I couldn't figure out how to use Print Artist's booklet template, and then, once I'd cracked that code, because I had to hand-feed the card-weight paper through my cheesy color printer; when it wasn't jamming on me, it was crashing my whole system.

But then, just when I was about to give up and sulk over a beer or two, everything started running perfectly. And before the brand-new $49.95 ink cartridges had breathed their last, I was actually able to print out thirty copies of the little twelve-pager, complete with color photos and a tiny reproduction of the Piet Mondrian house print I'd been hanging on to for thirty years, a house that I decided must be our heavenly home. If heaven really existed, of course.

I collated and folded the brochures, and then, around midnight, took a big glass of wine outside and sat on one of the built-in benches bordering our deck. I didn't turn on the light at the back door; I didn't want to take a chance on having an audience if I started crying again.

I looked up at the sky and thought about wishing on a star, but I wasn't paying attention and lost sight of the first one I saw. (The incantation is "Star light, star bright, *first* star I see tonight"—not "*one of many* stars I see tonight." I was quite sure that wishing on just any old star would be pointless.)

But there wasn't much else to see, so I kept looking up at the stars in the southern sky. There were several particularly bright ones. I wondered if my mother was even now sitting on just such a heavenly body. Or maybe—this was sort of a thrilling thought—had even *become* such a heavenly body.

I chose the third brightest of the group and locked my gaze on it. "Mom?" I said softly. "If that's you, wink at me."

The star winked, and my heart flip-flopped.

"Do it again," I said, and the star complied.

I repeated this experiment over and over, varying the time between commands to see if it was blinking randomly.

It wasn't.

I don't know how long I sat there telling the star to blink, but by the end of this session, I was halfway convinced that my mother was either living on that star or had been transformed into that star.

I pursued this kooky idea for at least a few weeks before replacing it with sounder theology.

But for months afterward I kept one eye on the heavens, just in case.

❦

NUMBED BY THE wine and invigorated by the chilly night air, I finally tiptoed back to my office and took a fresh look at my paper-and-ink tribute to Ethel Boehm Foth.

It really *was* cool, even if I did have to say so myself.

The cover was definitely slick. Against a deep blue-green, yellow, and black abstract design, I had inset a box that said "Ethel Boehm

Foth" and "1912–2000" and then inserted between these two lines a great snapshot of her and my dad—one taken in the late 1950s.

Even today this picture makes my heart ache with grief and gratitude. They're sitting close together on a beach in Door County, Wisconsin, crazy-happy smiles on their faces, their heads touching, my mom's hand tucked into my dad's. It must have been chilly out—Jacksonport is on the colder Lake Michigan side of the Door County peninsula, and my dad is wearing a casual jacket over an open-collared shirt—a rare event in the life of a man who almost always wore suits, even when he was vacationing. My mom is wearing a cardigan sweater over a lavender dress with a wrap-style bodice and sunglasses that would be in style today.

The second page featured a snapshot of a very young Ethel with a lapful of puppies and an oft-used quote from Rossiter Worthington Raymond: "Life is eternal; and love is immortal; and death is only a horizon; and a horizon is nothing save the limit of our sight."

There were similar treasures throughout the piece. I had included a studio portrait of Mom sporting a flapper style do, most likely taken when she was in her late teens, and a strip of four Photo-booth pictures of her, smiling gaily, probably from the 1940s. There was a shot of her feeding the pigeons in front of St. Mark's cathedral in Venice; another of her sitting at a picnic table with her best friend, Cecil; and a studio photo she'd had taken just a few years ago, so we'd have something to remember her by as she really was, she said: old.

The rest of the pictures were of her and Dad. One, taken in the 1960s, showed the two of them posing on a sidewalk in Madrid, he in his ubiquitous business suit, she in a smart red and black plaid wool coat. There were some faded black-and-white snapshots taken in a park when they were students at UW in Madison, in the 1930s. And there was a shot of them on the passenger ship *Berlin*, sailing home from Europe in 1963; it must have been a special night, because she was wearing a gorgeous lacy black dress, and they were walking along, holding hands and beaming, a bevy of smiling men and women in formalwear in their wake.

Amid the photos were poems—some that she'd written, and others that she'd clipped from magazines over the course of her life.

Of the latter, the one that best described her life had been penned by Jan Struther of *Mrs. Miniver* fame. It was entitled "Biography." The poet said, in essence, if you're going to comment on my life once I'm dead and gone, just say this:

"'Here lies one doubly blest.' Say, 'She was happy.' Say, 'She knew it.'"[1]

⁂

A WEEK AFTER my mother's death, I followed a well-wisher's advice and bought myself a study Bible in the easy-to-read New Living Translation. I started at the beginning, in the Old Testament book of Genesis. It was fascinating . . . but I was left scratching my head, unable to figure out what Christianity was all about.

I kept plugging away, but weeks passed before I told a longtime friend of my struggles. One of several "surprise" Christians in my life—I'd never even suspected!—she advised me to jump ahead immediately to the book of John, the last of the four New Testament gospels describing Jesus' life.

And that's just what I did the following Saturday morning after mowing the lawn and deadheading my early roses and late irises. I sat down on our deck in the sun, breathing in the vanilla scent of a Japanese tree lilac in full bloom, and was immediately entranced even by the prosaic language of this modern translation.

The apostle John didn't beat around the bush. He opened with this: "In the beginning the Word already existed. He was with God, and he was God. He was in the beginning with God. He created everything there is. Nothing exists that he didn't make. Life itself was in him, and this life gives light to everyone."[2]

The study notes explained this passage: "John shows Jesus as fully human and fully God. Although Jesus took upon himself full humanity and lived as a man, he never ceased to be the eternal God who has always existed, the Creator and Sustainer of all things, and the source of eternal life."[3]

Well, that was cool! I read on, alternating between the text and the notes, pausing every few verses to take it all in.

"But to all who believed him and accepted him," verses 12 and 13 said, "he gave the right to become children of God. They are reborn! This is not a physical birth resulting from human passion or plan—this rebirth comes from God."[4]

My eyes darted to the note below:

> All who welcome Jesus Christ as Lord of their lives are reborn spiritually. Through faith in Christ, this new birth changes us from the inside out—rearranging our attitudes, desires and motives. Being born makes you physically alive and places you in your parents' family (1:13). Being born of God makes you spiritually alive and puts you in God's family (1:12).[5]

The more I thought about it, the more incredible this seemed. Imagine, being a child of God! But that word, *reborn*—I wondered if it had anything to do with the phrase "born-again Christian." I hoped not; they were pretty much zombies, as far as I knew.

I plunged ahead, unable to put the Good Book down.

I came across this "reborn" idea again in John 3, but—I knew it!—it was phrased as "born again" and was apparently presented as a prerequisite for getting into heaven. My heart sank. But there was no turning back; I steeled myself for the details.

In this chapter, the apostle John described an exchange between Jesus and a man named Nicodemus, "a ruler of the Jews." Coming to Jesus at night, perhaps to avoid being seen with Him, Nicodemus had commented that Jesus must be from God because of all the miracles He had performed.

Jesus delivered the strangest reply: "I assure you, unless you are born again, you can never see the Kingdom of God."

With a sinking feeling (could these born-again dorks possibly be right?), I read the study note: "This was a revolutionary concept: the Kingdom is personal, not national or ethnic, and its entrance requirements are repentance and spiritual rebirth."[6]

This didn't help me too much. Another clue appeared in the same note, a few lines later: "[P]eople don't enter the Kingdom by living a better life, but by being spiritually reborn."[7]

That didn't do it, either. I kept reading. At the end of chapter 3, Jesus is quoted as saying, "And all who believe in God's Son have eternal life. Those who don't obey the Son will never experience eternal life, but the wrath of God remains upon them."[8]

The study note said in part, "To receive eternal life is to join in God's life, which by nature is eternal. Thus, eternal life begins at the moment of spiritual rebirth." A few lines later, after talking about how it's our responsibility to decide whom we will obey, the note said, "To put off the choice is to choose not to follow Christ. Indecision is a fatal decision."[9]

Whoa! I didn't want to be caught in a fatal decision; I wanted to be with my mom forever. I remembered what she had written in the beginning of her own Bible: "Jesus Christ is the light of my life and I see my way clearly." Apparently she had made the decision to follow Him. I decided to do so myself, then and there, and told Him so.

Pending, of course, the outcome of my investigation into Christianity's truth.

✂

WHEN YOU'RE A child of the '60s thinking about becoming a born-again Christian, you hesitate. You may even resist.

After all, born-again Christians are creeps, aren't they? Aren't they the ones who parade around busy streets with signs saying, "Jesus loves you"? Who sooner or later snap and murder their own families?

That's certainly the impression our culture gives us, anyway.

The born-again pastor of a mainline Protestant church recently told me he asked the fourteen members of a Bible study how many of them had been born again. One woman raised her hand.

He then asked how many of them had sorrowfully acknowledged their sinfulness, recognized that Jesus died to pay their sin debts, confessed their sins to Him and repented of them, asked for His forgiveness, and made Him their personal Lord and Savior.

They all raised their hands.

"Then," he said, "you've all been born again."

No report on their reaction to this news, but I'll bet more than one or two were a teensy bit horrified to hear it.

✂

DID MY DECISION to follow Jesus make me born again? I didn't have a clue. That evening I called the friend who had suggested I read the book of John in the first place and asked her.

"That's a great question," she said. "Check out 1 Peter 1:23."

"Check out what, now?" I asked, flustered, reaching for my New Living Translation Study Bible. "Why can't it just say it up front, in one place?"

She told me patiently to look for 1 Peter toward the back of my Bible, right after the book of James.

"I'll look," I said doubtfully. "Hold on—I'm lost in this thing!"

"Don't worry," she said, "you'll be able to find your way around pretty quickly if you just keep at it. And then you'll understand why it's not written like an operator manual; God is turning us into the likeness of His Son, not teaching us how to run a computer. Trust me; it'll soon start taking your breath away."

"Okay, I trust you. And I found 1 Peter. Now where?"

"Read chapter 1, verse 23."

"Let's see," I said, humming "A Mighty Fortress" to keep her from hanging up. "Okay, here goes: 'For you have been born again. Your new life did not come from your earthly parents because the life they gave you will end in death. But this new life will last forever because it comes from the eternal, living word of God.' And that would mean—?"

"Read the last sentence in that chapter," she suggested.

"'And that word is the Good News that was preached to you.'"[10]

"Do you understand now?"

"No," I said, quite sure that I never would.

"It means we are born again by the inspired, inerrant, and eternal Word of God. Keep reading it, Kitty—you'll see."

﹅

I DID AS this friend suggested and kept reading my Bible. It was no burden: it was better than any thriller I'd ever read. On the one hand, I wanted to read it as fast as I could; on the other, I wanted to pause at each verse and read the study note and think it over.

But always, in the back of my mind, I was looking for more clues to this "born again" business. Specifically, I wanted to know how you know when you've been reborn.

The answer came in the form of a lecture that aired toward the end of 2000, one of dozens that I'd taken notes on over the years. It was a program I joined late, so I didn't jot down the name of the lecturer or his topic, and I don't remember seeing him again. Still, I don't think I'll ever forget the content of his talk.

"Fruits of being born again," I had written at the top of the page, underscoring the words with a flourish.

Then a list of words and phrases, followed by Bible verses.

"Loving God," was the first phrase, followed by the notation Luke 10:27: "So he answered and said, 'You shall love the LORD your God with all your heart, with all your soul, with all your strength, and with all your mind,' and 'your neighbor as yourself.'"

I remember thinking that I hadn't even come close to doing these things, and wondering if anyone ever did.

"Repentance," was next, followed by 2 Corinthians 7:10: "For godly sorrow produces repentance leading to salvation, not to be regretted; but the sorrow of the world produces death."

Repenting was something I'd been doing a lot of ever since my mother died. It was effortless: every time I turned around, I was facing some other grievous action or word or even thought I'd been guilty of. And I was indeed sorrowful over all of it—not to mention horrified and ashamed and wishing time and again that I could start all over again at about the age of three.

"Obedience" was the next word, and 1 John 2:3–5 was the passage I'd marked down: "Now by this we know that we know Him, if we keep His commandments. He who says, 'I know Him,' and does not keep His commandments, is a liar, and the truth is not in him. But whoever keeps His word, truly the love of God is perfected in him. By this we know that we are in Him."

That was another toughie for me, especially in those early months when I was uncertain what His commandments entailed. But by the time I heard this lecture, I at least recognized them as potentially authoritative and nonnegotiable. That was a start; and as I listened, I vowed to waste no more time trying to justify lies or greed or gluttony by calling them something more palatable.

"A transformed life," was the last phrase in my notes; 2 Corinthians 5:17 was the passage. "Therefore, if anyone is in Christ, he is a new creation; old things have passed away; behold, all things have become new."

Hmmm. I was certainly feeling brand-new by then, at least between those sorrowful episodes of repentance. But was I?

I remember calling a new girlfriend that very night, a woman I'd met at church, and asking her the big question: How do I know if I'm born again?

"Well," she said, "I believe it's like this: When you repent and make Jesus your Lord and Savior, you are saved—and you are born again. Then He changes you, bit by bit, which is what they call sanctification. You start seeing changes in your life and your attitudes toward everything."

"Such as?" I prompted.

"Well, things like you can't get enough of His Word. You want nothing more than to obey Him and to tell everyone you know what He's done for you. You stop thinking about what *you* want, and start thinking about what He would want you to do. You feel real joy and peace for the first time. You suddenly find people you would've once done anything to avoid absolutely charming—and find the people who were once a gas not so much fun anymore. And you find yourself talking to God a lot, which is praying, and—hey, is any of this sounding familiar?"

"Yes, I think so," I said, almost embarrassed. I had that "killing me softly" feeling again, like this near-stranger was seeing some of my most personal thoughts. "But I'm a long way from being perfect in any of this."

She laughed. "Of course you are—we all are! We don't get perfect in this life, girl!"

"Oh."

"Let me ask you this," she said. "Have you noticed any dramatic change recently—say, since you started reading your Bible? Something effortless?"

"Yes," I said, astonished that she knew. "I woke up one morning unable to swear—isn't that weird?"

"That happened to me too," she said. "One day I was Miss Potty Mouth, and one night I bowed my knee to Jesus, and the next day I couldn't have cussed if you'd paid me to do it. It was just totally gone!"

"That's it exactly," I said. "What a coincidence!"

"I don't think so," she said. "I suspect that He makes some obvious change in some of us so that we'll know for sure that He's real, and acting on our hearts. I heard some famous pastor saying that this very same thing happened to him too. James Kennedy, I think."

"Wow. So do you think that means I'm born again?"

She sighed. "You know, I really can't say—that's between you and the Lord. You have to ask Him to let you know, I guess. But it sounds like He's starting to change you whether you like it or not, and it sounds like the fruit of the Spirit to me."

"Fruit of the Spirit?" I was learning a whole new language, it seemed.

"Galatians 5:22," she said, sounding just like my book of John girlfriend. "Look it up!"

EVANGELIST RAY COMFORT gave a vivid description of what it means to be born again in an essay distributed in March of 2006—too late for my quest but wonderful just the same. He was explaining what happened to a sinful first-century martyr-in-the-making who had, several years earlier, repented and believed in the gospel and called upon the name of the Lord, just as the Bible says we must all do if heaven is our goal:

Almighty God . . . made him a new creature. He was born again, with a new heart and new desires. . . . This man, who once lived for sin and drank it like water, suddenly found that he thirsted for righteousness, and wanted, above all things, to please the God that gave him life. It was a miracle. One day he had no thoughts of God. Not for a second. The next day the love of God was shed abroad in his heart. The Holy Spirit made His abode in him. . . .

When he prayed, he had an inner conviction that God heard his every whisper. It was as though he had been given the gift of faith. He believed without effort. The Name of Jesus was sweet to his ear, and Jesus Christ became more important to him than his own life. . . . He bubbled with an unspeakable joy and relished a peace that passed all understanding.[11]

✦

OF COURSE, SUCH outcomes depend upon Scripture being trustworthy. Emboldened by what I'd learned about its apparently flawless historical record and accurate, centuries-spanning prophecies, by fall 2001 I was studying the Bible with full confidence that it is God's own revelation of who He is, who we are, how He has intervened and continues to intervene in our lives, and what His ultimate purpose is for us. I was studying it with full assurance that it answers the questions of where we came from, what we're doing here, and where we're going.

In fact, the Bible was teaching me all I was dying to know. For instance:

- That reincarnation is not true. "And as it is appointed for men to die once, but after this the judgment, so Christ was offered once to bear the sins of many."[12]

- That upon death, God's children go directly to heaven to be with Him—no stops for purging, no deep sleep. "We are confident, yes, well pleased rather to be absent from the body and to be present with the Lord."[13]
- That I must live a God-honoring life, but that, as a born-again believer, I needn't worry about losing my salvation when I slip up. "My sheep hear My voice, and I know them, and they follow Me. And I give them eternal life, and they shall never perish; neither shall anyone snatch them out of My hand."[14]

So far, I haven't come across anything to discourage me from trusting the Bible implicitly. On the contrary, everything I learn, everything I observe, everything I experience, further solidifies its position in my spirit as the inspired and inerrant Word of God.

CHAPTER 25

To die is gain:
Women living on the edge

2:00 p.m., June 3, 2000

The day of my mother's funeral was sunny and warm. Not what I'd been hoping for. I wanted storms so severe that we would have been forced to cancel the whole thing.

But this God of hers had given us perfect weather, and now here we all were, at St. Peter's, Carrie and David's little church in the lake country nearly an hour west of Milwaukee. It's a gem of a building, at least one hundred years old, maybe more. Built of cream-city brick, its architecture is Norman, if I'm remembering my art history properly, with a touch of Gothic. Inside, it's quite plain, with thick, white walls, stained-glass windows set deep into pointy-topped arches, and dark wood everywhere, from the pews to the beamed ceiling.

I stood in the musty vestibule with my little brochures and gave one to everyone who came in. I didn't know many of these people, except for a couple of aides from the nursing home. They must've been friends of my sisters. For my support group, besides Dave, only my girlfriends Brenda and JoAnn and JoAnn's husband, Ben, were there. I'd told everyone else that it was to be a small, private service; I wasn't up for being sociable.

Brenda and I had grown up together, and I sat between her and Dave for the service. It was comforting that they'd both known my mom so well for so long, way back to when she was mobile and merry and ready for fun. They sat there silently with me, grieving.

At some point, the funeral home staff marched my mom's closed casket in and set it in the aisle to our right, not ten feet from us. I couldn't stop stealing glances at it. I wondered what in the world it was doing there, anyway—why haul a closed coffin all this way? Then I started wondering other things, like how we could know for sure that her body was really in there, and if, as smart consumers, we should demand to see it.

But then the service started, relieving me of the need to act on any of these thoughts. I don't remember much of what was said, other than someone commenting on how shocked my Protestant mother would've been if she had known her funeral would be held in an Episcopal church—which, according to St. Peter's own Web site, walks "a middle way between Roman Catholicism and Protestant traditions." But I don't suppose it really mattered. She was gone, and what we did with the body she'd left behind wasn't going to change the fact that she was now, as one of the aides assured me on her way into the church, absent from the body and present with the Lord.

There were some scripture readings—the 23rd Psalm, of course, but also the 121st, which I would later come to love, when I heard the Brooklyn Tabernacle Choir put it to magnificent music:

> I will lift up mine eyes unto the hills, from whence cometh my help. My help cometh from the LORD, which made heaven and earth. He will not suffer thy foot to be moved: he that keepeth thee will not slumber. . . . The sun shall not smite thee by day, nor the moon by night. The LORD shall preserve thee from all evil: he shall preserve thy soul. The LORD shall preserve thy going out and thy coming in from this time forth, and even for evermore.[1]

Someone read a passage from the Old Testament book of Isaiah, a passage that included the promise that the Lord Himself would be sent "to comfort all that mourn . . . to give unto them beauty for ashes, the oil of joy for mourning, the garment of praise for the spirit of heaviness."[2]

I may not have understood much of what was said that day, but the part about ashes, mourning, and spiritual heaviness hit home. This passage from Isaiah gave me another glimmer of hope to add to the collection I'd begun the night before Mom's death.

There were hymns too: "Holy, Holy, Holy" and "Lead on, O King Eternal," which I had chosen because they were the only two I could remember from my childhood, as well as "Amazing Grace," which naturally reminded me of Reggie White and Lambeau Field and that transcendent moment in the highlight reel of my life.

A young man and woman from this church, who'd visited my mother at the nursing home a number of times, sang a couple songs—one of which was "In the Garden." I didn't know this song, but it was apparently one of her favorites. Written in 1912, the year she was born, it describes an intensely personal relationship with Jesus Christ:

> And He walks with me, and He talks with me,
> And He tells me I am His own.
> And the joy we share as we tarry there
> None other has ever known.

I guess the listener can decide what this song is about. But I would later learn that the man who wrote it, C. Austin Miles, said it was about Mary Magdalene and the joy she felt when she saw her resurrected Lord, whose death she had been mourning.

Then there was my brother-in-law David's sermon. Alas, my mind is a blank; it must have been wandering at that point, perhaps back to

Siegen, or maybe all the way back to Jacksonport in Door County. At any rate, to happier times.

But I'm sure it was a wonderful message; David is an excellent speaker, and he'd been very fond of his mother-in-law.

⁕

By Fall 2001, when I was 100 percent convinced of the Bible's truth, and therefore of Christianity's, I'd begun to grasp what the apostle Paul was saying in Philippians 1:21–23: "For to me, to live is Christ, and to die is gain. . . . For I am hard-pressed between the two, having a desire to depart and be with Christ, which is far better."

We are all living on the edge of eternity, it seems. The difference is that, for the Christian, death is nothing to be feared. Clothed in the atoning sacrifice and righteousness of Christ, he knows where he's headed, and he knows it's for the kind of happily-ever-after that fairy-tale fans can only dream about.

And here's the most important take-away: there's *nothing* stopping every last person on earth from heading for the same joyful end.

⁕

As I learned more about the things of God, I naturally wanted to share His wonderful news with everyone I cared about so we could all rest in the blessed assurance of the same glorious eternity.

I thought they'd all say, "Oh, wow, that's great. I never thought of these things. Where do I sign up?"

Amazingly, many, if not most, declined. And not always politely.

No surprise, as it turned out. Jesus warned us more than once to expect rejection, and said we should actually be happy about it:

Blessed are you when men hate you, and when they exclude you, and revile you, and cast out your name as evil, for the Son of Man's sake. Rejoice in that day and leap for joy! For indeed your reward is great in heaven.[3]

Still, I figured my friends would be different. Surely they all had enough respect for my intellect to figure there had to be something to this Christianity business if I'd found it so persuasive. Surely they would at least want to know what I found so compelling.

But, no. Mostly they expressed absolutely no interest in eternity or ultimate truth and quickly changed the subject if I brought it up. Sometimes they simply yelled at me or ridiculed me. The rest of the time, they'd rather stay home and cut their toenails than be with me.

And so I simply follow Christ's advice and rejoice.

✂

"YOU ACTUALLY *BELIEVE* the Bible?" the atheist girlfriend I'd known the longest asked not long ago, over lunch at a trendy restaurant near downtown Milwaukee. "Doesn't it promote war and slavery and child sacrifice? Not to mention all that eye-for-an-eye stuff, so that in some countries they chop off your hands for stealing bread to feed your family?"

I sighed inwardly. I knew from experience that she wasn't looking for even a five-minute refutation of these ideas; I'd be lucky to get a solid minute in before she grew weary of the subject.

"Good questions," I said, spearing one of five little hunks of avocado in my $12.95 salad. "If I'd known enough before I became a Christian, I would've asked them myself. You know quite a bit about it, don't you?"

I really meant this, so I didn't feel guilty when I saw her face soften.

The avocado was perfectly ripe, and I savored it before continuing.

"But it turns out that when you take a closer look," I said, "you find that these things aren't quite true. Like this war business. It's true that the Old Testament records military action that God directed in order to get the children of Israel into the promised land and to rid it of pagans. He also used war to chasten or punish them. But it all seems to have a definite purpose; there isn't any random war-mongering going on as far as I can tell."

"Oh," she said, attacking her prime-rib sandwich ($14.95) with enthusiasm. I suppressed a pang of jealousy; she's one of these perennially thin creatures, whereas I've spent my life watching my weight creep up, up, up. "Okay, I'll buy that. Not that it proves anything. But what about the child-sacrifice issue? And slavery?"

For once I was on top of two subjects in a row.

"Child sacrifice is one thing I noticed in particular," I said, "because the idea is so horrific. But here's the thing: God clearly condemns this practice; it was the pagans who were sacrificing their children, not the Israelis."

"You're making that up."

"No, I'm really not. If you want, I'll find you the passages."

She looked at me suspiciously.

"I'll get you a list," I added.

"Okay," she said, popping a fry in her mouth. "And I suppose the Bible actually condemns slavery, too?"

"No. But it talks about slavery as a fact of life, which it was then and still is in some parts of the world. Just as Scripture talks about murder and adultery and theft as facts of life. That doesn't mean God condones any of these things."

"Not good enough," she said. "If this is God's book, why wouldn't He use it to condemn slavery?"

She had me there. Why hadn't He made it the eleventh commandment: "Thou shalt not buy or sell another human being"? I remembered something in the Old Testament about the year of Jubilee and freeing slaves, but that was only every fifty years or so.

"I don't know," I said truthfully. "Maybe because it's no big deal in the greater scheme of things. Maybe because we're all slaves to something or someone, to our jobs or our bad habits or our looks or material possessions. And only a relationship with the Lord gives us true freedom, the kind that transcends every form of human slavery."

"I have to tell you, that sounds pretty weak," she said, munching.

I shrugged. "I suppose it does if you haven't experienced it. I'm no expert on this subject, but I'll look into it and get back to you."

She dabbed at her lips with her napkin. Cloth, of course. "If you want. Now—what was my other question? Oh, right: eye for an eye."

I nodded, working on a big bite of my salad. It struck me that she'd kept pretty good track of her questions, as if she'd made a little "attack the Bible" list for herself before heading out to meet me. Maybe she'd even done a Google search for "proof against the Bible." That would explain her questions about fairly obscure facts. I really couldn't blame her; it was just the sort of thing I would've done in my pre-Jesus days, if I'd thought of it. Although more likely I would have just dumped her at the first sign that she'd found God.

"So, eye for an eye," I said. "That one's pretty easy—and it's a good illustration, I think, of how we sometimes look at the Bible crossways."

She raised a brow at me. "Do tell."

"Well, it turns out that 'an eye for an eye, a tooth for a tooth' was actually God's way of preventing the Hebrews from overreacting in their punishments. So if you knocked out someone's tooth, you wouldn't lose your life; you'd just lose a tooth. When you read through this law—I think the part I'm remembering is in the book of Exodus—it's really quite compassionate."

My friend chewed, looking at me with big eyes. I didn't know whether she thought I was an idiot or a genius. Trying not to care—she had asked, after all—I continued.

"God even set up certain cities as refuges, so that if you killed someone accidentally, you had a place you could go where you could live safely without threat of retaliation." The waiter showed up then to fill my coffee cup—one thing these fancy restaurants do well is coffee—and I paused to thank him. "So, yeah, the Bible is strict in the standards it sets, but it's also very fair. Just like God Himself: perfectly holy, perfectly just, perfectly merciful."

She grinned at me. For a fleeting moment I thought she was about to ask me to tell her more. Instead, she switched the subject abruptly back to work.

I wanted to scream at her.

"The Bible is trustworthy!" I wanted to yell. "It's trustworthy and perfect, and your ideas about it are all perversions of the truth! It's God's life manual for us, and it tells us all we need to know to spend eternity in heaven, and you are *ignoring* it! Why won't you listen to me before it's too late?"

"So," I said instead, "are you still doing a lot of Web work?"

❧

SOME PEOPLE CLAIM that the Bible has changed over the years.

"It's like the telephone game," another girlfriend explained patiently over dinner a year or two into my quest for God. (You can see why I have some weight issues, given the fact that most of my socializing takes place in restaurants.) "They didn't write in those days, you know; they told stories around campfires. So you can imagine the inaccuracies that crept in as these stories were handed down from generation to generation."

I'd learned by that time that written language had existed long before Moses, who wrote the first five books of the Old Testament, and I told her so.

She just shrugged, so I added that I didn't think the "telephone game" analogy was a good fit.

"The Bible wasn't transmitted by partiers who'd had a few drinks too many," I said. "It was copied painstakingly by professionals who devoted their lives to this task."

"Right. And they couldn't make mistakes?"

"Of course they could have," I said, able to keep my cool because she sounded just like me a couple years earlier. "But consider this: the Dead Sea Scrolls, which were found in the 1940s, contain nearly the entire Old Testament, and scholars have dated them to the first century BC—before Jesus was even born. Yet they match almost perfectly the next-oldest existing manuscripts, which were produced in the AD 900s. So the text survived intact over a thousand years of hand copying."

Apparently my girlfriend was not impressed. "You're really getting boring, you know that?"

Her comment stung. But I couldn't see any way around it. I had stumbled upon truth. And even in those early days, I could see that I wouldn't have been much of a friend to her if I'd just adopted a "take it or leave it" attitude, falling into injured silence the moment she expressed her disinterest or displeasure.

"YOU KNOW, THERE *are* contradictions in the Bible," the girlfriend I'm calling Anne informed me when we met for drinks at a mall restaurant in Brookfield. It was just after Christmas 2003, as I recall, and a couple months after our evolution-laced golf game. "Tons of contradictions," she added.

"Really?" I asked, trying to hide my excitement over the turn our conversation was taking—and the fact that she was the one doing the turning. "Tell me about them."

"For one thing," she said, "I understand that Genesis tells two different creation stories." She lifted her eyebrows and wine glass to the bartender. "Don't try to pin me down—that's all I know about it."

"Rats," I said. "I actually know the answer to that one, and now you're telling me you don't want to hear it?"

"It would be meaningless to me," Anne said, smiling. "But you're saying there are answers?"

"Definitely," I said, "across the board. For instance, very often if you look at the larger context, it's intuitively obvious. Which is the case with the Genesis issue you mention. Not that it's always so easy; I guess there are still things that have yet to be explained. But there are enough things that have already passed such challenges that it's a risky sort of charge to level against the Bible."

"The Hittites," she said, helping herself to the snack mix the bartender had set down with her fresh glass of wine. She chewed, glancing at me briefly, maybe to gauge my reaction to this piece of knowledge. "They really existed."

"Well my goodness," I said, truly impressed. "You've done your homework! Does this mean you're becoming a Christian?"

She laughed. "Don't hold your breath."

✺

MY FRIENDSHIP WITH several hyper-feminists were among the casualties of my conversion.

Maybe I should have just kept my mouth shut. But I figured that a friend doesn't let a friend live without hope; a friend shares the gospel with the people she cares about.

Trouble was, with these women, I ended up having to explain why being a Christian meant abandoning feminism.

"Well, it's like this," I said to each one in separate conversations. "As a feminist, I was concerned exclusively with myself. 'I want,' 'I need,' 'I have a right'—that's pretty much all I thought about. Whereas Christianity teaches me to say, 'What can I do for you?'"

Two out of three of these friends greeted this pronouncement with a good roll of the eyes.

"The way I practiced it, feminism was all about me," I said, "not about what is objectively true. It was about self-knowledge and self-righteousness and self-glorification."

All three responded to this with a sigh of disgust.

Surliness emboldens me. "Feminism is by definition competitive," I continued. "There are winners and losers and since I intend to win, you'd better get out of my way. Whereas faith is all about God and his perfect holiness, love, mercy, justice, and power. And there's no contest; compared to Him, we're all slugs, and if there were a race to righteousness, none of us would get much past the starting blocks."

Amazing: In three isolated conversations, each of my soon-to-be-ex-friends glanced at her watch the moment I said "righteousness."

"Feminism says the only absolute truth is that women are equal or superior to men," I added, speaking quickly because time was obviously running out. "Faith says there are many absolute truths, with the common denominator being the Lordship of Jesus Christ."

At this point, each one stood up, apparently having heard enough.

But I wasn't quite done. "Feminism says she who dies with the most toys or money or power or lovers wins. Faith says she who dies in Christ wins the only prize worth having—the kingdom of heaven."

If I were looking for a way to dump a friend, this would be ideal. Because none of these women has time for me anymore.

Which is a relief, in a way. It's no fun being around someone who has an obvious distaste for everything you stand for. And I'm sure they feel the same way about me.

꿎

SUCH EXCHANGES WITH my contemporaries stood in sharp contrast to the conversations I was having at the nursing home where my mother had lived and died.

Within a few weeks of her death, I started spending a morning there each week, visiting with seven or so women that the Activities Department assigned me, bringing them flowers from my garden, and—at least at first—clinging emotionally to them because I managed to find in each one some trait that reminded me of my mom.

One of my favorites was a woman whose name was Ida Mae, but who preferred to be called Johnny. She was ninety-seven when I met her, tall and slim and strong as a horse. She'd been a professional woman herself for many years, a private-duty nurse. She had met her husband-to-be quite late in life, in her early fifties, as I recall, but had been married to him for nearly forty years before he passed away. Or, as Johnny said, before he "went on ahead."

Johnny was a lifelong Christian who loved the Lord and never tired of talking about Him. She delighted in telling me about all the times He had intervened in her life, and in the lives of her loved ones. And she loved to talk about what heaven was going to be like.

"I'm very blessed," she would say. "I don't have any pain and the girls are really very nice to me." Then she would lean forward in her wheelchair and lower her voice. "But I'll tell you, I am very much looking forward to going home to my Lord."

Johnny had made good money in her day, and she and her husband hadn't had expensive tastes, she said. "That's why I can afford to have my own room in a place as nice as this one. But you mustn't let yourself get too carried away over money, you know. It's not all that important, and if I have to have a roommate one of these years, well, that will be just fine."

That wasn't a sacrifice Johnny had to make, however. One day in her ninety-eighth year, she felt sick to her stomach, and the next night she died in her sleep.

I began to understand, for the first time, how my mother was able to greet her friends' deaths so peacefully. Because I was certain Johnny was home at last, where she wanted to be. And that made me very happy.

Besides, she had helped me to realize some very important things. Most notably, perhaps, that it's foolish to have as your goal raking in just as much money as possible.

"Christians must not fall into the trap," wrote Nancy Pearcey, "of assuming that paid employment is the only thing that will give a woman a sense of dignity. That's a mistake secular feminists often make."[4]

She was right. I felt more useful after a morning spent with my "old ladies" than I ever had after a morning of pounding out brochure copy. And a lot more at peace.

⁂

ONE OF THE best friends I ever made at the nursing home was Helen, a beautiful little lady from Missouri. In her mid-eighties when I met her, she'd been raised by a mother and later a grandmother who hadn't had much use for religion. But she was curious, and in her teens started taking herself to church to learn about this Jesus that people were talking about. And along the way she became, forever-more, a Christian.

Helen's children loved her a lot, and they were always bringing her not only beautiful clothes but also reading material of all kinds, including books and magazines about her faith. We talked endlessly about these things, she in her quiet drawl, and I with unfettered enthusiasm that she, at least, seemed to appreciate.

One day she said excitedly that she'd read a wonderful little story about a silversmith, and that she wanted me to read it aloud so we could both enjoy it. But then she couldn't find the publication it was in, so she told me about it instead, even though she sometimes had a hard time finding even everyday words.

"It was like this," she said, smiling shyly. "There were these lady friends who were reading the Bible together and came across a verse they didn't understand. I think it was in Malachi—can you look it up?"

I reached for my New American Standard Bible, my translation of choice at the time, and began searching for the Old Testament book of Malachi.

"I think it was chapter 3," she added.

Finding it at last, I started reading in verse 1. She sat in her wheelchair, pressing her lips together and looking at the ceiling or the heavens, listening intently. It didn't take long: when I started verse 3, she cried, "That's it! Start over again."

"'He will sit as a smelter and purifier of silver,'" I read, "'and He will purify the sons of Levi and refine them like gold and silver, so that they may present to the LORD offerings in righteousness.'"

"Yes, that's the one," she said. "So these ladies didn't understand that verse, because they didn't understand how silver was made. So one of them decided to find out. She went to a silversmith and asked him to show her exactly what he did. And so he did!"

Helen reached for her water cup and took a good, long drink. She certainly wasn't having much trouble with her words today.

"This lady's idea was that this verse, the one you just read, had to do with the—" And she was stumped. She looked at me and shook her head. "You know what it is. When He changes us."

"Sanctifying?"

"Yes, that's it," she said, smiling at me gratefully. "Sanctifying. This lady thought this verse was intended to get that idea across, that God will purify us the way a silversmith purifies silver. And then two things."

She paused to make sure she had it right.

"Yes. First, he told her that he just sits and watches the furnace every minute that the silver is in there, because it mustn't go a moment longer than is needed or the silver will be hurt."

We grinned at each other.

"He does that with us, you know," she said. "He lets us go through trials but not more than—" She stopped again and looked at me sadly.

"More than we can bear," I said, nodding at her encouragingly. I looked at the verse again. "He will sit as a smelter and purifier."

We grinned some more.

"You said there were two things, didn't you, Helen?"

We both laughed; it was a rare visit when one of us didn't forget something important we'd wanted to share.

"And it's the best part," Helen said. "You will love this. The lady asked the silversmith how he knew that his silver was ready. And he said—" She looked at me with the giddiest expression on her face, as if she was about to deliver the greatest punch line of all time. "Do you know what he said, Kitty?"

I shook my head.

"He said, 'It's done when I can see my image reflected in the silver.'"

"Wow."

"I knew you'd love it. I do too."

CHAPTER 26

Joy for mourning:
It's going to be awesome!

9:00 a.m., August 5, 2000

My mother's urn had been sitting on our dining room table for more than a month before my sisters, Jenny, and I could find a mutually free weekend to bring it up to Pine Grove Cemetery in Wausau. I didn't mind; it was pale green marble and looked almost like a beautiful cookie jar, except the top didn't come off, and I kept telling myself that what was inside was just the remains of her earthly tent. No big deal.

It was on a hot August morning that Carrie, Jen, and I set out from Milwaukee in my brand-new black PT Cruiser—a sure sign of the crawling-out-of-my-skin anguish I was feeling that summer. I hadn't needed a new car; my eleven-year-old Blazer may have been rusting out, but it was still running. Maybe I was trying to spend my way to perfect peace.

We picked up Andy and her younger son Eric in Appleton and headed northwest for the two-hour drive. The closer we got to Wausau, the slower we went; the land had become quite hilly and I had the air-conditioning on against the practically unbearable heat and humidity. The added strain of carrying five adults was almost more than the four-cylinder engine could handle.

But we chugged along and finally made our way to the cemetery.

We found the office in the massive brick tower at Pine Grove's entrance. It was like walking into a time warp. The building had to be at least a century old, and the office was dark and damp and dreary, with nary a computer in sight. Saying she had been expecting us, the lone soul in the office immediately headed over to an ancient wooden cabinet with dozens of little drawers. She opened one without pausing to peer at the tiny labels and pulled out an index card.

"Here we are," she said, leading us to a colossal old desk. She found a map of the cemetery in a drawer and circled a spot on it with a magic marker. "If you go back out the door and follow this road straight back"—and here she traced the road on the map—"you should see John back there, getting your mother's plot ready."

We climbed back in the car and drove slowly down the tree-lined dirt road, keeping an eye out for a grave-digger.

A couple lines from the 1982 film noire *Body Heat* popped into my mind and stayed there. They were delivered by Kathleen Turner and William Hurt right after they had agreed to murder her husband.

Turner: "It's real, then?"

Hurt: "It's real, all right."

And this was real too—the end of the road. As long as my mother's urn was sitting on my dining room table, there was still some unfinished business to her life.

Now even that was about to end.

Within moments, we saw on our right an older fellow standing with a shovel next to a hole in the ground, mopping his brow with a handkerchief. He saw us too, and lifted his hand in greeting.

It's real, all right.

I stopped the car and we piled out and introduced ourselves to the man. We studied the grave marker before us for a time:

Herbert S. Foth
1910–1970

Then, while Eric fetched Mom's urn from the hatch of my car, we all stood there and looked at the hole John had dug right next to our father's marker. I don't think any of us spoke. What were we supposed to say? "Nice hole, John"?

"Well, there you go," John said when Eric returned with the urn, already encased in what they called a burial container. "You can set it in there, and then I'll come back and bury it." And he disappeared into the trees.

I hadn't thought through what we were actually going to *do* here, other than sing "In the Garden." Dave had given me an Anne Murray inspirational CD that happened to include that song, and my new car had a CD player, so I opened the doors and played it at full volume while Eric lowered the container into the hole.

Whereupon I lost it. So much for this being no big deal.

Four years later, when Ronald Reagan died and the news media spent days tracking his widow and his casket from place to place, I saw what might have been a similar scenario playing out in her heart: in spite of her obvious sadness, she was under total control through it all, from a service at Washington's National Cathedral through a sunset ceremony at his library in California.

It was only at the very end, when the casket arrived at its burial site, that she broke down and wept, stroking the casket, unwilling to leave it behind.

She had been losing him for years, as Alzheimer's disease ravaged his mind and body. When he died, at least she still had his body and his casket to shepherd from coast to coast. But now, they were taking even that away, and the pain was finally unbearable.

I think I understood exactly how she felt.

※

SOME MONTHS LATER, I read for the first time what is sometimes called "the great Resurrection chapter" of the Bible, 1 Corinthians 15.

In this wonderful passage, the apostle Paul talked about Christ's death for our sins and the five-hundred-plus brethren who had seen Him resurrected, most of them still alive at the time of this writing to confirm what Paul had written. A bit later, he addressed what had to be as burning a question for the ancient Corinthians as it is for us today: What about our resurrected bodies? How will all of this work? Here's what Paul wrote:

> But someone may ask, "How will the dead be raised? What kind of bodies will they have?" What a foolish question! When you put a seed into the ground, it doesn't grow into a plant unless it dies first. And what you put in the ground is not the plant that will grow, but only a dry little seed of wheat or whatever it is you are planting. Then God gives it a new body—just the kind he wants it to have. A different kind of plant grows from each kind of seed.[1]

The more I thought about this passage, the more amazed I became. Of course seeds must fall apart in order for the living plant inside to grow! And as many seeds as I'd planted over the years, I could vouch for the fact that the plant that emerges bears absolutely no resemblance to the lowly little seed.

So if this analogy holds, it would mean that our earthly bodies are nothing like what our resurrected bodies will be. That they exist only to temporarily house the spirits within. And that those spirits will ultimately be manifested in far more magnificent bodies.

All of which Paul seems to imply a few verses later:

> Our earthly bodies, which die and decay, will be different when they are resurrected, for they will never die. Our bodies now disappoint us, but when they are raised, they will be full of glory. They are weak now, but when they are raised, they will be full of power. They are natural human bodies now, but when they are raised, they will be spiritual bodies.[2]

And then, skipping down a few more verses, I saw that Paul described how this will occur, for dead and living Christians alike:

> But let me tell you a wonderful secret God has revealed to us. Not all of us will die, but we will all be transformed. It will happen in a moment, in the blinking of an eye, when the last trumpet is blown. For when the trumpet sounds, the Christians who have died will be raised with transformed bodies. . . . When this happens—when our perishable earthly bodies have been transformed into heavenly bodies that will never die—then at last the Scriptures will come true: "Death is swallowed up in victory. O death, where is your victory? O death, where is your sting?"[3]

I would later learn that what Paul described here and in 1 Thessalonians 4 may be what Christians call "the Rapture," from the Latin word *rapere*, translated from the Greek *harpazo* for being snatched away. Awesome thought! But the first time I studied this chapter, I was simply overjoyed to have been given a distinct vision of our earthly bodies being as disposable as seed husks, to be replaced by glorified bodies that will last forever.

✻

IN HONOR OF our trip to Wausau with my mother's ashes, Jenny had given me a CD by a Christian singer named Crystal Lewis. Jen pointed especially to the title song, "Beauty for Ashes," which reassures the child of God that He heals all sorrows: "He gives beauty for ashes, strength for fear, gladness for mourning, peace for despair."

It took me a while to make the connection, but I finally realized that this chorus was based on Isaiah 61:3, part of that hope-tinged passage that someone had read at my mother's funeral.

I listened to this song again and again. It was true: He *was* giving me beauty and strength, gladness and peace.

But it's only the beginning of what promises to be the happiest ending of all.

✻

AS I READ the Bible and books about the Bible, I found out that most of what we think we know about heaven is wrong. There's nothing in Scripture about angels hanging out on clouds, nothing about anyone playing harps, nothing about St. Peter serving as Admissions Director at the Pearly Gates. In fact, the Bible doesn't tell us much at all about what it will be like—perhaps because it's simply beyond our ability to imagine.

But there are, perhaps, intriguing hints. For instance, Ephesians 3:18 talks about the "width and length and depth and height" of God's love. Notice that this verse mentions *four* dimensions, not just three; could this mean that there are four dimensions in heaven, with the fourth being not time, but something entirely beyond our imaginations?

I recently heard someone talking on the radio about how the Bible says we're made in God's image, and how maybe that is analogous to someone looking at his reflection in a pool of water. This 4D idea popped into my mind, and I wondered: If a 3D person looks into a pool and sees a 2D reflection of himself, does that confirm a 4D God who created us as 3D reflections of Himself?

Interesting ideas, all—but, of course, impossible to grasp, anymore than we could imagine a new color or a critter with new body parts that we don't already see in the world around us.

⁂

MAYBE IT'S AS difficult for us to comprehend what heaven will be like as it would be for an infant in the womb to imagine what the world outside is like. And maybe that's why the Bible is silent on the physical aspects of eternity. Maybe a description would only confuse us.

But Scripture does tell us some things. For instance, in addition to having the new bodies mentioned in 1 Corinthians 15:

- Christians will be there with Jesus[4] and will be like Him.[5]
- We will be unlimited by earthly physical properties[6] in an entirely new environment.[7]
- We will be forever free of death, sorrow, crying, and pain.[8]

No wonder some people talk about death as the gateway to the greatest adventure of them all.

⁂

I DO HAVE some ideas about people and places and things I hope will be in heaven. And the Wilhelm Tell restaurant in Munich is one of them.

It was on our second trip to Europe together in the 1970s that Mom and I discovered the Wilhelm Tell.

Instead of the grand old hotels we had stayed in on our guided Caravan tour the previous year, we were staying in cheap places that were just a step above pensions—all humble but clean, all featuring a bathroom down the hall that we shared with other guests. The name of our Munich hotel is lost to history—and here I thought I'd never forget these details—but it had a stucco exterior, painted a pale salmon pink, and our room was stark white and very austere.

The Wilhelm Tell was a tavern just down the street and around the corner from our hotel. It was dark and smelled of beer and cigarettes and a roast in the oven, and we loved it. Although we really weren't all that fond of German food generally, we ate lavishly here, feasting on pan-fried pork chops and carrot salad with a vinaigrette dressing and quite possibly the best french fries in the world. (The Germans really know their way around a potato.) And it was cheap to boot, especially for Americans in those days of favorable exchange rates.

This was no tourist spot; the neighborhood was pretty far from Munich's major attractions. It was noisy and not exactly spotless, but the waiters were friendly and smiled encouragingly as we spoke in broken German (delivered with a Polish accent, one insisted), making us feel like part of the crowd.

We stayed in Munich three nights on that trip and ate all three of our dinners right there at the Wilhelm Tell. I suppose, in retrospect, that Mom might have been bored with that, or, for that matter, less than thrilled with our accommodations. After all, she had traveled through Europe extensively with my dad on his business trips, staying at luxurious hotels and dining at some of the finest restaurants. But if she was unhappy, she never let on. In fact, she seemed to thrive on rubbing shoulders with the locals, laughing with them as she explained in her floundering German that her husband had been in Deutschland *geboren* and that we had beloved *freunden* in Siegen.

My mother had her dreams of heaven, dreams that included the "strange and lovely" streets of Salzburg and a crisp October morning and a 10 a.m. glass of beer.

I have mine too, and one of the best takes place in a dark little restaurant called the Wilhelm Tell.

۶

AND YET THE question persists: What will heaven be like?

I have my own ideas about my arrival there, anyway—ideas firmly grounded in earthly things, however, so they probably aren't even remotely true.

Still, it's all I have to work with. And so my fantasy begins with suddenly finding myself walking down a dirt road on a perfect summer day, surrounded by fruit-laden shrubs and big old trees and zillions of flowers. The birds are singing, and the butterflies are flitting, and there are bunnies and foxes and horses all over the place.

As I stroll along, I suddenly notice a cat coming toward me—a white cat, it seems. As we get closer to each other, I notice that the cat has gray paws and ears and amazing blue eyes. And then, in the blink of an eye, I realize that it's my precious Siamese Sam, who died in November of 2001. He races up to me and leaps into my arms, his purrs the background music to a joyful reunion.

And my dream goes on, with me meeting each of my beloved pets along the way—including basset Woody, who died just months after Mom—until I finally see, in the distance, the Piet Mondrian house whose picture hangs on the wall of my home office. And as I get closer I can see my first yellow lab, Thumper, and standing behind him, my mom and dad and Granny.

My fantasy always ends there, however. I can't seem to get any closer. Maybe there are simply some joys that are too overwhelming for an earthly heart to handle.

CHAPTER 27

In the twinkling of an eye:
Let the butterflies begin

4:00 p.m., December 1, 2007

Today is my mother's birthday; she would have been ninety-five. I miss her. But I'm absolutely certain that she's better off in heaven. My nursing home visits underscore that point. Physical pain is too often the only constant companion of the elderly; modern pain management is not all it's cracked up to be. And while some folks get along just fine as their disabilities multiply, when failing eyesight leaves a lifelong reader unable to make out even giant-sized type, and immobility turns every trip to the toilet into a major project, many Christian old folk begin longing to leave their earthly tents behind, to be with their Maker, in the place He has prepared for them.

As the author of the book of Hebrews wrote, "For this world is not our home; we are looking forward to our city in heaven, which is yet to come."[1]

I'm certain of a lot of important things these days: that the Bible is the inspired and inerrant Word of God. That it answers almost every possible question we could have. And that it gives believers a glimpse of an eternity so wonderful, we human beings can't even begin to imagine it.

This earth is fine for now; but thinking about eternity gives me butterflies.

※

"HOW LONG IT takes to die."

That's how my mother opened an April 1992 entry in her journal.

"I thought my life would be over when Herbert died," she continued. "But I had many happy years after that."

She sketched it out: visiting Andy and her family in Appleton. Laughing with Carrie. Traveling with me to Europe, where we "walked—I really walked—from dawn till dusk."

She mentioned some of the people who remained dear friends of hers even after my dad's death—people who didn't require a foursome for friendship. She treasured them especially; as a young widow of just fifty-seven, she had experienced the sting of being dropped after six months or a year by people she thought were her friends, simply because she was alone, and they were not.

But by 1992, she was wheelchair-bound and living in this nursing home near us. She still appreciated kindnesses and attention, but the good times had clearly run out for her; she felt like a burden, no doubt because I made her feel like one some of the time.

In the Ten Commandments God gave us two types of directives.

The first four commandments have to do with our relationship with Him. We are to love Him above all, reject idols, refrain from taking His name in vain, and keep the Sabbath holy—that is, separate.

The last six are all about our relationships with each other— refraining from lying, stealing, adultery, murder, and coveting others' possessions.

But the first of this group—the fifth commandment—tells us to honor our father and mother. No exceptions: no "unless he is a nasty man" or "unless she becomes too sick to be fun" or "unless you have something better to do." I find it fascinating that the Lord put this one first—even before telling us not to murder or commit adultery.

Perhaps it was because He knew that these relationships are the foundation on which our characters are built, and the keys to our attitudes toward authority. Perhaps because they are, in the end, our most fundamental human relationships, foreshadowing in earthly terms our relationships with Him.

I'll let the theologians figure that out. All I know is that the fifth commandment made it almost unbearable for me to read my mother's thoughts during the last chapter of her life.

"How long it takes to die."

⁂

THE SUMMER BEFORE my ninth birthday—the summer of Nikita Khrushchev and the Berlin Wall and all the circumstances that would turn Mrs. G. into a terrifying false prophet—my parents traveled to Europe for the summer with my sister Andy, then seventeen.

Since I was too young to appreciate such a trip, they took me to Madison, about 150 miles southwest of Green Bay, to spend the weeks with their dear friends Arlene and George.

In most ways, it was a heavenly place to await their return. Arlene and George were among my favorite people in the whole world, kind and loving and happy just like my own parents, and they never failed to lavish some of their love on any children in their vicinity. They lived in a tree-lined neighborhood very much like our own, full of charming older homes and kids and family dogs, in a neat white two-story house.

They had one daughter who was still at home—a girl who was probably an exotic thirteen or fourteen at the time, and who was much nicer to me than I would have been to a summer-long intruder. And Arlene, no doubt anticipating how homesick I would be, gave me a gift every Friday to help me celebrate making it one week closer to Mom and Dad's return. I've forgotten what almost all of those gifts were, except for an Etch-a-Sketch—a drawing toy so new that I'd never even seen one before, so enchanting that I spent many hours that summer learning how to draw with it.

Arlene even found a playmate for me. Her name was Maureen. She was my age and lived up the hill from Arlene's house. Her house was exotic, too: it had no upstairs, and her backyard was all wooded, and there were these beautiful flowers in front, in a bed framed by split-rail fencing. I remember in particular stunning orange blossoms with freckles, which my new friend called tiger lilies.

Maureen and I spent lots of long summer days together, exploring the neighborhood and the woods beyond, playing games like Sorry and Old Maid, piecing together jigsaw puzzles, packing lunches, and taking off on our bikes—Arlene's daughter let me use hers!—to destinations unknown. You could do that in those days; adults didn't worry if the children in their charge disappeared for six or eight hours, as long as they were home in time for supper.

Thanks to this wonderful, warm cast of characters, it was one of the best summers of my childhood. Except that I wasn't at home with my parents, and I ached for them. And so it was also the only unhappy summer of my childhood. Good and bad, rolled into one.

In the end, though, the good outweighed the bad, because I knew the bad would come to an end. I had no doubt that my parents would come get me eventually and take me home, and, in fact, when I thought about that, when I pictured them pulling up in front of Arlene's house, I could barely contain my joy.

It's kind of the way I feel now that I'm a heaven-bound Christian whose parents and Granny have gone on ahead.

Others, even some other Christians, seem to think I'm crazy and quite possibly suicidal. But I am neither. They simply don't understand, maybe because they never had a summer-of-1961 experience like mine.

Which is too bad, because it's a totally thrilling way to live.

On the one hand, I am surrounded by people I love—a fine husband and extended family, an array of good friends, a church family whose loving-kindness is astounding. I live in a nice house with a big garden and all the pets anyone could ever want. I enjoy my work most of the time, especially since my commute is about ten steps from the kitchen, and it can be traversed in warm slippers or bare feet, depending on the season. And I spend much of my free time studying mind-blowing books about all things related to the Lord, most importantly the Bible.

What more could I want?

I honestly can't think of a thing. Not even a lakeside cottage or a fat retirement account or an exotic vacation could add anything to my joy. Not even another Super Bowl season for the Packers.

Life is good.

And yet.

My mom and dad and Granny aren't here. They've already departed for our new home, leaving me behind, unable to get to them under my own power. And so I am at times consumed with a new kind of homesickness, a longing to be with them in the Lord's kingdom, a land where there are no tears, no aches and pains, no disease or death, hunger or thirst, just Jesus and joy that we can't even imagine in our earthbound 3D hides.

And so I ache once again. And once again it's mostly a good ache, one that's accompanied by butterflies and by capital-*H*, biblical Hope—not merely a wish but a confident expectation about what is to come.

Life is indeed good. But it's going to get a whole lot better one day. And it's all going to happen in the twinkling of an eye.

EPILOGUE

Enter by the narrow gate:
It's the only way to fly

*I*n March of 1993, with seven years left in her earthly journey, my mother wrote these words in her tattered journal:

> I look forward to death, except for one reason only. How can I possibly live in a world, no matter how heavenly it may be, if my little agnostic Kitty is not there?

She had reason to worry, it turned out. She knew that God makes no special allowances for theistic fence-sitters who neither deny nor admit His existence—that Jesus said in Matthew, "He who is not with Me is against Me."[1]

She also knew that by rejecting Him, by refusing to even acknowledge my sin, I'd been cruising along the road not to heaven but to hell—that He'd said, in Luke, "Unless you repent you will all likewise perish."[2]

When I finally read these warnings myself, I wondered why no one had ever sounded the alarm for me. Had I been so unapproachable on the subject? Or had I simply refused to listen?

I'd clearly spent decades galloping down what Jesus called, in Matthew, the "broad . . . way that leads to destruction."[3]

And my mother knew it.

I wonder if she now knows that just weeks after He called her home, I took the advice Jesus gave in the same passage: "Enter by the narrow gate . . . which leads to life. . . ."[4]

And I wonder if she knows that I was telling the truth when I whispered to her that last day, "I'll see you there, Mom."

I suppose a truly loving daughter would hope that her mother is too immersed in heavenly joy to even give the folks back on earth a thought.

Not me. I hope she knows. And I hope she's as excited about our happily-ever-after reunion as I am.

NOTES

Chapter 1
1. Isaiah 40:28–31 KJV.
2. John 14:1–3 KJV.

Chapter 4
1. http//www.worldnetdaily.com/news/article.asp?ARTICLE_ID=13008 (accessed December 27, 2007).
2. Betty Friedan, *The Feminine Mystique* (New York: W.W. Norton & Company, 1997), 15.
3. Ibid, 32.

Chapter 7
1. Study by Parents Television Council and National Religious Broadcasters, quoted in Creator's Syndicate, Brent Bozell, "Television's Problem with Religion," December 24, 2004.

Chapter 11
1. Allen Lacy, *The Gardener's Eye* (New York: Atlantic Monthly Press, 1992), 3.

Chapter 12
1. Reggie White, *In the Trenches* (Nashville: Thomas Nelson, Inc., 1996), 189.
2. Ibid., 122.
3. Ibid.

Chapter 14
1. Patrick Glynn, *God the Evidence: The Reconciliation of Faith and Reason in a Postsecular World* (Rocklin, CA: Prima Publishing, 1997), 22.
2. Ibid., 28–29.
3. Scott M. Huse, *The Collapse of Evolution* (Grand Rapids: Baker Books, 1997), 68–72.

4. Ibid.

5. Henry M. Morris and John D. Morris, *The Modern Creation Trilogy: Science & Creation*, vol. 2 (Green Forest, AR: Master Books, 1996), 323.

6. Ibid., 319.

7. Ray Comfort, *Scientific Facts in the Bible* (Gainesville, FL: Bridge-Logos, 2001), 26.

8. Leonard Miller, "The Ancient Bristlecone Pine," http://www.sonic.net/bristlecone/ (accessed December 27, 2007).

9. BBC Online, "World: Middle East Oldest Alphabet Found in Egypt," http://news.bbc.co.uk/1/hi/world/middle_east/521235.stm (accessed December 27, 2007).

10. Paul Halsall, ed., "Mesopotamia," in *Internet Ancient History Sourcebook*, http://www.fordham.edu/halsall/ancient/asbook03.html (accessed December 27, 2007).

Chapter 15

1. Richard C. Lewontin, "Billions and Billions of Demons," *New York Review of Books* 44, no. 1 (January 9, 1997), 31.

2. Aldous Huxley, *Ends and Means* (London: Chatto & Windus, 1938), 270–73.

Chapter 16

1. James W. Sire, *The Universe Next Door: A Basic Worldview Catalog*, 3rd ed. (Downers Grove, IL: InterVarsity Press, 1997), 197.

2. Ibid., 198.

Chapter 17

1. Sire, *The Universe Next Door*, 121–24.

2. 1 Corinthians 14:33 KJV.

3. See, for example, Syed Kamran Mirza, "Was Allah the Moon God of Ancient Arab Pagan?" http://www.faithfreedom.org/Articles/skm30804.htm (accessed December 27, 2007).

4. Dave Hunt, "Lamb of God," The Berean Call, http://www.thebereancall.org/node/2562 (accessed December 27, 2007).

Chapter 18

1. Isaiah 40:22a.

2. Job 26:7b.

3. See, for example, the Sloan Digital Sky Survey at: http://cas.sdss.org/dr5/en/proj/basic/spectraltypes/ (accessed December 27, 2007).

4. Jeremiah 33:22.

5. Hebrews 11:3.

6. Newton BBS (an electronic community for Science, Math, and Computer Science K–12 Educators), Ask a Scientist, Chemistry Archive, "Who Discovered the Atom?" http://www.newton.dep.anl.gov/askasci/chem99/chem99396.htm (accessed December 27, 2007).

7. Ecclesiastes 1:7 and Job 26:8.

8. Job 38:16.

9. Jonah 2:5–6.

10. See, for example, Answers In Genesis, "Geology Questions and Answers," http://www.answersingenesis.org/home/area/faq/geology.asp; and ibid.,"Fossils Questions and Answers," http://www.answersingenesis.org/home/area/faq/fossils .asp, (both accessed December 27, 2007).

11. Leviticus 12:3.

12. 2 Corinthians 3:14a, 15–16.

13. A. S. A. Jones, "Learning to Think Spiritually: How to Perceive God; Truth in Paradox," http://www.ex-atheist.com/Learning%20To%20Think%20Spiritually .html (accessed December 27, 2007).

Chapter 19

1. Randall Price, *The Stones Cry Out* (Eugene, OR: Harvest House, 1997), 169.

2. Acts 13:22.

3. D. James Kennedy, *Why I Believe* (Nashville, TN: Word Publishing, 1999), 20.

4. Price, *The Stones Cry Out*, 297.

5. Ibid., 307.

6. Josh McDowell, *The New Evidence That Demands a Verdict* (Nashville: Thomas Nelson, 1999), 61.

7. Isaiah 42:9 NLT.

8. Genesis 28:14–15.

9. 100prophecies.org, "100 Bible Prophecies Explained," http://100prophecies.org /page3.htm (accessed December 27, 2007).

10. Leviticus 26:7–8a.

11. "100 Bible Prophecies Explained."

12. John Ankerberg, John Weldon, and Walter C. Kaiser, "If Specific Prophecies Were Fulfilled by the Messiah, Does the Science of Probability Consider This Proof There Is a God?" excerpted from Ankerberg, Weldon, and Kaiser, *The Case for Jesus the Messiah: Incredible Prophecies That Prove God Exists* (Chattanooga, TN: John Ankerberg Evangelistic Association, 1989) and available at: http://www.johnanker-berg.org/Articles/apologetics/AP1299W1.htm (accessed December 27, 2007).

13. Clifford A. Pickover, *Wonders of Numbers: Adventures in Mathematics, Mind,*

and Meaning (New York: Oxford University Press, 2001), 196.

14. See, for example, Sandy Berger, "Internet Information Doubles," http://www. compukiss.com/populartopics/research_infohtm/article892.htm (accessed December 27, 2007).

15. See, for example, Jay Cross, "Who Knows?" *CLO Magazine,* cited on Internet Time Blog, http://internettime.com/blog/archives/001423.html (accessed December 27, 2007).

16. Henry M. Morris, annotator, *The Defender's Study Bible* (Iowa Falls, IA: World Bible Publishers, 1995), 1043.

Chapter 20

1. Ephesians 2:8–9.
2. 1 John 1:9.
3. 1 John 4:8.
4. Romans 6:23.
5. Isaiah 53:6.
6 John 3:16.
7. James 2:10.
8. Horatio G. Spafford, "It Is Well with My Soul," 1873.
9. Hal Lindsey, *The Late Great Planet Earth* (Grand Rapids: Zondervan, 1970), 115.

Chapter 21

1. James Hitchcock, *What Is Secular Humanism?* (Ann Arbor, MI: Servant Books, 1982), 10–11.
2. Ibid., 48.
3. Ibid., 75.
4. Ibid., 64.
5. Ibid., 66.
6. Nancy Pearcey, *Total Truth: Liberating Christianity from Its Cultural Captivity* (Wheaton, IL: Crossway Books, 2004), 341.

Chapter 24

1. Jan Struther, "Biography," *Betsinda Dances and Other Poems* (Oxford, 1931), quoted at http://www.zip.com.au/~lnbdds/home/janstruther6.htm (accessed December 27, 2007).
2. John 1:1–4 NLT.
3. *Life Application Study Bible* (Wheaton, IL: Tyndale House Publishers, 1996), 2030.
4. John 1:12–13 NLT.

5. *Life Application Study Bible*, 2032.
6. Ibid., 2040.
7. Ibid.
8. John 3:36 NLT.
9. *Life Application Study Bible*, 2042.
10. 1 Peter 1:25b NLT.
11. Ray Comfort, "Are You Ready for the Lions?" (February 2006), http://www.christianworldviewnetwork.com/article.php/496/RayComfort (accessed December 27, 2007).
12. Heberw 9:27–28a.
13. 2 Corinthians 5:8.
14. John 10:27–28.

Chapter 25
1. Psalm 121 KJV.
2. Isaiah 61:2b–3 KJV.
3. Luke 6:22–23a.
4. Pearcey, *Total Truth*, 345.

Chapter 26
1. 1 Corinthians 15:35–38 NLT.
2. 1 Corinthians 15:42b–44a NLT.
3. 1 Corinthians 15:51–52a, 54–55 NLT. See also 1 Thessalonians 4:15–18 and John 14:1–3.
4. John 14:2–3.
5. 1 John 3:2.
6. John 20:26.
7. Revelation 21:1.
8. Revelation 21:4.

Chapter 27
1. Hebrews 13:14 NLT.

Epilogue
1. Matthew 12:30a.
2. Luke 13:3b.
3. Matthew 7:13b.
4. Matthew 7:13a, 14a.

BIBLIOGRAPHY

There are many junky or downright dangerous "Christian" books out there today, and I've read my fair share of them. Some say we can name our wishes and they will be granted. Others tell us all about God's perfect love and forgiveness without ever mentioning His perfect holiness and justice. And still others teach us how to "Christianize" occult and pagan practices.

A girl has to be very careful what she reads these days.

These are among the books I recommend most highly for understanding the biblical worldview. That doesn't mean I agree with everything each author writes, or that they would agree with what I have to say. But each one helped bring me closer to the conclusion that the Bible is the inerrant and inspired Word of God—that, as the apostle Paul wrote in 2 Timothy 3:16–17, "All Scripture . . . is profitable for doctrine, for reproof, for correction, for instruction in righteousness, that the man of God may be complete, thoroughly equipped for every good work."

Special thanks to Thomas Nelson for letting me include this list. In the often ruthless business world, it is truly astonishing that a company would, in essence, promote its competitors' products; clearly the folks at Thomas Nelson are more concerned about following Jesus' instruction to "Go into all the world and preach the gospel to every creature" (Mark 16:15) than they are about the bottom line. Amazing!

Bones of Contention: A Creationist Assessment of Human Fossils, Marvin L. Lubenow (Grand Rapids, MI: Baker Books, 1992). Think the fossil "record" proves evolution? You won't after you've read this extraordinary book. If you want to cling to popular views of our origins, you won't like it at all. But if it's truth you're after, don't miss it.

The Case for Christ: A Journalist's Personal Investigation of the Evidence for Jesus, Lee Strobel (Grand Rapids, MI: Zondervan, 1998). I stumbled across Lee Strobel's books early on in my quest. Armed with a master's degree from Yale, Strobel was a hardened investigative reporter for the *Chicago Tribune* when he set out to prove his wife's newfound Christianity a crock. But his investigations led him to the opposite conclusion.

The Collapse of Evolution, Scott M. Huse (Grand Rapids, MI: Baker Books, 1997). If I had to choose just one book for an overview of how real science supports Genesis rather than Darwin, this would be it. Dr. Huse covers an amazing amount of territory in relatively short order, using language that anyone can understand.

Created for His Glory: God's Purpose for Redeeming Your Life, Jim Berg (Greenville, SC: BJU Press, 2002). This book's stated purpose is to help us find the peace and joy that the Bible describes. I guess Dr. Berg has done a great job, because it was after I read it that I started viewing just about everything with eternal eyes and therefore experiencing what the apostle Paul called in Philippians 4 "the peace of God which surpasses all understanding." Totally life changing.

Darwin on Trial, Phillip E. Johnson (Downers Grover, IL: InterVarsity Press, 1993). The Harvard-educated author is a lawyer, a law professor at the University of California at Berkeley, and an outstanding writer who makes the case against Darwinism irrefutable. I finally set aside my pen, because I was underlining just about every sentence.

Darwin's Black Box, Michael Behe (New York, NY: The Free Press, 1996). I don't think one should have an opinion on bio-chemical evolution—or on evolution in general—until one has read this incredible book. Okay, if you already reject evolution, I guess you're off the hook; but for everyone else, this is a must-read.

Darwin's Enigma, Luther Sunderland (Green Forest, AR: Master Books, 2002). If I were to rate my favorite books according to the amount of ink I used to underline and star vital passages, this one would be near the top. It was here that I first learned critical facts about evolution—and read the admissions of prominent evolution-ists, including the late Stephen J. Gould of Harvard, that there really are no transitional forms in the fossil record. Oops.

Death and the Afterlife, Dr. Robert A. Morey (Minneapolis, MN: Bethany House, 1984). What does the Bible say about death and eternity? Who'll be resurrected, and to what end? Will everyone be saved, or might some people simply pass into nonexistence upon death? This book explores these subjects in depth, comparing bibli-cal teachings to other views, from the occult to the universalist.

The Defender's Study Bible, Henry M. Morris, annotator (Iowa Falls, IA: World Bible Publishers, 1995). This is a wonderful edition of the King James Version for anyone with an interest in science. Dr. Morris provides highly readable and eye-opening explanations of many passages—especially gripping when he unveils the science behind such passages as 2 Peter 3:4–7.

Evangelism Explosion, D. James Kennedy (Carol Stream, IL: Tyndale House Publishers, 1996). This book not only communicated the gospel to me in a nutshell, in the process pointing me to support-ing biblical passages and providing solid analogies; it also delivered some noteworthy new pieces for the puzzle of absolute truth.

Every Prophecy of the Bible, John F. Walvoord (Colorado Springs, CO: Chariot Victor Publishing, 1999). They say that nearly one-third of the Bible involves prophecy. This book, written by an acknowledged prophecy authority, is essential for grasping the significance of the hundreds of predictions that have already come true, and watching for those that have yet to be fulfilled.

The Genesis Flood: The Biblical Record and Its Scientific Implications, John C. Whitcomb and Henry M. Morris (Phillipsburg, NJ: P&R Publishing, 2003). This is the book that started the modern creation science movement in 1961. The authors cover everything from arguments against the Genesis Flood to the overwhelming evidence confirming it. It's not lightweight; the discussions of geology, hydrology, and archaeology were challenging for me. Still, outside of the Bible itself, it may be the most significant book in my library.

God the Evidence: The Reconciliation of Faith and Reason in a Postsecular World, Patrick Glynn. (Rocklin, CA: Prima Publishing, 1997). This is the book whose outstanding discussion of the anthropic principle led me to conclude that there is indeed an intelligent designer behind our universe. If you're not convinced, this might be a good place to begin. Author Glynn holds a PhD from Harvard and is associate director of the George Washington University Institute for Communitarian Policy Studies, so not even a superintellectual has to feel embarrassed to be seen with his book.

Hard to Believe: The High Cost and Infinite Value of Following Jesus, John MacArthur (Nashville: Thomas Nelson, 2003). This book blew me away. The author (one of my very favorite preachers) starts with Luke 9:23, in which Jesus is quoted as saying, "If anyone desires to come after Me, let him deny himself, and take up his cross daily, and follow Me." He then proceeds to tell it like it is, explaining that while salvation is a free gift of God, there is a cost to following Christ—a willingness to deny self and submit to His will.

Help! I'm Turning into My Mother, Becky Freeman and Ruthie

Arnold (Eugene, OR: Harvest House, 2002). We all need to laugh now and then—especially when we're in the midst of all this heavy-duty reading. This book, written by my agent's very cool wife and her apparently equally cool mother, warmed my heart and kept me smiling for days. (Not to mention proving that Christians can have a great sense of humor!)

The Holiness of God, R. C. Sproul (Wheaton, IL: Tyndale House Publishers, 1998). I read this book fairly early in my investigation and need to read it again. I believe it was here that I first encountered unabashed reverence for the Lord and His holiness. It was here, too, that I got my first inkling of things that are so seldom discussed today in polite company—including His wrath and what the burden of our sins did to Jesus, the Lamb of God. A real eye-opener!

How to Give Away Your Faith, Paul Little (Downers Grove, IL: InterVarsity Press, 1988). It was not long after a group of girlfriends laughed in my face over my changed life that I picked up this book, billed as "the classic guide on evangelism." Not only did it turn out to be a big help for sharing my faith, it also gave this baby Christian a better handle on the teachings of Christianity.

In Six Days: Why Fifty Scientists Choose to Believe in Creation, John F. Ashton, PhD, ed. (Green Forest, AR: Master Books, 2000). We keep hearing that real scientists believe in evolution. This book proves that claim to be a lie, as fifty PhDs from virtually every branch of science explain why they believe in a literal six-day creation by the God of the Bible.

The Indestructible Book: The Bible, Its Translators, and Their Sacrifices, Ken Connolly (Grand Rapids, MI: Baker Books, 1996). This book is a must-read for anyone who thinks that all sacred books are alike; it demonstrates conclusively, in less than two hundred beautifully illustrated pages, that the Bible stands alone. Consider this chilling quote: "Some people were so committed to the belief that [the Bible] is God's book that they were even willing to die for that proposition. And strangely, others have been willing to put them to death." Read it and weep. Literally.

In the Trenches, Reggie White (Nashville: Thomas Nelson, Inc., 1996). Where would I be today without the late Reggie White? I suppose the answer is that God would have used someone or something else to crack open my hard heart, but I will still be eternally grateful to Reggie—not only for writing this excellent book, but more important for always wearing his heart for the Lord on his sleeve, in plain sight for any observant fan.

The Kingdom of the Cults, Walter Martin (Minneapolis, MN: Bethany House Publishers, 1985). This 500-plus-page volume is considered the definitive book on cults—not only those that are allegedly "Christian," but also the overtly non-Christian, all of which deny the deity of Jesus Christ and the all-sufficient atoning power of His death on the cross.

The Late Great Planet Earth, Hal Lindsey with C. C. Carlson (Grand Rapids, MI: Zondervan Publishing House, 1970). I wish I'd picked up this book on the amazing truth of biblical prophecy when it was first published. It might have changed everything. Even now, it's an exciting read.

Lies Women Believe and the Truth That Sets Them Free, Nancy Leigh DeMoss (Chicago, IL: Moody Press, 2001). This book was written for Christians, but I can't imagine that any woman could read it and remain unchanged. Author DeMoss takes on the lies that ruin our lives and destroy our peace—lies about ourselves, our relationships, our emotions, our circumstances, our sin, and most important of all, God Himself. And then she tells us the truth. Forget "women's liberation"; this is the real deal.

Life Application Study Bible (Wheaton, IL: Tyndale House Publishers, 1996). This was the first Bible I read from cover to cover. It uses the New Living Translation, which is a "thought by thought" translation rendered in language that a sixth grader should be able to read—especially good for someone who's intimidated by the prospect of doing more than looking up a verse here and there. It also contains great maps and sidebars, plus extensive notes that explain how specific words, phrases, and verses pertain to our lives.

The Long War Against God, Henry Morris (Green Forest, AR: Master Books, Inc., 2000). When I was an atheist, I figured evolution was a radical new (and well proven) discovery of modern science. Then I read this brilliant book and learned that this idea has been around practically since the beginning of time. I also learned it's been foundational to just about every ugly thing that man has ever done to man, especially in the twentieth century.

The MacArthur Study Bible, John MacArthur, general editor (Nashville, TN: Thomas Nelson Bibles, 1997). I'm not sure it gets any better than this: the Holy Bible rendered in the readable yet reverent New King James Version . . . with study notes provided by the inimitable John MacArthur. He has included a number of excellent articles on subjects ranging from how the Bible came into being to how to recognize genuine saving faith. And he provides sound advice on how best to study Scripture—critical for someone who no longer has all the time in the world left.

The Modern Creation Trilogy, Henry M. Morris and John D. Morris (Green Forest, AR: Master Books, Inc., 1996). If I were stranded on a desert island and could only have the Bible and one other book, this might well be that other. (Sure, it's a three-part set, but it's my little contest, so I set the rules.) The Drs. Morris look at scripture, science, and society in terms of biblical creation—and demonstrate beyond the shadow of any doubt that real science supports the Genesis account of our universe's origins.

The New Evidence that Demands a Verdict, Josh McDowell (Nashville: Thomas Nelson Publishers, 1999). This book fell into my hands early on in my search—and I'm so glad it did. McDowell covers it all, demonstrating in minute detail why we can trust the Bible as well as Jesus' claim to be God. He also answers the most common questions skeptics raise, including how the Bible's books were chosen and how we can be sure that the Scripture we read today is faithful to the earliest manuscripts. Indispensable.

The New Tolerance, Josh McDowell and Bob Hostetler (Wheaton, IL: Tyndale House Publishers, 1998). If you become a Christian, you're going to be accused of being arrogant, self-righteous, hate-filled, fanatical, extreme, bigoted, and perhaps most horrific of all in today's culture, intolerant. You'll feel better about the accusations once you've joined these authors for a bird's-eye view of how our entire culture has been brainwashed into calling good evil and evil good.

Occult Invasion, Dave Hunt and T. A. McMahon (Eugene, OR: Harvest House Publishers, 1998). Hunt and McMahon are among my favorite authors, in no small part because they expose the waves of false teachings that are pounding our culture in general and the church in particular. As a result, they not only alert their readers to spiritual dangers; they also provide us with logical explanations for phenomena, from UFOs to near-death experiences, that might otherwise appear to discredit biblical Christianity.

Our Created Moon, Don DeYoung and John Whitcomb (Green Forest, AR: Master Books, 2003). I love this little book. Its authors not only told me everything I've ever wondered about the moon and then some, but they also put this information into biblical perspective, so that for me its primary take-away is just this: "What an awesome God we have!"

Scientific Facts in the Bible: 100 Reasons to Believe the Bible Is Supernatural in Origin, Ray Comfort (Gainesville, FL: Bridge-Logos Publishers, 2001). Ray Comfort covers, in a nutshell, subjects from medicine and biology to astronomy and archaeology—all in his entertaining style. For its quick overview of the Bible's shocking scientific accuracy, this little book is on my top ten list. But then, in my humble opinion, Ray Comfort is one of the best writers ever.

The Search for Significance, Robert S. McGee (Nashville: Word Publishing, 1998). This must have been one of my bargain finds, because I was searching for my mother, not personal significance. But what a happy discovery! It was here I first learned principles both foundational and pertinent to my quest—for instance, that the focus of the Christian life is Christ, not rules and regulations, and that trying to make up for bad deeds with good ones does nothing more than send us into a useless "guilt-and-penance spiral."

The Source of My Strength: Relying on the Life-Changing Power of Jesus Christ to Heal our Wounded Hearts, Charles Stanley (Nashville, TN: Thomas Nelson, Inc., 1994). I stumbled across Charles Stanley preaching on WVCY-TV early on in my quest, and almost immediately came across this heartwarming book at a local bookstore. I'd heard the phrase "Let go and let God" before; with this volume, Dr. Stanley showed me how to do that.

The Stones Cry Out: What Archaeology Reveals About the Truth of the Bible, Randall Price (Eugene, OR: Harvest House Publishers, 1997). Who says the Bible is myth? And who says archaeology is boring? This is a captivating book, one that has turned my travel fantasies from Germany and Austria to the Holy Land.

Streams in the Desert, Mrs. Charles E. Cowman (Los Angeles, CA: The Oriental Missionary Society, 1925). My niece Jenny gave me my first used edition of this wonderful devotional, still in print, and I've given copies to many others since then. For each day of the year, it contains a Bible passage, an essay on that passage by someone who loved God, and often a poem on the same subject. It's not only water for a thirsty soul, but it also taught me a great deal about applying the teachings of the Bible to everyday life.

Things Unseen: Living in Light of Forever, Mark Buchanan

(Sisters, OR: Multnomah Publishers, 2002). *Things Unseen* is a book not about heaven itself, the author tells us, but about "heavenly-mindedness." He observes that this world is not enough for us. He writes about feelings that are both "laughter and mourning, spring and winter, homecoming and exile," longings that are really home-sickness for heaven. He points out that we're all dying, and that we'd best all look up. This is not the only Mark Buchanan book I've thoroughly enjoyed, but it's probably my favorite. He really gets it.

Thinking Against the Grain, N. Allan Moseley (Grand Rapids, MI: Kregel Publications, 2003). Subtitled "Developing a Biblical World-view in a Culture of Myths," this book showed me what it means to hold "an intellectually coherent and biblically faithful worldview." I was already a Christian when I read it, but I didn't know what to do with that fact. Dr. Moseley provided compelling direction.

Total Truth: Liberating Christianity from Its Cultural Captivity, Nancy Pearcey (Wheaton, IL: Crossway Books, 2004). Even if you're not a believer, this would be an engrossing read—especially if you think Bible-believing Christians have checked their brains at the door. It is, in fact, an astounding book that unveils in painstaking historical detail how our worldviews shape our beliefs, often to the detriment of truth. Already thoroughly marked-up, it's on my list of books demanding a second reading. And probably a third.

The Universe Next Door: A Basic Worldview Catalog, James Sire (Downers Grove, IL: InterVarsity Press, 1997). If your question is, which God? this is a great place to begin. If it weren't for this book, I might still be floundering around in search of the truth.

What Is Secular Humanism? Why Humanism Became Secular and How It Is Changing Our World, James Hitchcock (Ann Arbor, MI: Servant Books, 1982). When I first started wondering how I could have been so blind to everything related to Christianity, Dr. Hitchcock explained it in terms of the culture I grew up in. I love this book and am sorry that it seems to be out of print, but you can pick up a used copy for a song. Beware: a prominent atheist has re-cycled the main title for his own 2007 book. Coincidence?

What Your Counselor Never Told You, William Backus (Bloomington, MN: Bethany House Publishers, 2000). Talk about eye-openers! Dr. Backus claims that most of our problems are the result of (brace yourself; I'm going to use that ghastly word) sin—pride, envy, anger, greed, sloth, lust, gluttony, and all the rest. Believe it or not, he's right.

Why I Believe, D. James Kennedy (Nashville, TN: W Publishing Group, 1999). This terrific little volume summarizes some of the most compelling evidences for Christianity. Nearly all the chapter titles begin with "Why I Believe in . . ." and conclude with every-thing from the Bible, Creation, Heaven, Hell, and Moral Absolutes to Christ, the Resurrection, and the Return of Christ. I try to keep several on hand to give away to seekers, because Dr. Kennedy makes a very persuasive case in language the layman can easily understand.

The World That Perished, John C. Whitcomb (Grand Rapids, MI: Baker Book House, 1999). "If the universal Flood concept explains far better than other concepts many of the significant fea-tures of the earth's crust, why is it not more generally accepted by geologists?" Good question, Dr. Whitcomb—and I thank you for both posing and answering it (as well as scores of others) in this fas-cinating follow-up to *The Genesis Flood*.

Zondervan NASB Study Bible, Kenneth Barker, general editor (Grand Rapids, MI: Zondervan, 1999). This New American Standard Bible was the second study Bible I read, and my first for-mal, word-for-word translation of the original text—as exhilarating as graduating from a tricycle to a two-wheeler! Its study notes opened up new worlds to me: they talk about what various passages mean to the reader, of course, but they also provide extensive historical and geographic references, pertinent cross-references, and explanations of everything from theological phrases to ancient Hebrew idioms.

ABOUT THE AUTHOR

Kitty Foth-Regner was a freelance copywriter with big-name clients, an enviable portfolio, an unusual knack for translating complex technical topics into simple terms, and a business built entirely on referrals. A summa cum laude journalism graduate, she had talent, brains, lots of friends, a great boyfriend, a cool house west of Milwaukee, Wisconsin, all the pets she could handle, and a really good cleaning woman. She had just one published novel but plenty of other ideas in the hopper, just waiting for her undivided attention. She was, in short, a feminist in full and happy control of her life. And then her beloved mother developed a fatal illness, reducing all those achievements to dust and sending her off on a frantic quest to see if her mother's Christian faith might by any chance be true.

The coauthor with Amy Ammen of *Hip Ideas for Hyper Dogs* (Howell Book House, 2007), she lives near Milwaukee with her husband, dogs, and cats.

ACKNOWLEDGMENTS

Many thanks to Greg and Becky Johnson for taking this story from a 300-page rant into a simple "what happened to me" story.

To Nancy Miller for inspiring me to put it down on paper.

To Pastor Marsha Headley not only for her invaluable editorial suggestions, but also for being the first to show me what it means to be a passionate follower of Jesus Christ, to pray unceasingly, and to trust Him with my life.

To the once-and-future pastoral staff of Brookside Baptist Church (www.brooksidebaptist.org), including Drs. Sam Horn, Joe Helm, and Bill Lincoln, pastors Dan Herman and Ken Keltner, and evangelist Steve Pettit for helping me to see the Bible for what it truly is: the Lord God's revelation of Himself, lovingly provided to give every last person the opportunity to know Him and His will; and to pastors Jonathan Albright and Steve Sauers for music befitting the King of kings.

To Beth Horn and Lana Lee Helm for their kindness, love, and support, as well as outstanding proofreading.

To Dr. Vic Eliason and his team at the VCY America broadcast

Acknowledgments

network, for presenting consistently and compellingly biblical programming to reach those who are searching for truth, as well as those who have found it.

To Paula Haberman for teaching me to take Scripture seriously—*very* seriously.

To JoAnn for listening endlessly, Brenda for her enthusiasm, and Dave for his patience and proofreading help.

To Jenny Reese, Mike Cronin, Leigh Gott, Victor Oliver, and Kristen Parrish for excellent editorial suggestions.

To Heather Skelton for patiently and expertly shepherding this book through to completion.

To Norma Rome for her incredible proofreading and feedback.

To Karen Grishaber for helping me get over my knee-knocking stage fright.

To Chris Corsbie for providing steady copywriting work to keep the wolf from the door as I worked on this book.

To Dr. Dan Killian for keeping me feeling spry enough to sit at the computer hour after hour after hour.

And above all, to my Lord and Savior Jesus Christ, who bore my sins on the cross so that I might live with Him forever, not so incidentally relieving my mom of the prospect of "heaven without her."